ON
BELONGING

Library of Congress Control Number: 2022933712

ISBN: 978-1-4197-5303-9
eISBN: 978-1-64700-231-2

Printed and bound in the United States

10 9 8 7 6 5 4 3 2 1

Abrams books are available at special discounts when purchased in quantity
for premiums and promotions as well as fundraising or educational use.
Special editions can also be created to specification. For details, contact
specialsales@abramsbooks.com or the address below.

Abrams Press® is a registered trademark of Harry N. Abrams, Inc.

ABRAMS The Art of Books
195 Broadway, New York, NY 10007
abramsbooks.com

ON BELONGING

FINDING CONNECTION
IN AN AGE OF ISOLATION

KIM SAMUEL

ABRAMS PRESS, NEW YORK

To Caitlin and Charlotte,
my joy

CONTENTS

INTRODUCTION

ON A GENTLE SPRING EVENING in May 2002, I was invited to a small dinner in New York City honoring Nelson Mandela and Graça Machel. I had gotten to know Graça personally years earlier and had been moved by her potent presence, her grace, and her sense of the world. Her work in Mozambique, South Africa, and internationally around humanitarian issues had touched thousands of lives, and I was happy and excited to be seeing her again. And I was about to meet Mandela for the first time, a true beacon of hope for our whole human race. As you might imagine, I was overcome by joy and jitters at the same time, in equal measure.

It had been two years since my father, Ernie Samuel, had died from complications related to a brain injury he had sustained five years earlier. He had been one of the shining lights of my life, a man whose kindness and compassion remained constant and unwavering throughout his life. I was thinking how much I wish I could have shared this moment with him.

As Graça introduced me to her husband, she asked, with radiant warmth: "How have you been doing since your daddy passed?"

"I miss him every day," I told her. I spoke about how his journey at the end of his life was one of resilience and tenderness.

Following his injury, my father fell into a three-month coma, then awakened, very slowly. But he was whole as ever. More than anything, he loved his family and his life. He met his physical and social challenges with determination and grace, even as he experienced increased isolation and was treated as if his identity was defined only by his medical condition and his age. The insurance company would not consider paying for rehabilitation because he had reached the age of sixty-five—in their words, he was in his "sundown years." Instead, they offered to put him in a nursing home where he would live out his days without hope of regaining his independence.

Caring for my father alongside my family in what turned out to be the final years of his life, I had witnessed the isolation he felt as a result of systemic and relational failures to treat or see him as a whole person. This gave me important insights into the nature of social isolation and connectedness. I began to realize that it wasn't disability that causes isolation. It's the way people *perceive* disability that leads them to treat people with disabilities differently, often rendering them invisible or not seen for the whole person they are. Same with older people; it's not about age, but rather ageism.

Mandela, who had spent almost three decades in prison with long periods in solitary confinement, was watching quietly as I shared these reflections on the isolation my father experienced.

I turned to him and said, "Of course, you would know all about isolation."

He paused. "No, I have never been isolated."[1]

In that moment, I thought back to when I visited the prison on Robben Island in Table Bay off the Western Cape of South Africa. This was where Mandela spent so many years sequestered, deprived of freedom, and unable to see his children grow. I remember the thunder of the door to his cell as it closed, the tiny window he would have had to lift himself up to just to get a glimpse of the outside world.

"Never isolated—not even on Robben Island?" I asked.

"No," he replied, with quiet conviction. "On Robben Island, we were all brothers working together with a common purpose. I was never alone."

He continued, "I have seen isolation. I have seen it in the child with AIDS whom no one in the village will love or care for or touch or feed or shelter. I have seen isolation—and it is very bad."

This exchange marked me deeply. Here was a man who had been physically isolated in the starkest of conditions, yet more than twenty-seven years of imprisonment, he stayed connected with his community through a shared sense of purpose. Each day, he and his brothers served the cause of his people's freedom, understanding their personal struggles against repression and racism as a microcosm of their wider struggle. Together, they built a powerful sense of solidarity and belonging that endured the harsh conditions of prison.

Mandela never lost sight of the traditions that gave him a strong sense of his place in the world, the love of his homeland, or the wisdom transmitted to him from his elders. His faith greatly influenced his compassion for all people, including those who oppressed him. He drew from these foundations as he developed a sense of how to emerge from prison undiminished, how to conserve and replenish his beliefs.[2]

In 1941, the philosopher Erich Fromm, a German Jew who fled the Nazis, wrote about the paradox of belonging within conditions of physical isolation: "An individual may be alone in the physical sense for many years and yet he may be related to ideas, values, or at least social patterns that give him a feeling of communion and 'belonging.'" There are also those, Fromm observes, who live among people and yet are overcome with feelings of isolation.[3] What leads us to these different experiences?

Even from prison, Mandela turned isolation into a sense of belonging within himself and moreover for millions of other South Africans. Although the structures of apartheid cut off most formal routes of belonging for him and many of his countrymen and women in white-ruled South Africa—where those labeled "black" and "colored" were told they didn't belong to a place where their ancestors had lived for thousands of years—Mandela fought with conviction to ensure they knew that they did, indeed, belong.

My conversation that night with Mandela and Graça had moved me profoundly. It would continue to change my life in ways I couldn't foresee at the time. That night with the two of them, I felt the affirmation of my journey to understand social isolation and connection in real, concrete ways in the world. *This is what I will be doing for the rest of my life,* I remember saying to myself.

I'VE SPENT MUCH TIME since that night thinking about belonging and its absence, social isolation. Not long after my father awoke from his coma and began his long rehabilitation, I began to imagine social isolation as the feeling of sitting all alone at the bottom of a well, enveloped by damp air and impenetrable walls, unable to escape the darkness. Many people who are socially isolated experience feelings of invisibility and hopelessness, as well as a lack of agency and choice over their situation.

Long before my father's brain injury, I had been familiar with feelings of isolation of a different kind. Many times in my childhood, I felt like I didn't fit in or that I wasn't worthy. I was highly sensitive to what was going on in the world around me. I struggled to put those observations and feelings into words.

Not knowing how to make sense of the world and my place in it, I turned to books, in my case to the nineteenth-century poet, painter, and printmaker, William Blake. I took refuge in Blake for his commentary on the interwovenness of light and darkness, and the way his *Songs of Innocence and Songs of Experience* guided me to realize that there is light even at the bottom of a dark well. Blake's poems helped me understand that the darkness is also part of the whole, and that we can relate to it skillfully. Ultimately, as I began to pursue my life's purpose in helping others find belonging themselves, I found the sense of connection I was looking for, too.

Sleepers Wake!
Wachet auf, ruft uns die Stimme
—JOHANN SEBASTIAN BACH[4]

At the beginning of 2003, I met a remarkable woman, Kathleen Raine CBE, in London. She was one of Britain's foremost poets, a renowned scholar who wrote extensively on William Blake, and a founding member of the Temenos Academy, dedicated to offering education in philosophy and the arts in the light of the wisdom traditions of East and West. I marveled at how her poetry spoke to the theme of belonging. In her poem "Message from Home," she urges the reader,

Recollect more deeply, and the birds will come,
Fish rise to meet you in their silver shoals,
And darker, stranger, and more mysterious lives
Will throng about you at the source
Where the tree's roots drink from the abyss.

Sleep at the tree's root, where the night is spun
Into the stuff of worlds, listen to the winds,
The tides, and the night's harmonies, and know
All that you knew before you began to forget,
Before you became estranged from your own being.[5]

For Kathleen, the act of remembering the deepest parts of ourselves is a return to others, and to the earth. There's a continual sense of the animals and beings in the natural world actively responding to our journey of recollection, back to belonging.

Kathleen became one of my greatest teachers. We spent many afternoons together in her home, discussing how human beings have grappled with overcoming feelings of separation for thousands of years. I had found in Kathleen a kindred spirit and a guide. She could see as directly as anyone into the essence of the work I felt called to do.

I saw Kathleen for the last time in a hospital on a Saturday morning in June of that year. She knew that she was going to leave the world. She put her hands softly on my face when I told her that I would see her on Monday, and, as tears welled in my eyes, she told me that she wouldn't be there.

"This is goodbye," she said. "But only for a while."[6]

Kathleen's spirit remains close, and I often reflect on her wisdom. Perhaps more than any other, I find myself returning to one core idea that permeated our conversations: There is crisis all around us, people have been left behind, and our society must be woken up to what it has forgotten.

Social isolation and the inequality that both drives it and results from it is a structural, relational phenomenon. As we'll see throughout this book, cycles of social isolation and inequality result when wider socioeconomic, political, and cultural structures and processes create conditions in which people—including distinct groups of people—are denied access to systems that support inclusion and belonging.

These structures of isolation are often based on differences we see in another person or group that we then use to "other" them—to distance them from ourselves and claim they aren't like us. Othering on the basis of gender, race, ethnicity, religion, sex, age, disability, sexual orientation, and so on is deeply woven into the very fabric of our societies.

As Nelson Mandela suggested in our conversation, structural issues rooted in historical forms of othering—social, economic, and political—deny many human beings the experience of belonging. Moreover, many of the social and spiritual foundations that have historically provided a sense of belonging have eroded over time.

We are at a moment of heightened importance in the history of our human family. We're facing significant crises that will require our united effort to overcome. Climate change is accelerating at a breakneck speed, citizens are losing faith in their elected officials and institutions, and healthcare systems around the world have been pushed to the brink—and in many cases, totally devastated—by the COVID-19 pandemic. While we're more connected than ever before in terms of sheer technical ability, we're currently living in an age of isolation. Inequality and polarization contribute to this isolation, and much of humanity is grappling with myriad forms of alienation, disenfranchisement, and feelings of separation. This age of isolation has created and fueled insidious and toxic digital spaces, contributed to the rise of mental health challenges across the board, especially among young people, and has left us feeling lonelier than ever. Many of us feel an inherent, desperate desire to belong in deeper and more sustaining ways.

This convergence of crises has resulted from a long-standing accumulation of neglect of the deepest responsibilities core to belonging—our responsibilities toward each other and the earth. Against the backdrop of climate change, species loss, pandemics, increasing inequality, and poverty, humanity is facing a reckoning. Yet these deep fissures are also potential openings for us to reconnect, regenerate, and reimagine what kind of world we want to live in. From this crisis of social isolation, we can build the belonging for which we so desperately yearn.

LATER IN 1997, after my father returned home, I became involved with wider issues of social isolation and connectedness through the Special Olympics movement, whose founder, Eunice Kennedy Shriver, changed the world. In her office one day over tea, she gave me sage advice. "Kim," she said, "don't spend your life chasing other people's dreams. Follow your own dream, work hard, and invite people to join you there."

During dinner five years later in New York, Graça and I spoke at length about the connections between my work on social isolation and her work with the United Nations on the impact of armed conflict on children, including child soldiers, across the globe. She proposed that we work together to bring the issues of social isolation and connectedness more explicitly into the work of her organization, the Foundation for Community Development (*Fundação para o Desenvolvimento da Comunidade*, or FDC).

This initial idea turned into many years of collaboration and partnership with FDC, the Nelson Mandela Children's Fund, and the Synergos Institute, a global organization that takes a decentralized approach to solving complex issues of poverty through partnership, trust-building, and collaboration across sectors and among grassroots communities.

My work in southern Africa led me eventually to the Oxford Poverty & Human Development Initiative (OPHI) at the University of Oxford's Department of International Development. I became a visiting scholar at OPHI working with a team of development economists studying multidimensional poverty, which understands poverty to consist of multiple deprivations beyond income, including health, safety, education, and living standards. My time there has been important in exposing me to new ways of thinking about social isolation and measurement.

My research progressed into the honor of being named Professor of Practice in Social Connectedness at McGill University's Institute for the Study of International Development. This gave me the opportunity to create and teach a new course in the field of international studies, addressing social isolation and social connectedness through the dual lens of program and policy development.

The community of belonging I found with my students was rooted, in part, in the Social Connectedness Global Symposia program, whose idea came to me in 2013 on a trip to Grabouw, a town located in the Western Cape province of South Africa, while visiting our colleagues at the National Association of Child Care Workers (NACCW), along with team members from Synergos and OPHI. When I looked up, I saw a medicine wheel, and later learned it was being used as a community healing tool, resembling those I had seen in Indigenous communities across Canada. In that moment, I had the spark of an idea—might there be a way to bring together people who were already doing the work of building belonging, who wouldn't otherwise have met? Quincy Jones, whom we'll spend time with later in the book, once told me that "coincidence is God's way of remaining anonymous." Seeing that medicine wheel felt like that kind of divine coincidence.

The first global symposium on "Overcoming Social Isolation and Deepening Connectedness" took place the following year. Elders and youth from several Indigenous peoples in Canada joined, and childcare workers from South Africa were among the first to be invited; in all, people came from thirteen different countries to a beautiful, natural space called the Evergreen Brick Works in my hometown of Toronto, Canada, for three days of engaging sessions and open dialogue in a safe space.

Those who attended included civil society leaders, students, educators and policymakers, human rights activists, artists, advocates, and athletes. We'll meet many of them in the pages of this book. Sessions pulled together individuals who likely would not have met otherwise—some experts in their field, others simply passionate or curious about building a better world. People were encouraged to bring their whole selves to the global symposium, meaning that they would be accepted and celebrated for their various gifts and abilities and, equally, accepted for their vulnerabilities. They were invited to gather in a spirit of connectedness and belonging, with the goal of identifying real and actionable pathways of change. Everyone had a contribution to make, a story to share.

Since the beginning, the biennial Global Symposia have illuminated what's already within us and our communities. By the time of the second global symposium in 2016, the initial vision for social connectedness had begun to open up to a deeper vision—one of a co-created movement that has the potential to shape a new future, a new humanity centered around what it means to belong, in theory and in practice. My own life experience, the success of the first two symposia, and the passion and brilliance of my students inspired me to create a nonprofit organization focused on this work of this building belonging. With the support of two of my students from 2016, Celine Thomas and Jessica Farber, soon to be joined by a core group of other recent graduates, we started building the Samuel Centre for Social Connectedness (SCSC). Named in honor of my late father, SCSC was officially launched in 2017. This "think-and-do" tank is grounded within three core values: respect, recognition, and reciprocity.

SO, WHAT IS BELONGING EXACTLY? It is one of those things that we know how to feel, but may not always know how to describe. In the simplest sense, belonging is wholeness. It's the experience of being at home in ourselves as well as the social, environmental, organizational, and cultural contexts of our lives. It's the basis for human flourishing.

The purest forms of belonging enable us to exist as unique, authentic beings within a larger whole, and yet to experience that whole within the multiplicity. The following lines in Walt Whitman's epic poem "Song of Myself" in his evoke this feeling:

> I CELEBRATE myself, and sing myself,
> And what I assume you shall assume;
> For every atom belonging to me as good belongs to you.[7]

When we are a part of true belonging, the boundaries of our limited sense of self expand to encompass others: our neighbors, the members of our communities and countries across all lines of identity, the animals, and oceans—all inhabitants of our shared planet—and the earth itself.

This "I" isn't an individual "I" as we typically think of it. It's an "I" that inhabits a consciousness of belonging, an "I" that belongs to everything.

Belonging has been such a fundamental driver in human culture that nearly all major wisdom traditions of humankind—which contain the oldest stories of who we are—point the way back to it. Mystics such as Meister Eckhart and Jalāl ad-Dīn Muhammad Rūmī speak of a belonging so elemental that no "inside" or "outside" exists, no self that is separate from the other, no Lover separate from the Beloved.

But what does belonging look like in practice? Ultimately, belonging involves a reciprocal give-and-take within our many relationships—those that we have with one another, with the lands on which we live, with systems of governance and decision-making, and with structures of meaning. Through the course of my work, I've come to define several different dimensions of belonging that interact with each other to create a whole greater than the parts. These are dimensions of people, place, power, and purpose.

Belonging manifests perhaps most obviously through our relationship with *people*—with one another. We are social beings. There's an evolutionary dimension to our inherent need for human connection; evidence for this exists in humanity's common historical origins, and our biology. The survival of human beings in traditional hunter-gatherer societies—which typified human life for the vast majority of our history—depended on small communities of families joining to forage, hunt, and fend off shared threats together.[8] Although our societies have changed dramatically since then, and will continue to do so, this fundamental reality remains the same: We require connection with one another.

Our connection to *place* happens through a relationship with nature, with the lands on which we live, whether in a forest or a city neighborhood. In an ideal relationship of belonging to place, this relationship is reciprocal: We care for the places where we live and they, in turn, care for us. We have a responsibility toward our lands, which is ultimately a responsibility for our own well-being. When we feel a sense of belonging in a physical place or a natural ecosystem, we feel at home. We feel peace. We don't simply feel a need to extract whatever we can for our short-term personal benefit.

It means we live in reciprocity with nature, and it entails a commitment to honoring, preserving, and enriching this relationship.

Belonging is also found in our relationship with *power*, and our capacity to participate meaningfully in the decision-making structures of the broader whole. Our agency, the ability to make choices in shaping our circumstances, and our capacity to collectively determine our shared future, are all bound up in this dimension of belonging. This also involves the inner power of knowing one's self, and the outer power of having agency in the world in meaningful ways. The Reverend Dr. Martin Luther King Jr. emphasized that power—which he defined as the strength to "bring about social, political or economic changes"—must be undertaken in order to "implement the demands of love and justice."[9]

Belonging through *purpose*—the ability to create meaning in our lives and to share our gifts with the world—provides a vital sense of "why." It helps shape our perspectives on where we should be headed and what is right and good. Our sense of purpose is formed, in part, by the cultural and social norms and narratives about ourselves in relation to each other and the world around us. While religion has often informed these perspectives, we can also find belonging by encountering a calling, a personal sense of faith, or an ethical orientation outside of formalized religious structures or institutions.

These four dimensions of belonging—people, place, power, and purpose—interweave with each other and function in relationship to one another.

Psychologist Abraham Maslow identified "belongingness" as one of our most basic needs in his Hierarchy of Needs, coming just after physiological needs (such as air, water, and food) and safety (health, personal security).[10] I reach beyond this and suggest that belonging—as the antithesis of social isolation—is not only a need; it is a right as well. Indeed, in the pages of this book I will argue that we all possess a foundational Right to Belong.

I believe that every person, by simple virtue of the fact that they are born, has the Right to Belong. I envision the Right to Belong not as a new formal legal right, but rather as an undercurrent of established international human rights, a modern moral framework that inspires and informs social movements that span diverse sectors of society.

I've been working with many others to build a global movement around the Right to Belong. In May 2020, in the early months of the COVID-19 pandemic, I brought together more than forty changemakers and leaders across diverse fields for an online meeting of minds to explore the Right to Belong and its role as a unifying narrative as we confront the most pressing challenges of today.

I feel a renewed sense of urgency in the present moment as we see deepening inequality, climate- and conflict-driven displacement, and a worsening crisis of social isolation. Belonging is missing, and it's the only way forward.

Only Connect!

—E. M. FORSTER, *HOWARD'S END*[11]

In this book, we'll learn that belonging is manifested in our connection to people, place, power, and purpose, and we'll examine why those things are important. We'll learn what happens to both the individual and society when that belonging is neglected or, worse, exploited. We'll learn how to build more-inclusive communities, better systems, and stronger relationships rooted in reciprocity. And finally, we'll imagine what a twenty-first-century rights framework—the Right to Belong—could look like, both in theory and in practice.

We are living in an age of isolation, and it's only been made worse by the COVID-19 pandemic. This twenty-first-century problem requires a radical rethink about what we choose to value as a human species. Our only way back to wholeness—as individuals and as communities—is to build belonging for ourselves and for each other. We will not be able to abate or solve the most pressing problems of our world until we first recognize the truth of our interdependence. We must widen the circles of our belonging to include all people. We must acknowledge a fundamental truth: that we are all interconnected—*we only belong if we belong together.*

This is a book about innovative solutions and practical new possibilities for our future. It's about the power of belonging to heal a fractured world.

CHAPTER ONE

PATTERNS OF BELONGING

THE GREAT BEAR RAINFOREST on Canada's west coast is a magical place. With 25,000 square miles of pathless woods, rushing rivers, and bountiful salmon runs, Great Bear is one of the last great old-growth temperate rainforests on earth. It's a place of enormous abundance, and I can only imagine what it has been like for the peoples who have lived there for thousands of years, harvesting from both the lands and waters.

In Great Bear, sitting amid these woods, is a Sitka spruce tree, in a mist-shrouded covering of lichen and moss, resting atop a magnificent network of lateral roots interconnected with roots of other trees. It's difficult to discern where one ends and the others begin.

At the beginning of September 2006, I came across this particular tree one day while hiking with my then-fourteen-year-old daughter Caitlin Samuel, my sister Tammy Samuel-Balaz, and her family. That day we walked up the Elcho River Valley, located in territories of the Nuxalk and Heiltsuk Nations, for a half-day hike. It was the first time I really understood the difference between a walk in the woods and a walk in the wilderness—true, unadulterated wilderness of the kind you rarely find these days—a wild place in the best sense of the word.

My sister Tammy had been diagnosed with terminal cancer two years earlier. As she and I walked together through the woods, I felt a tenderness, a heightened sense of the preciousness of existence, that left a profound imprint on my memory.

Tammy was absorbed in being alive with her kids and her family in the middle of a rainforest teeming with life. In the Great Bear Rainforest, that meant life in all its cycles of change, with species evolving and adapting with the seasons, with whole ecosystems ebbing and flowing with the elements, and whose trees had been birthed from seeds into saplings into giants several hundred or a thousand years ago. She experienced the birds and animals with wonder and seemed to relish every step she took in the forest.

Sitka spruce trees spread their great branches alongside silver and white firs, red cedars, and western hemlock. Red alders lined the forest estuaries we waded through, forming the threshold between ocean and forest.[1] Where the estuaries gave way to solid ground, the understory of the forest was covered with elderberry, twinflower, and wild currants, which fed black-tailed deer and black bears. Salamanders wriggled among the ferns on the ground story, tracked by the glistening paths of slugs and snails.

Tammy sought to take in all of it—from the bear scat to the porcupines in the estuary shallows to the great blue herons that lifted their slate-colored bodies into the air from the riverbanks. She didn't want to miss a single thing. It was through Tammy's eyes that I experienced much of that time in the rainforest, and this brought me joy.

Impermanence was also all around us in the forest. I was conscious of having to make a choice in those months and years when my sister was sick. These moments could be about the sadness, or they could be about the living. I decided to affirm life despite the pain and grief at the prospect of losing my sister.

Sometimes, it's in the darkest moments in our lives that we receive the most light. I think back often to those moments in the rainforest with Tammy—the radiance in her smile, her strength and steadfastness for her kids as she faced the unknown, her sense of peace.

We climbed over the roots of many Sitka spruce trees as we navigated alongside the Elcho River together in the rainforest. The network of roots, exposed above ground, helped us find our balance as we placed our hands on their soft bark. When we finally paused for a rest after half a day of strenuous hiking, I walked to a Sitka spruce and sat down.

Resting under the shelter of the giant tree, surrounded by the canopy of the ancient forest, I was struck by the connectedness of the roots extending out before me, and how fallen trees had become nursery beds for young tree seedlings and saplings.

Below my feet in the ground, miles of fungi and pods of bacteria wove through the unseen world of the soils, forming a sheath around every root, exchanging nutrients and protection. Scientists have discovered that root tips communicate with other species in this forest network, transmitting signals from one plant to another through the fungi, carrying messages about possible stressors to life.[2]

The Sitka spruce sits in relationship within a wider network of ecosystems—ocean, estuaries, and freshwater rivers—whose ecological processes are intricately interwoven. Temperate rainforests like the Great Bear Rainforest support the greatest salmon runs on Earth. Trees that fall into the river provide nutrients for aquatic life. Salmon carcasses plucked from the water by grizzly and black bears and then discarded on the ground return nutrients back into the soil, which in turn feeds the roots of the Sitka spruce trees. And the trees in the forest seed the sky with particles of aroma that, along with dust and exhaust from elsewhere in British Columbia, coalesce mist into droplets, forming rain that feeds back into the Sitka ecosystem.[3]

As I sat there, held within the immensity of the roots, everything slowly came to rest. A stillness settled inside me, my breath slowed. Time stood still. I was part of the trees, the soil, the sun. My sense of self gave way to an expansiveness that permeated every particle of my being. I was part of everything.

THE ROOTS OF WHOLENESS

AN AWARENESS of wholeness and unity is shared by many Indigenous knowledge systems. It's found in the worldview of many of the diverse Pacific coastal First Nations peoples who have inhabited the land that forms the Great Bear Rainforest for thousands of years. It's embedded in many of their social, ecological, material, and spiritual structures and customs, which reflect the complex relationships that have developed over millennia between the human and more-than-human world.

For the Nuu-chah-nulth peoples of the Pacific Northwest, this awareness of oneness and interconnectedness is encapsulated in *Tsawalk*, which translates in English as the word "one." As Dr. Eugene Richard Atleo, Hereditary Chief of the Ahousaht First Nation, writes, "Nuu-chah-nulth peoples today, in concert with many other Indigenous peoples, embrace the phrase that is variously translated as 'everything is one,' 'everything is related,' or 'everything is connected.'"[4]

I spoke recently with Albert Marshall, an Elder from the Moose Clan of the Mi'kmaq Nation, whose land is located on the other side of Canada, in the community of Eskasoni in Unama'ki in Cape Breton, Nova Scotia. I wanted to get his take on the interconnectedness between humans and the living planet they inhabit. Albert is a native Mi'kmaq speaker, a father of six, a teacher, and a skillful advocate for the protection of the natural world.

Albert contemplates how his people have survived for more than 18,000 years, maintaining balance with the world around them. He asks, "How can this group of people live here for thousands and thousands of years, and not once have they compromised the ecological integrity of the area? I believe there's only one answer to that: when they act and work together as a group. If you look under the trees, you'll see all these roots. What are the roots doing? They're holding hands. They're supporting each other. There are great lessons there, looking at the different species of trees. They are helping each other in so many different ways."[5]

Like the roots Albert speaks of, everything on this earth is knit together in a web of kinship. Robin Wall Kimmerer, professor of environmental biology and member of the Potawatomi Nation, wrote about the interconnectedness of trees and fungi in her book *Braiding Sweetgrass*. "They weave a web of reciprocity, of giving and taking. In this way, the trees all act as one, because the fungi have connected them. Through unity, survival. All flourishing is mutual. Soil, fungus, tree, squirrel, child—all are the beneficiaries of reciprocity."[6]

Speaking about the social, ecological, political, and cultural aspects of belonging—about people, place, power, and purpose—Albert observed that when any one strand of this multidimensional and interconnected web suffers, so do we. "These four domains are the main ingredients of life as we understand it. In order for any of us to feel well, then all those four domains have to be maintained in a healthy and balanced way. And if any one of them is compromised, then the whole being of us is affected," he said.[7]

For Albert, the experience of wholeness starts with rootedness in a particular community and place. This sense of home and belonging to one's land creates a sense of responsibility and a duty of care. "I am from We'koqma'q, the territory of the Mi'kmaq," he tells me. "That's where my focus is at, where all my energy has to be because that's part of my home. If I don't look after my home, where am I going to live? Hopefully, one day this will resonate for the rest of our non-Native brothers and sisters. That this is our home."

As Albert describes it to me, the feeling of being rooted in a particular place isn't just a foundation for good psychological health. It's a foundation for everything. You love a place and care for it. And your place takes care of you, too. "Your environment will provide your every need," he tells me, "Your dwelling, your food, your medicines, your knowledge, and everything else. And in that environment is our Mother Earth."

Over several decades, Albert and his wife, Murdena Marshall, who passed away in 2018, have advocated an approach to viewing the world that seeks to integrate apparently opposing viewpoints called "Two-Eyed Seeing," or *Etuaptmunk* in Mi'kmaq. Albert explains that Two-Eyed Seeing refers to learning to "see from one eye with the strengths of Indigenous ways of knowing, and from the other eye with the strengths of Western ways of knowing, and to use both of these eyes together, for the benefit of all."[8]

It's the gift of multiple perspectives cultivated by many Indigenous peoples, Albert says, and it asks that we bring together our different ways of knowing to motivate people, Indigenous and non-Indigenous alike, to use all of our gifts and teachings to leave the world a better place and not compromise the opportunities for our youth—extending forward to seven generations—by forgoing our responsibilities of stewardship toward each other and the Earth.[9]

Albert and Murdena were both involved with the Mi'kmaq studies curriculum at Cape Breton University (CBU) in Nova Scotia. Observing the failure within mainstream science to acknowledge Indigenous knowledge in science and science curricula, Albert, who is an advisor and lecturer, and Murdena, who was an associate professor, asked, "If we can integrate our ways of knowing into the system, what would happen?"[10]

"So we developed an integrative science program which did exactly that," Albert told me, "where you actually integrate two forms of science: the Western science and the Aboriginal science." Students from that program now work in fields throughout the sciences, constantly integrating the Indigenous ways of knowing with scientific ones.

For Albert, belonging to a greater whole is a concept that speaks to our responsibility to ourselves, to others, and to the earth. "Embedded in our consciousness is an awareness of how we are interdependent and interconnected with every living entity."[11] This recognition is essential for humanity right now. Albert told me, "If we expect some transformative changes, I don't believe we can do it within the current structure. The new path, the journey, has got to be based on the laws of nature."[12]

The laws of nature Albert is talking about include interdependence, interconnectedness, love, harmony, and reciprocity. Many cultures around the world also orient themselves around these values. As Cherokee businesswoman Rebecca Adamson explains, the Hopi express this being in harmony with the laws of nature as *novoiti*; for the Tlingit, she says, this is *shagoon*.[13] As Anishinaabekwe activist and author Winona La Duke writes, Anishinaabeg and Cree people call this *minobimaa tisiiwin*, or "the good life," which also translates, she continues, to "continuous rebirth."[14]

THE MEASURE OF BELONGING

AS I STATED AT THE OUTSET, I see belonging manifest in four essential dimensions; it's our connection to one another, to the land, to our capacity to make meaningful choices, to a sense of shared meaning or mission. Indeed, to people, place, power, and purpose. I believe that we can bring these deep principles of wholeness and connectedness into the realms of public policy, urban planning, education, healthcare, and community organizing. The pattern of interdependence that manifests throughout nature can flourish in our everyday lives. As it is with the great trees and root systems, so, too, it is with human beings.

If we want to make this fundamental truth matter in real and tangible ways, we must find ways to define it and understand its significance. If belonging is to become "seen" by governments and communities, it must be measured. Policy changes can then be developed from what indicators tell us about the nature and extent of social isolation and how it relates to other elements of poverty and inequality.

What we measure reflects what we value. We see what societies value through the laws they enact, the rights they uphold, the ways they allocate resources—and in the nature of the statistics they measure. Every decision a business or a government makes is a reflection of those underlying values. Every important trend that transpires in the history of a society—for example, the decline of the family and the community relative to the economy and the state—reflects a society's underlying values.

What we measure determines not only the content of laws, regulations, and resource allocation, but also the historical narratives by which we understand ourselves and our relationship to the world. "What are people for?" asks philosopher, poet, and farmer Wendell Berry, writing about the deterioration of human relationship with the land in the context of rising mechanization.[15] If people are for storing grain, that's how we'll measure history. If people are for making war, that's what will be glorified and sanctified.

As the old adage goes, we measure what we treasure. What that means is that we put the effort into tracking the things to which we assign value. But in this case, "we" does not reflect everyone but, rather, those in positions of economic and political power. Stock valuations, GDP numbers, real estate prices? Those numbers are at our fingertips, nearly always. But stats on police brutality, sexual harassment, and depression among the most impoverished? Harder to find, because they aren't deemed valuable by those in power.

We need to change the conversation and push for governments and organizations to instead measure what *we* value. Things that make a real difference in our day-to-day lives. Things that impact our ability to belong

7

in our communities as our whole selves. And as we seek to measure what we—as a human collective—value, we must also rethink how we gather that data.

Belonging, specifically, is difficult to measure because it is deeply personal and intersectional. The United Nations' Sustainable Development Goals (SDGs), adopted in 2015, were hugely important in driving the conversation about intersectionality in measurement. They were groundbreaking in that they deviated from traditional metrics of developmental success, treating environmental sustainability and social inclusion as equally important to economic growth.

Kathy Calvin, former president and CEO of the United Nations Foundation, once shared with me, "I think the SDGs were born out of a couple worldviews that weren't necessarily present even in the last ten or fifteen years. One is intersectionality: how interrelated the SDGs all are, and that you can't really keep a girl in school if you haven't dealt with her health and you haven't dealt with some issues under her rights, or you don't anticipate that she can become a fully functioning member of a productive economy."[16]

With a lens to leave no person behind and instead pursue what Calvin refers to as its "flip-side"—social inclusion—the SDGs shine a light on, for example, the interrelated concerns of poverty, inequality, humanitarian crises, and rights abuses. Calvin has identified inclusion and belonging tying most clearly into two of the SDGs: Goal 3 ("Ensure healthy lives and promote well-being for all at all ages") and Goal 10 ("Reduce inequality within and among countries").

Still, I see belonging in each of the SDGs. Cherie Nursalim is the special advisor on climate for the government of Indonesia, and the founder of United in Diversity, which connects Indonesia's private sector with civil society organizations and government to advance sustainable development priorities and improve citizens' quality of life. Cherie is completely transforming financing and investing in Indonesia through innovative partnerships. Throughout her cross-sector work, she brings forward the Balinese philosophy of "Tri Hita Karana," or "Three Ways to Happiness," which she describes as "the harmony or the whole, the trinity of people, nature, and also the spiritual."[17]

Each of the seventeen SDGs, for which Cherie is a major advocate, encompasses an aspect of this trinity, creating what she calls an "SDG Pyramid to Happiness." She shared her understanding of belonging as the undercurrent to all of the SDGs: "Every part of the SDGs—I think it's a right. It's a right not to be hungry, to not be able to have access to something to survive. It's a right to get education. Belonging is the glue to all this."

I take inspiration from Kathy Calvin, Cherie Nursalim, and the foundational work of the SDGs as I reflect on belonging and continue to ask the pivotal question: How do we measure what we value, and how do we build belonging for everyone?

Dr. Sabina Alkire has been a colleague and friend for many years. She is the director of the Oxford Poverty & Human Development Initiative (OPHI). As Sabina and I have discussed, when it comes to belonging, it's difficult to pin down the data. "One of the challenges for thinking about belonging is that it seems to mean quite different things to different people," she said in a recent conversation.[18]

"To an introvert, belonging might mean being loved and cherished by one person. To a monk it might mean being rooted in a community. To a hermit it might mean being in a cell. And to an extrovert it might mean being liked by 2,000 people on Facebook." She went on, "So, one of the challenges for writing about and measuring social isolation is recognizing that the people's need for belonging also has to do with their personality type. Each person, in a sense, has to arrive at their own definition of what does it mean to belong and what could take that sense of belonging away from me."

Lord Richard Layard, professor emeritus of economics at the London School of Economics, is founder-director of LSE's Centre for Economic Performance and Wellbeing—the latter of which can be understood broadly as "a state in which all aspects of a person's life are good."[19] Layard is also co-editor of the World Happiness Report (WHR). Published annually since 2012, this report assigns a "happiness score" to more than 150 participating countries. Variables that are scored in the report include income, freedom, trust in government, healthy life expectancy, and social support from family.

In discussing the difficulty of building out data sets related to belonging, Layard recently shared with me that we tend to default to measuring that which is easily captured: "We go into a situation where money, which is the easiest thing to measure, becomes the measure of all things."[20]

John Helliwell, professor emeritus of economics at the University of British Columbia, professor emeritus of the Canadian Institute for Advanced Research (CIFAR) Programme on Social Interactions, Identity, and Well-Being, and co-editor of the WHR with Layard, offered this reflection on the nuance of measuring belonging: "Belonging, almost like happiness or fear or pain, is something that you don't have to ascribe a meaning to, its meaning is intrinsic. So, if you say you feel you belong somewhere, it's a feeling as primal as being in pain or feeling happy. It doesn't have to have a description, it simply is."[21]

Indeed, while we know that they exist, and that they are vitally important, can social connectedness and belonging be measured?

Over the course of 2020 and 2021, I teamed up with the Social Progress Imperative, a global nonprofit organization, based in Washington, DC, which amalgamates data on the social and environmental health of societies. The organization created an index—the Social Progress Index (SPI)—which digresses from other indices that overwhelmingly focus on the economic development of countries and engage other measures of progress only superficially. Michael Green, CEO of Social Progress Imperative, explained the rationale this way: "Fundamentally, we know that social progress outcomes are not explained by economic variables alone. There is some mix of institutions, culture, relationships that is driving these outcomes."[22] And so, the SPI instead emphasizes tracking the social outcomes of economically rising and developing countries. However, while the SPI is outcome oriented, it keeps in mind that these outcomes are driven by social structures and economic factors. Rather than looking at what was invested in a community or country, the SPI measures what actual change has come out of it.

Our goal with this collaboration was to understand how "belonging" might be measured within the SPI. We focused on integrating the 4Ps framework that I introduced earlier—people, place, power, and purpose.

The SPI measures twelve components of social progress—carefully selected outcome-oriented measures, categorized into three dimensions of four components each: Basic Human Needs, encompassing components of nutrition and medical care, water and sanitation, shelter, and personal safety; Foundations of Wellbeing, comprising access to knowledge, access to information and communications, health and wellness, and environmental quality; and Opportunity, comprising personal rights, personal freedom and choice, inclusiveness, and access to advanced education. All of these components might conceptually be seen as enablers of belonging, especially as they are underpinned by the ideal of inclusive societies. For our collaboration, these twelve components were regrouped into three main categories of Enablers of Belonging, as well as a separate category of Outcomes (which represent the results of "being enabled to belong"). The SPI examined these enabling conditions, then measured whether the outcomes of these enablers were met.

Our research showed that communicating with others, having a healthy and safe neighborhood, and being surrounded by positive physical environmental conditions can help individuals achieve a greater sense of belonging. It also revealed a specific tension: While increasing connectedness may present opportunities for people to meet wider communities, it does not guarantee or mitigate feelings of loneliness.

Another key finding of this collaboration was the link discovered between Enablers of Belonging and Outcomes. When looking at the Enablers of Belonging framework, which measures different areas in which countries can enable belonging for their citizens, we noted that they are strongly related to the Outcomes dimension. Not only that, but our research found that countries with higher Belonging scores tend to have higher Outcomes scores and vice versa: Countries with lower Belonging framework scores tend to have lower Outcomes scores.

We also found that the relationship between "Social progress" and "Belonging" is complex. Societies can progress, for example, by improving access to communication and information for citizens, while the sense of isolation and loneliness that people feel can increase. The increasingly common image of a group of friends or family members gathered together, each one focusing on their phones instead of connecting with one another, epitomizes the friction we so often experience in an age of hyperconnectedness and simultaneous isolation. The mutable nature of belonging is illustrated by the fact that many people, Millennials and Gen Z especially, might find a sense of belonging through social media, on the very same platforms and devices that cause others to experience loneliness and social isolation.

Experiencing a sense of belonging results in better outcomes for people. Though the data-collection stage is still in its infancy relative to more traditional "progress" metrics and frameworks, we are committed to figuring out the best way to measure belonging for individuals and their communities. This partnership with SPI to develop a Belonging Framework was an important first step.

THE PRACTICE OF BELONGING: ŌGIMI VILLAGE

WHAT IF WE COULD CONSCIOUSLY build the underlying value of belonging into the structures of daily lives, our community life, our systems of care and social services, even into our economies, governments, and international institutions? What would it look like to live in a community that's built on a deep vision of wholeness?

In the summer of 2018, I visited the Japanese prefecture of Okinawa, one of the world's "Blue Zones," regions where people live exceptionally long and healthy lives, and where diseases like heart disease, cancer, and diabetes are quite rare.[23] My research brought me to Ōgimi Village, a collection of small rural hamlets on the Northern Okinawa Main Island that are nestled among richly wooded peaks and bright green rice fields with an almost ever-present ocean breeze. Ōgimi is also known as the "village of longevity."[24] However, what I came to see wasn't just about longevity. It was about belonging. I wanted to understand how older people there experienced belonging in the community. I knew from what I'd heard and read that older people in Ōgimi had a strong sense of connectedness, rootedness in the natural world, self-reliance, and ongoing life purpose.

In Ōgimi, I found a modern community that thrives by reflecting the patterns of interconnectedness that abound in nature. Surrounded by a national park and governed by strong rules against widespread development, the community is incredibly committed to environmental preservation. People largely prize local sustainable agriculture and praise what they call *Bunagaya*—the spirit of pristine wilderness. The location of Ōgimi in a protected nature reserve helps to safeguard belonging through connection to place.

The residents of Ōgimi showed such a strong commitment to the stewardship of cultural lineage, of the traditional arts and practices of a specific place. Whether it's *Eisa*, the local folk dance, or playing the *sanshin*, a traditional stringed instrument, parents in the community pass local art forms down to their children as part of a kind of line of succession, starting at a young age. Ōgimi is the modern home of *Bashofu*, a renowned practice of ornate banana leaf textile weaving, once common across Japan. I saw centuries of shared tradition and human generations in these intricate tapestries.

I noticed in this village made up of small hamlets located at the southernmost tip of Japan a special appreciation of the little joys in life. Almost everywhere I went, people talked to me about a sour green citrus fruit called shequasar, rich in antioxidants, harvested in the early fall as the centerpiece of a community harvest festival. The fruit is seen as essential to longevity, and it strikes me as one element in a larger whole that sustains and replenishes the life force and health of the village.

One of my most memorable encounters in Ōgimi was with Sumi-san— a formidable 102-year-old woman with six children, sixteen grandchildren, and thirty great-grandchildren, and a beloved member of her community. When we met, she was getting ready to go and labor in the fields. At age 102. Surprised, I asked her, "Why do you go out and work in the fields every day?"

Sumi-san looked at me as if the answer were obvious, but replied all the same. "Because there's a lot of fields, and they need weeding and watering. I go out there every day to pick the weeds."[25]

More than a century old, her commitment to an intense physical daily work practice astonished me; for Sumi-san, this strength and commitment was entirely unremarkable.

Woven into life in Ōgimi, I noticed, was a deeply ingrained sense of purpose. It's an integral part of the community's culture. Okinawans have a word for it: *ikigai*. It's the idea of "why I wake up in the morning."

On my last day in Ōgimi, I was invited to share a meal with a group of older people, many of whom had known each other their whole lives. I noticed something as we sat there together: The octogenarian and nona-genarian women were almost always holding hands. What was more, they took my hand in theirs as well. We sat together, holding hands, interlinked like the roots of the tree of which Albert Marshall spoke.

For much of our meal, 91-year-old Kikue Okushima and 89-year-old Yuki Nakaima stayed connected in such a caring way. The two women had known each other their whole lives, attending the same school in the same hamlet, never moving away. Both were grandmothers, and both were ambassadors to the residents of their community.

Holding hands that day felt full of meaning on many levels. The women and men whose hands I held had held the hands of each other through shared births and passings, joys and hardships. Their hands had grown strong in the fields and yet were capable of working fine paper into the most intricate origami.

When one travels around the area, poverty is not evident, and there are no displays of conspicuous wealth. A tradition called *moai* is woven throughout social and kinship relations, in which Okinawans form strong kinship bonds through a peer group that they turn to for companionship, advice, social activities, and, if need be, for financial help. The *moai* is an extended circle of belonging that is created by parents when the child is very young. Many people keep their *moai* strong into their later years—much like Kikue and Yuki had. It's a circle to which they always return.

Yoshihisa Shimabukuro, another local octogenarian and former mayor of Ōgimi, told me more about *moai*, describing it as "a structure of associ-ations and groups to guide peoples' activities and create an atmosphere of welcoming, where it's easy for people to feel like they can join in." He con-tinued, "A big part of that is trust, creating an atmosphere where people feel they can trust one another and work together on some shared endeavor."[26]

In the hamlets, there are service days for the elders to get involved in the community in a number of ways—for example, caring for those in need. Shimabukuro describes how, when people don't show up, "we visit them and ask why they didn't come." If they're facing memory challenges or some other difficulty, he says, "we go pick them up and accompany them the next time. We don't think even for a second that it's OK, they don't need to come. No, we make sure to take them with us." What's more, these events are organized *by* the older people *for* the older people of Ōgimi; they are actively creating spaces of belonging for one another.

These are lived values. It's not just about people declaring what their values are, but rather bringing the circles of reciprocity into the basic structures of life. People are connected and embedded in circles of belonging.

I saw in Ōgimi a community of true belonging. As I left, I thought about the incredible commitment it takes to keep our social connections fresh and strong, dedicated to reciprocal caring. I also thought about how rewarding it is when these connections are fostered and maintained. I pondered what it could take to bring these dimensions of connection to people, place, power, and purpose into other societies and communities—including the big urban centers where, steadily, much of the world population increasingly flocks. We can and should take inspiration from cultures around the world for which cultivating wholeness is not the exception but the norm. My visit to Ōgimi affirmed that this state of connection is fundamental to our ability to thrive.

I'm reminded of the longitudinal Harvard Grant Study, which followed 268 Harvard-educated men beginning in the 1940s and spanning their entire lives. Robert Waldiger, the fourth director of the study, said in a 2015 talk, "The experience of loneliness turns out to be toxic. People who are more isolated than they want to be from others find that they are less happy, their health declines earlier in midlife, their brain functioning declines sooner and they live shorter lives than people who are not lonely." He continued, "The clearest message that we get from this 75-year study is this: Good relationships keep us happier and healthier."[27]

I saw this firsthand in Ōgimi. There are many factors that contribute to the long life of the people in the "Blue Zone" of Okinawa. Dan Buettner, author and National Geographic Fellow who popularized the concept of Blue Zones, has identified nine factors, commonly referred to as the "Power 9."[28] Among this list are the diet and exercise factors one would normally associate with good health—regular moderate exercise, moderate caloric intake, and a mostly plant-based diet, including antioxidant-rich foods like the little green citrus fruit beloved in Ōgimi.

And still, some of the Power 9 are clearly and directly linked to belonging—things like deeply-rooted and long-held social connections, the presence of and commitment to loved ones, and having a sense of purpose. This lines up with what I witnessed in Ōgimi.

During my short visit, I saw all dimensions of belonging at play—strong commitments to people, place, power, and purpose. I saw a community talking, working, and laughing together, prioritizing social connections that have been empirically demonstrated to lower stress.[29], [30], [31] The people in Ōgimi prioritize engagement in family life, in spiritual practice, and social activities that reinforce these bonds. Over the past decade, several major studies from researchers in psychology, neuroscience, and medicine have found loneliness to be associated with increased risks of depression, anxiety, and even early death—attributable to associated health risks including coronary heart disease, high blood pressure, stroke, and dementia.[32] Scholars have also found strong associations between personal perceptions of loneliness and lower-quality sleep, weaker immune system function, impulsive behavior, and impaired decision-making and judgment.[33] Other recent—and timely—research shows that social isolation could lead to reduced expression of genes that are responsible for immune response to viruses.[34]

Albert Marshall underscores that real connection in community is about taking care of each other, showing up for each other, creating the conditions in which we can live in truth and show up as whole people. Of course, Sumi-san—hard at work in the fields at age 102, laughing, being in reciprocal relationship with the natural world and her friends—doesn't need scientific studies to explain the importance of community, rootedness, the sense of agency, and the experience of shared meaning.

Scientific research has played a vital role in examining causal relationships among a variety of factors affecting human psychological, neurological, and physical health, and continues to be important in understanding these issues. When Albert told me of the roots of the trees "holding hands, supporting each other"—and how this served as the foundation for tens of thousands of years of cultural and ecological continuity in his people's way of life—he was passing along a teaching about the importance of interconnectedness.

WHAT I FELT THAT DAY under the Sitka spruce tree in Great Bear Rainforest—in the presence of my sister, held by the roots of the tree, experiencing union with all that exists—is the same interconnectedness I recognized on a structural level in Ōgimi. It's laid bare in the SPI research. It's the wholeness we find in Two-Eyed Seeing. This wholeness isn't always easy to sense or experience in a world that's seemingly defined by fragmentation. Yet these shared experiences reflect states of wholeness that are possible for us to experience as individuals and communities. We can feel our place in the great scheme of things. As Albert attests, we must.

William Blake asks us to return to a sense that "every thing that lives is Holy." He invokes the divine body in every being, which is infinite and eternal. "It includes the whole cosmos," says Kathleen Raine. "It is a totality of which every particle is, as it were, one way into that totality, so that each of us possess this totality."[35] Ultimately, we all seek to return to and experience this, to know it and embody it in ourselves—and, if our societies determine that they value this depth of belonging, in our societies as well.

Franciscan priest Richard Rohr is the founder and dean of the Living School for Action and Contemplation in Albuquerque, New Mexico. As we grow toward this deeper knowing, he says, "we discover that we are not as separate as we thought we were. Separation from God, self, and others was a deep and tragic illusion."[36] For millennia, the wisdom traditions of the world have given individuals and communities a place and a context to experience this belonging. Religion, myth, and storytelling have offered people across cultures a roadmap for reconnection to the deeper pattern of the cosmos, reinforcing our belonging to community, to the place we live, and to the greater universe. These methods and traditions have recognized the tendency of humans toward estrangement, and have offered a way back home.

If this is the case, how did so many of us get to where we are today, desperately lonely, and dangerously isolated?

CHAPTER TWO

UNDERSTANDING
SOCIAL ISOLATION

THERE'S A SOFTNESS to the word "belonging" that belies its larger implications for our human family. Our ability to solve the most difficult challenges in today's world is related not only to the structural problems that underlie conflict, for instance, but also to the more subjective elements of human experience: whether people feel togetherness, a sense of shared mission, a place in the larger whole. These qualitative elements can determine our quantitative outcomes—whether we succeed or fail in the economy, public health, or achieving environmental sustainability. Our collective sense of belonging will determine whether we have the resourcefulness and resilience we need to flourish as a species.

My understanding of these issues has evolved over time. What began as a study of social isolation became a deeper exploration of social connectedness and ultimately, the larger framework of belonging. The conventional wisdom today is that we are living in the age of connectivity. In some ways, we are more connected than ever. We can send a message through virtual channels to people on the other side of the planet instantaneously. The proliferation of online social networks has meant we can have thousands of virtual "friends" who can know whatever we would like to share with the Internet. We can join online forums concerned with an apparently limitless number of interests and access information about almost anything.

Yet many of us are facing a deficit in belonging, increasingly isolated from deep relationships with other people, from the places we inhabit and the natural world around us, from effective power and decision-making structures, and from a sense of shared meaning and purpose. Even before global pandemics elevated issues of social disconnection in societies across the globe, the basic reality of our situation had already been clear: A deep fragmentation is at work in our world that leaves many adrift. We are living in an age of isolation, and the current status quo of inaction will only send us deeper into the abyss.

IF BELONGING IS CENTRAL to who we are, and key to our enjoyment of our time on this earth, then why do we so often experience its opposite—loneliness and social isolation? These are different but not mutually exclusive concepts. Let's start with loneliness.

Loneliness is a subjective, individual experience. It is a deeply felt, personal aspect of social isolation. It's also a relatively recent phenomenon. The British historian Fay Bound Alberti suggests that the term "loneliness" initially appeared in the English language around 1800. Prior to that, the closest word approximate was "oneliness," or the state of being alone, which wasn't associated with emotional distress.[1] Of course, it's not that people weren't at times lonely. As American historian Jill Lepore summarizes, there existed widows and widowers, outcasts, people in extreme poverty, and those suffering illness prior to the nineteenth century. Certainly they were lonely. It's rather that it just wasn't possible to survive in those times without living closely among other people. Aptly described by Lepore, loneliness used to be, largely, a passing experience.[2]

It was only with the onset of industrialization, the growth of the consumer economy, the declining influence of religion, and the popularity of evolutionary biology—which all served to elevate the individual as the primary locus of value and orientation rather than a society where everyone had a place—that loneliness began to be recognized as a widespread and chronic condition among individuals. "Many of the divisions and hierarchies that have developed since the eighteenth century—between self and world, individual and community, public and private," she observes, "have been naturalized through the politics and philosophy of individualism."[3] As Alberti claims, loneliness developed as a result of "the commercialization of the individual, at the expense of the social" that "was dominant from the late 18th century in Britain," a force which continues to drive the "modern social individualism" we see on social media today.[4]

In 1959, psychiatrists began talking about loneliness, with German analyst Frieda Fromm-Reichmann stating, "Loneliness seems to be such a painful, frightening experience that people will do practically everything to avoid it." She continued, "The longing for interpersonal intimacy stays with every human being from infancy through life," she wrote, "and there is no human being who is not threatened by its loss."[5] In the 1980s, medical literature on loneliness began to emerge.[6]

In their widely used social psychology framework on loneliness, social psychologists Daniel Perlman and Letitia Anne Peplau define loneliness as "a subjective, unwelcome feeling of lack or loss of companionship. It happens when we have a mismatch between the quantity and quality of social relationships that we have, and those that we want." This discrepancy leads to negative feelings or distress of feeling socially isolated even when among family or friends.[7]

Being alone may trigger feelings of loneliness, one may also feel extremely lonely while surrounded by people, and those with few social contacts may not feel lonely at all—indeed, many people enjoy their solitude and value it. This apparent contradiction highlights that the crucial issue for the feeling of loneliness is not the number of social connections one person has but, rather, how meaningful they are.

Loneliness is a significant component of the broader issue of social isolation, which is a structural, relational phenomenon. Social isolation isn't only about our individual lives but, rather, entire groups of people and the systems that fail to support them. Social isolation occurs when wider socioeconomic, political, and cultural structures and processes create conditions in which people, including distinct groups of people, are isolated from systems that support belonging and inclusion. The result is often poverty, inequality, and discrimination. Indeed, when we apply the four dimensions of belonging—people, place, power, and purpose—to social isolation, we can see that this phenomenon is not merely "disconnection from other people." Yes, social isolation can be the result of a lack of connection to people, but we must also include the lack of connection to the other three dimensions of belonging. That's because with social isolation, we are really talking about the obstacles that impede us from experiencing things like meaningful relationships, exercising agency, engaging in authentic expression, and having a stake in collective outcomes. These obstacles can affect individuals and entire communities.

Contrary to the new phenomenon of loneliness, social isolation is a deep, insidious part of our history, woven into the very fabric of our societies. Consider ostracism and the practice of shunning, which is still employed by various religious and cultural groups to this day to enforce social order and maintain social cohesion. Or consider the extreme example of slavery, which, for various cultures around the world, had long served as a legitimized form of extreme social isolation and dehumanization. This type of social isolation still exists today when we look at pernicious examples like labor exploitation and sex trafficking. Historical and cultural sociologist Orlando Patterson tells us: "The degradation of slavery defines the slave as the ultimate 'other' in the eyes of non-slaves—someone beyond the pale, base and irredeemably dishonored—which, in turn, enhances her isolation."[8]

In the broader context of building a world where everyone belongs, we must address the growing threat of loneliness and social isolation. These are pressing challenges with serious health and societal impacts—on individual, community, and systemic levels.

LACK OF CONSISTENT and up-to-date metrics across countries makes it hard to paint a full picture of the prevalence of social isolation. However, even without a globally unified approach on this front, there are a few deductions we can confidently make: around the world, young adults[9],[10],[11] and older adults[12],[13],[14],[15] are consistently among the most socially isolated. Around the world, as many as 50 percent of people over the age of sixty are at risk of experiencing social isolation.[16]

Loneliness is also more prevalent among both younger and older people. For example, 11.3 percent of children aged ten to fifteen in Britain are often lonely, and nearly 10 percent of sixteen- to twenty-four-year-olds in the UK reported feeling "always or often lonely" according to official figures on child loneliness.[17] In every European country, at least 10 percent of people who are over the age of sixty report feeling frequently lonely.[18] Globally, it's estimated that approximately one-third of people over the age of sixty will experience loneliness.[19]

However, social isolation and the loneliness that often accompanies it aren't just plights suffered by the young and the old. From the 1960s onward, between 30 and 50 percent of people across multiple studies and cultures said that they felt lonely, and between 10 and 30 percent said they felt "intensely lonely."[20] Today, at any given time, roughly 20 percent of people in the US feel sufficiently isolated for it to be a major source of unhappiness in their lives.[21] In Europe, 18 percent of people can be classified as "socially isolated," with 7 percent feeling frequently lonely.[22] Canada has a loneliness rate of 20 percent.[23]

In Japan, which is known for the culturally-specific phenomenon of extreme social recluses known as *hikikomori*—which are most often young people—10 percent of the entire population report feeling often or always lonely.[24] Still, given the reliance on self-reporting, some experts think that this number could be higher.[25] Collecting data on loneliness and social isolation in Japan and elsewhere is difficult for exactly this reason—people may not want to admit to these feelings.[26]

AS OUR SYSTEMS AND STRUCTURES fail us, as we fail to maintain connection to the four dimensions of belonging, and as barriers hold us back from building that belonging that we so desperately need, we're seeing real impacts on our health and on the world around us.

While many of us instinctively appreciate that being connected to other people is one of our most basic human needs, the evidence shows that when we lack those meaningful connections with others, the consequences can be seen all the way down to the molecular level. Our cells inflame. Our hormones misfire. Our immune systems weaken.[27]

Neurological studies have confirmed that our brains experience social pain in a way that is similar to the experience of physical pain.[28] Research has established that chronic feelings of internal social isolation trigger a series of physiological events that have an impact on health comparable to the effect of high blood pressure, lack of exercise, and obesity, and can actually accelerate the aging process.[29] Further, Julianne Holt-Lunstad, professor of psychology and neurology at Brigham Young University, has found that the health effects of loneliness are the equivalent of smoking fifteen cigarettes a day.[30]

Dr. Holt-Lunstad analyzed 148 academic studies and found that the lack of meaningful social contact with other people is a predictor of all causes of death. Her research found that "people with a solid group of friends are fifty percent more likely to survive at any given time than those without one." She observed that one contributing factor to this trend may be that people who are socially isolated have weaker immune systems and can have exaggerated stress responses.[31]

Dr. Dhruv Khullar, a medical researcher at the Weill Cornell Medical College has found evidence that loneliness creates abnormal immune responses and accelerated cognitive decline. Dr. Vivek Murthy, the US Surgeon General, has argued that loneliness is associated with a greater risk of cardiovascular disease, dementia, depression, and anxiety.[32]

The consequences of social isolation and loneliness can be fatal. Recent research tells us that social isolation increases chance of mortality by almost 30 percent; similarly, loneliness increases chance of mortality by 26 percent.[33] A recent study attributes 162,000 deaths per year in the United States to loneliness—higher than the number of deaths caused by lung cancer or stroke in the US.[34] Social isolation is as dangerous for older adults as smoking and obesity, and those who are socially isolated often delay seeking care for medical ailments, which can sadly lead to premature or avoidable death.[35]

Of note, a 2018 meta-analysis shows that the connection between loneliness and all-cause mortality is slightly higher in men than in women.[36] There are a few theories as to why this might be the case. Among them is the fact that men may be less likely than women to admit to feeling lonely for cultural reasons.[37] Other researchers point out a tendency of men to have generally more negative attitudes than women when it comes to seeking care.[38] And things like alcohol and tobacco use are more prevalent in men than women—unhealthy habits associated with loneliness.[39]

The impacts of loneliness and social isolation on our physical and mental health are deeply interconnected. Loneliness increases the risk of depression, and depression increases the risk of loneliness.[40] In 2015, researchers from the Oregon Health & Science University found that people who have face-to-face social contact only "every few months or less" had nearly double the risk of depression when compared to people who meet with friends or relatives at least three times per week.[41]

In a recent conversation, Holt-Lunstad emphasized to me how critical belonging and social connectedness are to our very survival, and the devastating impacts of their absence. "Fundamental is the fact that humans are social species, and that we need others to survive. In essence, our brains have adapted to expect others and the proximity of others," she shared. "Throughout human history, being outside the group is very dangerous and threatening, whereas being part of the group provides a sense of safety. When we don't have safety, and we have cues of threats, we need to be constantly vigilant of those threats. Ultimately, this is reflected in our biology, which in turn influences our mental health, our physical health, our cognitive health. It's taxing on us when we have to be constantly vigilant to these threats."[42]

Our young people are particularly vulnerable. Recent studies show that children who have been separated from their parents for long periods of time, such as in the case of deportation, have lasting emotional trauma and are at increased risk of anxiety and depression.[43] For youth between the ages of fifteen and nineteen worldwide, depression is the fourth leading cause of illness and disability,[44] and in Canada, mental health issues will affect up to 20 percent of young people before they turn nineteen.[45]

The deep structural causes of social isolation mean that it can impact our health in incredibly nuanced ways. Psychiatrist Murali Doraiswamy at Duke University recently explained to me how a person's sense of belonging, or lack thereof, markedly impacts how they access health services. "If you don't feel like you belong to your community, or you have a lack of trust in your community, you will delay seeing a doctor for preventative care, and will likely end up in the emergency room, at which point it may be too late," he says.[46]

Dr. Doraiswamy also pointed out to me the differential treatment of patients when doctors believe a patient does not belong to his or her community. The stark disparities in health outcomes of minority groups in the United States reveal how these conscious or unconscious biases on the part of doctors can perpetuate social isolation.[47] African Americans, for instance, have a mortality rate 1.6 times that of white Americans, and Black children with asthma, for example, are 2.5 times more likely to end up hospitalized than white children with the same condition.[48]

Social isolation lies on the opposite end of the social continuum to belonging, impeding our ability to form meaningful connections to people, place, power, and purpose. Today, the ways in which we work and socialize tend to distance us from one another and our communities—this has only been exacerbated by the COVID-19 pandemic. Climate change, deforestation, sinking islands, and the decimation of soil and air quality create environmental refugees and forced displacement of people from lands, further eroding human connections to place. Inequality runs rampant, with countless categories of people denied access to power and agency over their lives—often along racialized or gendered lines. And we see denial of purpose when, for example, those with physical, intellectual, or psychosocial disabilities are institutionalized, fulfilling external assumptions that some people should be denied the experience of being a part of a common system of meaning.

The current state of denied belonging is not a problem unique to the twenty-first century; as we'll see in the following chapters, the fractures from our inherent wholeness have been metastasizing for a very long time. As our human family grows, systemic failures to uphold our responsibilities to one another and to our earth have grown more serious. These resulting problems, left unattended, have grown in scale and scope. Today's denials of belonging can be traced back to social isolation, and the systems that fail to support our human species. We are all interconnected to a greater whole, but we haven't created our societies with that fact in mind. The structural hurdles that we have created instead have led to a perfect storm of disconnection and a deprivation of belonging.

THESE DATA AND ISSUES are just the tip of the iceberg. Dr. Khullar believes there's a lot we don't yet know about the health impacts of loneliness because it's intrinsically difficult to study. He says, "Loneliness is an especially tricky problem, because accepting and declaring our loneliness carries profound stigma."[49]

The late John Cacioppo—a University of Chicago professor, author of the seminal book *Loneliness*, and a pioneer in the field of social neuroscience—once spoke of being embarrassed holding his own book in plain view while on an airplane.[50] Most of us don't want to appear lonely, whether in a small group or in a crowd. As Dr. Khullar remarks, "Admitting we're lonely can feel as if we're admitting we've failed in life's most fundamental domains: belonging, love, attachment. It attacks our basic instincts to save face and makes it hard to ask for help."[51]

The broader concept of social isolation is systemic and intersectional, and equally difficult to measure. However, we're making progress. In my research with the Oxford Poverty & Human Development Initiative (OPHI), we considered social isolation within the frame of the global Multidimensional Poverty Index (MPI)—an international measure developed jointly by OPHI and the United Nations Development Programme (UNDP) in 2010, based on OPHI's 2007 MPI framework, which covers more than 100 countries and expands the understanding of poverty beyond income to encompass other dimensions that constitute poverty.

In our work, we defined social isolation as the "inadequate quality and quantity of social relations with other people at the different levels where human interaction takes place, at the individual, group, and community levels, and within the wider social environment."[52] I further conveyed this definition of social isolation intuitively as an "experience in which a person feels like they are sitting alone at the bottom of the well: they feel as if no one knows they are suffering; that no one cares; if they call out they cannot be heard; they are invisible and outside all circles of concern."[53]

SOCIAL ISOLATION AND POVERTY

WHAT HAPPENS when we don't have enough opportunities to form meaningful social connection through face-to-face relationships? Dr. Amartya Sen—Indian-born Nobel Laureate in Economics, and professor of economics and philosophy at Harvard University—argues that our social connections are foundational for almost everything in our lives. Besides being of intrinsic value, social connections are also instrumentally important—affecting not just our social and emotional well-being, but also our opportunities to find employment and have a safety net. Sen has written about how social exclusion results in denial of a broad range of human capabilities that restrict our ability to thrive in the world.

Sen departs from traditional notions of economic development and progress to focus on developing the abilities of the entire individual, to look at them as whole people, and what they are capable of doing and being. As Sen rightly points out, however, our capacity for human flourishing, and our ability to exercise agency and enjoy real freedom, can happen only when we have the right social, economic, and political environments in place.[54]

Similarly, the celebrated University of Chicago philosopher Martha Nussbaum describes human connection—that which sits on the opposite end of the spectrum from social isolation—as one of the core human capabilities that are essential to human thriving. She writes that this capability of "affiliation" with other people "pervades the other capabilities."[55]

Nussbaum explains, "It pervades the other capabilities in the sense that when they are made available in a way that respects human dignity, affiliation is part of them—the person is respected as a social being." She goes on, "Making employment options available without considering workplace relationships would not be adequate; nor would forms of health care that neglect, for example, people's needs to protect zones of intimacy by provisions for personal privacy. Affiliation organizes the capabilities in that deliberation about public policy is a social matter in which relationships of many kinds (familial, friendly, group-based, political) all play a structuring role."[56] Nussbaum recognizes social injustice and inequality as a barrier to human thriving, arguing that the inability of people to develop and mobilize their capabilities is due to systemic barriers such as discrimination.

Barriers like this limit our ability to have meaningful social connection and exercise agency, which is a common occurrence in the experiences of both social isolation and poverty. In fact, social isolation and poverty are closely related.

Most countries in the world define poverty by income. In the United States in 2020, for a single adult under the age of sixty-five, the "official poverty definition" was an income before taxes of $13,465. For a family of four with two children under the age of eighteen, it was $26,246.[57] Yet people experiencing poverty often define their poverty much more broadly. "Multidimensional" poverty, for example, is defined not only by a lack of material means or resources to make ends meet, but also by other deprivations such as health, education, political enfranchisement, adequate housing, bodily and physical safety, and environmental health.[58] Yet even this definition falls short in capturing people's lived experience of poverty, including its more subjective, "softer" aspects related to belonging.

At OPHI, we've called attention to the "missing dimensions" of poverty that relate to belonging—including violence,[59] disempowerment,[60] informal work,[61] lack of safety at work, and deprivations of social connectedness comprising isolation, shame, and humiliation.[62]

In much of my work over the last two decades, I have found that conventional understandings of poverty often don't account for the impacts of social isolation and social connectedness on people's lived experience of poverty. For example, in 2013, I did field research in Mozambique and South Africa with OPHI. Listening to people there, we learned that social connectedness plays a critical role in their survival, and that social isolation, shame, and humiliation resulted in deprivations of this crucial social connectedness, ultimately worsening their experiences of poverty.

Being poor is one of the experiences that can make people feel like they are "less than," and are often treated as such: less significant, less valued—indeed, less human. Nobody should ever be made to feel that they are less than any individual or any group. Whether they are excluded by others, or feel compelled to withdraw on their own, the result is a downward spiral that is difficult to reverse. Ambassador Luis Gallegos Chiriboga, Ecuador's former minister of foreign affairs and human mobility, recently shared his thoughts with me on the linkages between barriers to belonging and poverty. "Many groups lack the sense of belonging that should be translated into the proper social safety nets and programs to protect them." As he observed, many people have been left behind.[63]

Consider the World Bank's groundbreaking 1999–2000 study *Voices of the Poor*, surveying over 60,000 poor people in sixty countries across the world, or the dimensions of poverty identified by Amartya Sen and fellow Nobel Laureates Joseph Stiglitz and Jean-Paul Fitoussi. In these and other contexts, one finding has come up over and over again: People name isolation as a component of their poverty. And they name social connectivity as part of their well-being.

Voices of the Poor helped make this clear. As one participant put it, "Poverty is pain; it feels like a disease. It attacks a person not only materially but also morally. It eats away one's dignity and drives one into total despair."[64] *Voices of the Poor* reminded me that it is essential to ask people living in poverty *how they* define their poverty, rather than taking the easy approach of relying on our preconceived, prescriptive notions of what poverty looks like.

Again and again, people's accounts of their lives and their perspectives speak to how deeply they value social connection. In my research, respondents ranked relationships with others as among the five most important aspects in their lives—alongside food, shelter, education, and work. For many people, however, living in poverty makes social connection more difficult to develop and retain. As one woman responded in the research I carried out with OPHI in Mozambique, "Poverty means being lonely, and not being able to get other things because you are lonely."[65] She felt isolated because she was poor, and poor because she was isolated.

In South Africa in the same study, one person told our research team, "Most of the people who get HIV are the most poor people, so we tend to say they were using their bodies to get food and money, so the stigma is there. That's why some people are not able to tell anyone they have HIV, and they end up dying because they can't ask for help because they are ashamed."[66]

Another respondent explained, "Even if you are hungry, you can't go to them to ask for food or money, because they are judging you that you are poor. They won't give you money, so it's better that you isolate yourself."[67]

Hearing these stories helps make clear why breaking the cycle of poverty isn't as simple as building a health clinic or providing free food or cash assistance. Assistance programs are prone to failure if humiliation and stigma persist or are caused by that assistance, and social bonds are frayed. Asking questions about what people value in their lives is essential to ensuring our dignity and our capacity for a full spectrum of requirements for human survival and thriving are made possible. And social connectedness and belonging are central to these full-spectrum requirements.

SOCIAL ISOLATION AND THE
LEGACY OF COLONIZATION

WE CAN SEE the intersecting impacts of social isolation and poverty—notably through colonization—in the case of tuberculosis in the Canadian Arctic, which is the land of the Inuit and the Inuvialuit, among other Indigenous Nations.

Tuberculosis (TB), an infectious disease that primarily affects the lungs, is what I consider a disease of isolation—one that either results from or contributes to social isolation. This type of disease can result from isolation in the way that poverty, inequality, and discrimination can prevent an individual or entire community from accessing clean drinking water, clean air, or affordable medicines. Likewise, certain diseases can contribute to isolation through stigma and ostracization, in cases such as TB, leprosy, or HIV/AIDS in the early decades of its existence.

The relative invisibility of the story of TB in northern Canadian history is a sad reflection of what the country values—southern Canada over northern Canada; non-Indigenous over Indigenous—and it speaks to the ways in which disparities in power have affected the health of Indigenous peoples of the Arctic for generations.

While tuberculosis is a curable and preventable disease, it continues to affect more than 10 million people worldwide and results in more than 1.4 million deaths per year.[68] The majority of these deaths occur in low-resource regions of countries like India, China, Pakistan, South Africa, Nigeria, and Bangladesh.[69] Canada, however, one of the wealthiest nations in the world, is an unlikely home for one of the epicenters of the global tuberculosis crisis.

In the northern territory of Nunavut, where 84 percent of the population is Inuit, more than one in one hundred infants (under one year of age) have TB.[70] By comparison, the rate in the rest of Canada is three infants per 100,000.[71] The distinction is not just geographic. The rate of TB among Inuit is approximately 300 times higher than the rate of TB among non-Indigenous Canadians.[72] As Natan Obed, president of the Inuit Tapiriit Kanatami (ITK), a federal organization that advocates for fifty-three Inuit communities, recently said, "There's no other way of putting it. It is a public health crisis and one that's sixty years in the making."[73]

The historical treatment of TB in the Arctic has been punitive in nature, prioritizing containment and control, and has been characterized by a top-down, unequal, and undemocratic colonial model imposed onto the Inuit that persists today. These systems of governance eroded Indigenous communities' connection to power in important ways that affect a broad range of measures of health.

An often-cited 1994 study provides a history of the development of the tuberculosis epidemic in the Arctic. Prior to the arrival of the European traders and explorers, TB was largely unknown to the Inuit. In the 1950s and '60s, when the first big epidemic hit the territory, the Inuit had little biological resistance to the disease and no medical services with which to fight it. By the 1950s, at least one-third of the Inuit population was infected with TB. During this time, thousands of Inuit were taken from their families and their communities and were sent south for treatment to a sanatorium in Hamilton, Ontario. On average, these Inuit were quarantined in the sanatorium for two and a half years, and by 1956, one in seven Inuit was in a sanatorium in southern Canada. Many died there or were never seen again, their families never notified.[74] This deprivation of belonging and disconnection to power and agency subsequently resulted in a disconnection to people—notably, the Inuit's ability and right to nourish relationships with people in their own communities, an inherent need of human beings everywhere.

It's no wonder that a legacy of fear and stigma around TB has persisted to today, and that the trauma of that time has been passed down through generations. Stephen Lewis, co-founder of the international advocacy organization AIDS-Free World, spoke of these enduring consequences of Canadian TB policy in the Arctic after visiting northern communities affected by TB. "To listen to the Elders was to understand how the haunting horror of those days lives on," he said. "The continuing memory of the mindless destruction of the family, the language, the culture, to add to the difficulty of dealing with TB in the present. It's like a level of stigma that can never be eradicated."[75]

The stigma that TB is a "dirty" disease—one that requires people to be sent away, that it comes from being poor—results in significant social isolation.

Patients with TB in Nunavut today are subject to quarantine in their homes for two weeks, despite medical evidence that they are no longer contagious after two to three days of treatment. The stigma, fear, and mistrust in the colonial health system that has been imposed in the North also means that TB is often diagnosed too late or not at all; many have faced discrimination in the healthcare system and, consequently, are reticent to say they have it.[76] Indigenous people today rarely see themselves represented in the healthcare system, and also face discrimination and racism in these structures, resulting in distrust of the systems that are supposed to serve and care for them. This is true for many marginalized communities around the world.

Tuberculosis is a communicable disease. The irony that TB can be both a "disease of isolation" on the one hand, and a "disease of overcrowding" on the other, isn't lost on me. In fact, it shows how complex this issue of social isolation can be—how people can live in close physical proximity yet be socially isolated, cut off from belonging, their community, their systems of governance, their language and culture, and their own pathways to healing.

There are other intersecting structural factors that affect the nature of TB in the Arctic as well. Fifty-two percent of Inuit over the age of twenty-five living in Inuit Nunangat (homeland of the Inuit in Canada) are food insecure.[77] These are issues of power that also affect the ability of the Inuit to be resilient in the face of communicable epidemics like TB, and which must be addressed in order to ultimately eliminate this treatable disease.[78] Addressing these elements of power and people cannot come without a fundamental questioning of what it is we value, as nations and communities.

"NOT WAVING BUT DROWNING"

I was much further out than you thought
And not waving but drowning.

—STEVIE SMITH[79]

THE FACTORS THAT CONTRIBUTE to social isolation are wide-ranging and include something as commonplace and seemingly harmless as social media and digital technology. Yet these technologies are in fact part of the changing face of social connection and isolation. Recent studies have confirmed what many of us may feel intuitively when we use social media: Often, it creates connectivity, but not necessarily connection. Although there are real advantages of social media and our ability to reach others across the world in a matter of seconds, on the whole, these platforms have failed to deepen our connections to ourselves, to the people around us, and to the places we inhabit.

Since 1975, the University of Michigan's Monitoring the Future survey has asked high-school-age teenagers about both their leisure-time activities and their levels of well-being. The results of the most recent studies, from the age of the smartphone, are concerning. Jean Twenge, a psychologist at San Diego State University who led one of these studies, has cautioned that "the twin rise of the smartphone and social media has caused an earthquake of a magnitude we've not seen in a very long time, if ever." Looking at a range of research metrics, she observes that rates of teen depression and suicide have risen drastically since 2011.[80]

According to Twenge's research, "Teens who spend more time than average on screen activities are more likely to be unhappy, and those who spend more time than average on non-screen activities are more likely to be happy."[81] She contends that just the opposite happens with face-to-face connection: "Those who spend an above-average amount of time with their friends in person are twenty percent less likely to say they're unhappy than those who hang out for a below-average amount of time."[82]

Although many of us may be able to count more people classified as "friends" on social media, this hasn't translated into a deepened connection to people, especially for young people. Social media platforms instead often spawn a mass of weak ties. Excessive online existence has been found to stem the natural development of a social identity and deep, committed relationships.[83] Generation Z and Millennials have been identified as the loneliest generations, in large part due to the heightened presence of social media in the world and their lives.

Indeed, a 2017 study from the University of Pittsburgh's Brain Institute surveying adults between the ages of nineteen and thirty-two found a significant association between increased social media use and increased perceived social isolation.[84] Respondents with the highest levels of social media use were three times more likely to be lonelier than those with the lowest levels of social media use. Social media presents a paradox, according to Cal Newport in *Digital Minimalism*: "Social media makes you feel both connected and lonely, happy and sad," he says. The key issue, he contends, "is that using social media tends to take people away from their real-world socializing that's massively more valuable."[85]

Social media is interfering with healthy social bonds all over the world. Marlene Ogawa is a program director with the Synergos Institute in South Africa. She once shared with me her perception of the impact of technology in the region. In some ways, she said, technology had been a clear plus—for example, cell phones made it much easier for people who had moved to the city to stay in touch with relatives in the village. But, at the same time, some people felt that "because of television, because of telephones, young people are not interacting with the elders the way they used to, and they are not talking to each other anymore."[86]

Marlene recalled to me a story she'd read about a wedding photographer in Mozambique, who had been at a reception where a great-grandfather was giving a beautiful speech, and then she'd looked around and saw that the younger guests were all busy on their phones. It wasn't just that they'd missed the beauty of the story the great-grandfather was telling; it was that they had missed *him* telling it. They'd missed the face-to-face connection—and the intergenerational celebration.

This is not a simple a matter of young people no longer communicating as in the past. Around the world, adults, too, are subject to the seductive powers of "individualizing" technologies from TV to Internet to smartphones for entertainment and productivity. Though an adult psyche may be less vulnerable than the psyche of an adolescent, the absence of quality in-person interaction takes a toll. The trends seem inexorable. It's more difficult to host a block party, join a book club, or simply invite friends over for dinner when there's so much electronic competition for our time and attention.

It's more difficult to do deep, immersive, sustained team building in our workplaces when our colleagues are scattered across global supply chains and our connection to place becomes more disparate and unrooted. As our nervous systems fixate on individualized and tech-mediated modes of being, there's a tendency to avoid face-to-face contact—even within the close quarters of an office setting. Dr. Vivek Murthy, US Surgeon General under both President Obama and President Biden, has written about how modern offices can be highly isolating environments in which people seek "shelter" in their devices.[87] We've been driven into further isolation by the COVID-19 pandemic and the rise of remote work.

The artificial intelligence (AI) revolution may add a new dimension to these challenges, as smart technologies that work at lightning-fast speeds can displace entire professions. To be sure, there is value in computers that can read X-rays from afar, or quickly absorb thousands of pages of published medical research to assist with a diagnosis. But as computer scientist and tech executive Kai-Fu Lee put it in a talk at TED 2018 in Vancouver, "AI is taking away a lot of routine jobs, but routine jobs are not what we are about." Machines cannot substitute for, much less improve upon, the human ability to love, empathize, or be creative. In Lee's words, "We can, we should, and we must, create jobs of compassion."[88] Again, we see dimensions of belonging at play here—human connection to both power and purpose.

There is no easy fix to this rapidly evolving challenge. Indeed, as Julianne Holt-Lunstad recently shared with me, "Digital means of connecting are incredibly complex. Tech is expanding at a very rapid pace. The key here is that this is part of the way in which we interact socially now. They're not going away. Ultimately, what we need is a better understanding of how these can facilitate social connection, and how they can hinder social connection. There is some evidence to suggest both; and we would be foolish to assume that it's all one or the other."[89]

Our answer to the question "What do we value?" must encompass a reassessment of how our design and use of social media and technology impact our ability to belong to ourselves, each other, and the world around us. This is especially true for our youth, who will be leading humanity as climate change alters our environment and our societies profoundly in the years to come. "It's important that the communities these young people are a part of take note and explore solutions," says Dr. Doug Nemecek, chief medical officer for behavioral health at Cigna, which released a large survey on the US loneliness epidemic in January 2020. He concluded, "It's critical that they have spaces where young people can connect face-to-face to form meaningful relationships."[90]

SOCIAL ISOLATION AND COVID-19

WHILE THE COVID-19 PANDEMIC has been a devastating challenge for communities around the world, one of its primary effects has been to exacerbate preexisting inequalities in our systems and societies that have long been in place—inequalities that only further our descent into social isolation. Some researchers have even described the existence of a parallel pandemic—one rooted in loneliness and mental health. Indeed, COVID-19—coupled with society's widespread unwillingness to prioritize connection to people, place, power, and purpose—has pushed social isolation to a breaking point.

While technology has been helpful in keeping people connected to one another in a time of mandated distancing—and while it's proven especially helpful for those in long-term care homes to remain in touch with family during facility lockdowns—it is no substitute for face-to-face connection. In a world where we are increasingly tied to our screens for work and entertainment, what little contact we had with other human beings has been largely prohibited during COVID-19, driving us further into our devices and providing us with only superficial levels of virtual connection. Not only that, but the reliance on technology to, for example, compensate in the delivery of education has been experienced unequally at best.

We've talked a lot as a global community about leaving no one behind in this pandemic, especially when it comes to our children. However, nearly half the world's population doesn't use the Internet.[91] Globally, it's estimated that more than 800 million students don't have a household computer, more than 700 million don't have home Internet access, and more than 50 million don't have 3G/4G mobile network coverage.[92]

The geographic inequalities we face in education are only heightened by this pandemic, with entire communities of young people—usually in the most impoverished regions—unable to participate in remote learning, falling further and further behind in their education and becoming more isolated from their peers with each passing year. Of the 9.7 million children who may not go back to school after dropping out during the pandemic, it's estimated that nearly 40 percent are refugees.[93] Indeed, our children are being hit particularly hard during COVID-19: A 2020 study showed that three-quarters of parents or caregivers in the UK are concerned that their children have been suffering from loneliness following lockdown.[94]

Inadequacies in healthcare systems have resulted in the relegation of older people to conditions of elevated mental and physical health risk and isolation. As of March 2021, more than 1.4 million residents and long-term care employees had contracted COVID-19. Of those, nearly 200,000 had died, which at the time accounted for up to 40 percent of all COVID deaths in the US.[95] In Canada, as of March 2021, 45 percent of long-term care homes had been impacted by COVID-19, with long-term care residents accounting for 67 percent of all pandemic deaths across the country.[96]

Those who have been spared are subject to increasingly harmful confinement and isolation. A recent study in Ontario, Canada, found a dramatic increase in the prescription of psychotropic medications to older people in the province's care homes. The study linked the increase to "the effects of prolonged social isolation during lockdowns," including restrictions on visits from loved ones and suspension of social activities and group dining.[97] The *Washington Post* reported in September 2020 that people with dementia were dying not just from the virus, but also from the physical isolation that was intended to protect them. Patients who had been previously stable were seeing an increase of falls, higher instances of depression, and increased frailty and pulmonary infections.[98]

Existing gender disparities in the workforce have intensified, resulting in disproportionate rates of job loss during the pandemic for women, and women of color more specifically.[99] A few sobering figures from the US alone: 865,000 jobs held by women were lost in September 2020 alone;[100] due to the pandemic, a quarter of women considered reducing their hours or leaving their jobs altogether;[101] and one in five childcare jobs have disappeared, affecting women of color disproportionately.[102]

COVID-19 has also pushed our food systems to a breaking point. Thanks to the pandemic, adult malnourishment could increase by up to 132 million people, and the number of people living in extreme poverty could increase by up to 115 million, according to World Bank estimates.[103] This, of course, also intersects with issues of climate change, which we know is a threat multiplier. While regions are ravaged by extreme weather events like drought, floods, and fires—often subsequently disrupting our food supply and distribution networks—this deadly pandemic is making it harder for international humanitarian groups and national agencies to adequately respond to the climate crisis, which as we know is multifaceted and only getting worse.[104]

The COVID-19 pandemic has exposed the structural and human choices we've made as societies over decades, often revealing underlying values that don't recognize belonging and instead have allowed social isolation to take root. In many cases, values of material progress based on economic growth for some but not all have been prioritized over racial and social equity, environmental sustainability, inclusivity of disadvantaged and marginalized populations, including migrants and refugees, and care for those unlike ourselves.

As we look at some of the factors behind historical and present-day separation and disconnection in our societies, we see that problems of loneliness, social isolation, and belonging are not fundamentally new: They are not just twenty-first-century problems. These challenges have been developing over centuries, through decisions about governance, power, and what we value about the people with whom we coexist. Decisions about the ethics and intent of technology matter, and have exponential impacts decades down the line. So do decisions about who receives healthcare and how, and the kind of healthcare that matters to us. The same holds true for the kinds of economies we create, who those economies serve, and the kinds of opportunities that are opened up to different communities of people.

Are our decisions creating disconnection, or are they creating the potential for unity, equality, and reconnection with our fundamental dignity, self-respect, and care for each other? These questions and their answers, through our actions and our choices, on individual, community, and societal levels, touch every part of our lives and our societies.

How do we reconnect the disconnect? How do we return home to ourselves? How do we restore our species to wholeness after such a prolonged period of social isolation? As we look to the future, we see that for belonging to take hold, we must address all levels and dimensions of belonging: inner and outer, and throughout the interactions between people, power, place, and purpose that feed and sustain us in our human journeys. When we fail in this effort, the consequences can be a matter of life and death.

CHAPTER THREE

THE SHADOW SIDE
OF BELONGING

Things fall apart; the centre cannot hold

—W. B YEATS[1]

IN 1917, amid the upheavals of World War I, the Bolshevik Revolution, and rapid global industrialization, the visionary Bengali poet, philosopher, and composer Rabindranath Tagore offered a warning: "Take away man from his natural surroundings, from the fullness of his communal life, with all its living associations of beauty and love and social obligations, and you will be able to turn him into so many fragments of a machine."[2] More than a century later, it's a warning we still need to heed.

What happens to human beings when the longing for belonging goes unfulfilled?

Rantsope Meshack "Rex" Molefe is an expert in the field of early childhood development, an educator, and a leader in a range of nonprofits in his home country, South Africa. In a recent conversation, Rex made it clear to me why he followed a professional calling focused on helping young people find "the fullness of communal life" that Tagore describes. As a child, Rex didn't have these conditions. He shared with me how he grew up in profound isolation, in an unforgiving home, where he felt little respect, appreciation, or love.

At age eleven, Rex ran away from home. He was soon conscripted as a child soldier, and wound up in military encampments in Tanzania, Zambia, and even as far as Libya. It was a brutal life. It's hard to imagine the atrocities he witnessed—and in which he was forced to be involved.

Yet there was a paradox in Rex's experience. For the first time in his life, as an early adolescent at war, Rex felt he had a home where he was heard, respected, and treated as a real person. He told me: "I found love in the military, because there I was given attention, and there that's where I began to realize who I am." Despite the awful realities, he describes how he was made to feel "appreciated" and "special," and how he found people with whom he "could connect easily."[3]

In a report on the impact of armed conflict on children, Graça Machel states: "Young people often take up arms to gain power and power can act as a very strong motivator in situations where people feel powerless and are otherwise unable to acquire basic resources."[4]

Children make up half of the multidimensionally poor around the world,[5] and the lack of access to education, services, and health, as well as to a loving environment, allows recruiters to prey on structural vulnerabilities. In 2019 alone, nearly 8,000 children were recruited as child soldiers.[6] Rex's story reveals the deep personal dynamics of this global geopolitical tragedy. He draws a direct link between the personal experiences of denied belonging and the horrendous real-world outcomes. "When those things are not there—appreciation, worthiness, love, compassion and so forth—and we are repeatedly being subjected to very tough discipline, it'll drive you to isolation." This, he tells me, "can turn you into a monster."[7]

Rex draws on these personal lessons for his work with young people today. "If we are told that we are useless, that we are not good enough . . . those are the files that get deeply embedded in your subconscious mind," he said to me, reflecting on his early life and the many years it's taken to heal. These conditions don't simply resolve themselves. Denied belonging is liable to metastasize over time. It can turn into hate. It can turn into outright violence.

Rex has witnessed, firsthand, how a deficit of belonging drives people into the most desperate situations imaginable. Looking to the contemporary global landscape, Rex is unequivocal: "The mayhem and social ills that we are confronted with today in the world actually stem from that lack of sense of belonging."

The belonging that Rex experienced as part of brutal militias of child soldiers is no justification for the violence and atrocities that the groups committed. He suffered immensely in that life, and he's grateful to be making amends for it today as a champion for children's rights in South Africa. And, still, the core fact is undeniable. He was drawn to that horrendous situation of life as a child soldier because it meant, for the first time in his life, escaping from isolation, and being connected, respected, and empowered as part of something bigger than himself.

This is the shadow side of belonging. It looks like belonging, it initially perhaps feels like belonging—home, love, family, community. But it is hollow, and ultimately unfulfilling. When we seek belonging in ways that do not acknowledge and honor our innate interconnectedness, we only stray further from wholeness, into the shadowlands.

The manipulation of our need to belong takes many forms, including economic and political inclusion for some through the exclusion of others, violent movements that cultivate meaning through an assault on the "other," or forced assimilation of a minority group. Whole nations have been built on these manipulations. If we fail to understand and address the shadow side, we risk it becoming our only experience of belonging.

WEEDA MEHRAN is both an astute academic and a gifted artist. She grew up in Afghanistan, amid the terror and repression of the Taliban, managing to excel in her studies in a society that systematically denied women and girls opportunities for education. Her mother's bravery made her schooling possible. With support from a community of teachers, Weeda's mother defied the Taliban's laws and taught all three of her daughters at home. She passed this drive for education on to her daughters. As Weeda underscored in a recent conversation: "My resistance against the ruling of the Taliban" pushed her to continue "to the highest level of education."[8]

Weeda became the first Afghan woman to earn a graduate degree from Oxford and then went on to get a PhD from Cambridge. Today, as a researcher and lecturer in politics at the University of Exeter, she takes a multidisciplinary approach to studying propaganda campaigns across a number of militant groups including the Islamic State (IS), the Taliban, and Boko Haram. Her research focuses on conflict resolution and peacebuilding, investigating the dynamics of radicalized online communities and the relationship between online and offline structures, social and political relations, and logic that produces and reinforces extremist ideologies among youth.

While the conventional wisdom is that people join militant extremist groups because of ideological fervor, Dr. Mehran finds evidence that recruitment is often driven by something more commonplace. It's not always the will to create a religious paradise or an ideologically pure political experiment; just as often, it is the drive for acceptance, respect, and shared meaning. It's about reestablishing a connection to people, place, power, and purpose.

A defining factor, Weeda told me, is "socialization." She has found, for example, that university students who describe themselves as isolated, without bonds to close friends or connections to family, are more prone to joining extremist groups. She described to me how recruiters for the Islamic State, for example, actively prey on a sense of "not feeling your belonging . . . not sharing values and perspective." What they're looking for, particularly in their online efforts, is social isolation—"the feeling that even if you share, people will not listen to you."[9]

As Weeda explained, an essential part of the Taliban's strategy is reinforcing isolation. The Taliban take youth from their homes and communities, severing their ties to family, forcing them to form distorted communities based on separateness and coercion. These "shadow communities," Weeda continues, "are rigid, exclusive, and cannot see beyond their own myopic ways."[10]

"Since the Taliban were outsiders," she tells me, "they felt they could do whatever they wanted since there weren't the same social restrictions or stigma associated with being a member of the community." The Taliban had forgone their connection to the people and place of Afghanistan, and adhered instead to a set of rigid ideological commitments. Responsibilities of community then matter only within the limited scope of the group. This is the foundation for a sense of in-group loyalty that enables violence.

In April 2021, President Joe Biden announced that US troops would pull out of Afghanistan by September 2021, ending a twenty-year military engagement triggered by the 9/11 terrorist attacks. In August, on the eve of US withdrawal, the Taliban swiftly took Kabul, toppling the Afghan government and assuming power in Afghanistan. The full impact of these recent developments on the shadow side of belonging remains to be seen, but we can already see that the extreme oppression of women and girls in Afghanistan through the neglect and active suppression of their rights and freedoms continues under this new era of Taliban rule.

Sabrina Sassi, a researcher working on violent extremism in urban environments at Université Laval in Québec, tells me about related dynamics of disconnection. Sabrina grew up in Montrouge, a suburb just five kilometers south of Paris. While it has historically been a tight-knit community of Turkish, North African, and sub-Saharan immigrant families, it's also been subject to harsh realities of Islamophobia and institutional racism. There's precious little economic opportunity and historically substandard education. People often feel cut off from the dominant society. Amid the economic breakdown, there's been a widespread decline of traditional community structures. Radicalization of the isolated and vulnerable has followed.

In recent years, France has been rocked by a series of terrorist attacks—most notably, on the thirteenth of November 2015. It was over the course of that evening that the bustling city of Paris was hit by coordinated Islamic State terror attacks. These attacks targeted the national sports stadium, several restaurants and bars, and, most infamously, Le Bataclan, a popular concert venue. The events of this night left 130 dead and 350 wounded.

Montrouge has not been spared from the violence. A police officer was killed there by a lone gunman during the *Charlie Hebdo* attacks in 2015. Sabrina can draw a direct line between her community's sense of isolation and disempowerment and the extremism that's manifested.

For Sabrina, the issue is personal. "I can't ignore it," she says. "It hurts so, so very much."[11] Growing up in Montrouge, she was told in ways both big and small that she didn't belong. Coming from a Muslim family with Tunisian parents, Sabrina was routinely told that her cultural and religious background would be a barrier to her success. School administrators told her, for example, that she could never attend a top university. However, with support from family and, among others, a teacher who believed deeply in her, Sabrina defied discrimination, arriving at an extraordinary career and an experience of greater belonging. Yet she is an exception.

Sabrina has a deep understanding of Rex's experience, and her work draws similar conclusions to Weeda's. In her analysis, violent groups grow and take hold by making outcasts feel socially included and empowered. She tells me, "A lot of terrorist groups, a lot of extremist groups bank on the feeling of belonging. That's how they recruit. It's really like it's a marketing strategy. . . . That's why they offer to people who do not get that in their home societies." According to Sabrina, those who do not experience belonging are "easier targets."

It's the very same dynamic as when young people, without close community bonds or economic and educational opportunity, are lured into gangs or other violent groups. It's usually not violent tendencies or a calling to join a particular fight. Rather, it's a need to be connected to support systems, to claim an identity, to share in a sense of meaning. They're not joining these groups because of an apocalyptic vision or a desire for bloodshed; rather, they are seeking to fulfill the most basic of human needs. They're seeking to fulfill the vital conditions of belonging that have been systematically denied. While it's certainly no justification for wrongs and atrocities they might commit, the fact is that most people in such situations are responding to this unfulfilled longing and right that we all share.

These same insights have implications beyond violent extremism. When we languish in conditions of denied belonging, the consequences can be visceral, even biophysical. Dr. Carl Hart is one of the world's foremost experts on the science of addiction. He is the first African American to be a tenured professor in the sciences at Columbia University, where he chairs the Department of Psychology and teaches and researches neuropsychopharmacology. Like Weeda and Sabrina, Dr. Hart has witnessed firsthand the realities of that which he studies. As he recounts in his book, *High Price*, Hart grew up in one of the poorest neighborhoods in Miami, Florida. His parents divorced when he was young, and he was raised by a single mother. He came of age in the 1980s during the depths of the crack-cocaine epidemic, and he came to know, on an intimate basis, the damage that crisis wrought. He came to know the personal pain of stigma and shame that often accompanies lack of resources. He came to know the pain of collective isolation, too: racism, mass incarceration, systemic barriers to participating in the economy. When we spoke in the summer of 2018, Carl described to me how, even in places of incredible wealth like Miami and New York City, there are places like Harlem, not far from Columbia University, where we spoke, where you have whole communities that "don't benefit from the fruits of the larger society: information, education, resources. . . . That's isolation."[12] That was his reality.

He remembers, "I fully believed that the crime and poverty in my community was a direct result of crack cocaine. . . . I reasoned that if I could solve or cure drug addiction, that I could fix crime and poverty in my community."[13]

Professor Hart's perspective on the underlying problem has since evolved. One of his defining insights as an academic researcher is that the assumption he once held so strongly—that drugs are to blame for social problems—was wrong. As he told me, "We act, as a society, as if drug addiction has to do with drugs. A drug addiction has almost nothing to do with drugs. The majority of the people who use drugs don't become addicted." Hart's research shows that the real issue behind addiction isn't the physiological or psychological power of the substance, but something else altogether.

Hart explained to me that, to understand drug addiction, we have to understand the environment in which addiction occurs. We have to look at whether there are what he calls "competing reinforcers" to drug use: factors like strong family bonds, a sense of place in the community, connection to nature, meaningful work, economic opportunity, a voice in shaping culture or politics, or connection to a spiritual life. When these reinforcers are weak or nonexistent, people seek socially and physically destructive forms of escape.

The real issue, in other words, is a deprivation of the experience of belonging. This leads to the social isolation that drives extreme substance abuse, and that substance abuse can, in turn, undermine the health and well-being of whole communities.

Through studies of neuroscience and pharmacology, Carl Hart arrived at the same core conclusion that Weeda and Sabrina reached in their studies of the sociology, psychology, and politics of violent extremism: When human beings are denied the experience of wholeness, we are subject to misguided, destructive, irrational behaviors. We desperately grasp for any semblance of belonging. He has studied how our bonds with other people play an important role in pathological drug use or the lack thereof. "The majority of people who avoid drug problems tend to have strong social networks," he writes. "A great deal of pathological drug use is driven by unmet social needs, by being alienated."[14]

As we spoke, Carl underscored that the real work of addressing addiction is about creating contexts conducive to the experience of belonging. In the face of judgment, shame, stigma, fear, dislocation, and disempowerment, he says that people will often find "refuge in psychoactive drugs—and they may overdo it."[15]

When we face the denial of our human birthright to belong, we're liable to pursue strategies that compound isolation. Sometimes it's substance abuse. Other times its social division. We'll do almost anything to fill the void, to deal with the emptiness, to find a way out from sitting all alone at the bottom of the well.

When we recognize the root causes of the shadow side of belonging, then we naturally must respond by expressing empathy and working toward systems change. Rather than focus on drugs, for example, we should seek to address the "competing reinforcers." Similarly, Weeda and Sabrina underscore that we can counter radicalization only by building belonging. In practice, this means policies and priorities that give people voice, meaning, opportunity, and connection. A growing body of research supports their observations. In the Organisation for Economic Co-operation and Development (OECD) member countries, for example, terrorism is correlated to lower levels of "social cohesion" and a lack of opportunity.[16] It is essential to build conditions of respect, appreciation, opportunity, and shared meaning if we are to overcome social crises. The tragedy is that our responses have so often been precisely the opposite.

THE CRISIS OF OTHERING

WHAT IS THE COMMON THREAD in the stories and insights that Rex, Weeda, Sabrina, and Carl share? They all demonstrate the consequences of denied belonging. Too often, we have systematically failed to deal with those consequences. In fact, across contexts, many societies have responded to complex issues of denied belonging by further undermining belonging—pointing fingers at the "moral failings" of marginalized groups of people, warehousing them in prisons, worsening the elements of economic isolation, willfully ignoring the underlying conditions of poverty, conflict, and hopelessness.

These tendencies run deep. We often fail to address the root causes of these conditions and invest instead in actions and values that widen the gaps between us. There is a temptation to see those who are not like us as less than—less than us and, in some cases, less than human. We dehumanize and distance ourselves from others, and, through this separation, we can deny our interconnectedness, deny our responsibilities to one another, and impose hierarchies to oppress each other.

This is the essence of othering.

It's a phenomenon that we see all around us in the twenty-first century, but it's certainly not new. Philosophers and literary voices have been illuminating and exploring the concept of othering for hundreds of years.

The philosopher Georg Wilhelm Friedrich Hegel, for example, wrote about the tendency of othering in the late eighteenth century. Hegel described how self-identity originates in the "exclusion of everything other outside itself" and that "other" is thus "unessential, negative."[17] That is to say, we see in the "other" all that we refuse to see in ourselves. What Hegel describes is a deep internal manifestation of the shadow side of belonging.

It's the tendency to seek to create and sustain our own identity by defining ourselves and defending ourselves *against* that which we perceive as different.

The American novelist and scholar Toni Morrison once asked: "What is the nature of Othering's comfort, its allure, its power (social, psychological, or economical)? Is it the thrill of belonging—which implies being part of something bigger than one's solo self, and therefore stronger? My initial view leans toward the social/psychological need for a stranger, an Other in order to define the estranged self."[18]

In practice, othering leads to societal imbalance and structural inequalities. We get hierarchies of control, founded in an insistence on separateness—on the notion that some are deserving and others are not. Whether it's in a retributive approach to policing and prisons that denies the possibility of restorative justice, or a winner-takes-all approach to economics that denies people dignity and decent livelihoods, these are systems that reinforce othering. They are founded in the notion that we can achieve belonging only by denying it to those we see as different.

The tendency to consider people "other" or treat them as "less than" can occur along racial, gendered, religious, economic, or countless other lines. While we can increasingly see this manifest in the outright intolerance of xenophobic, anti-immigrant, and neo-segregationist movements, it more often appears in a subtler form. Instead of addressing the root causes of addiction, poverty, and inequality, we tend to perpetuate and reinforce what causes the problems in the first place: shame, stigma, exclusion, inequality. Instead of recognizing our responsibilities to one another and our innate interconnectedness, we are often inclined to apply blame-based approaches of "us versus them." This manifests in things like mass incarceration and police brutality—strategies of control that disproportionately impact those most perceived as "other" by political authorities, including young people of color.

When Carl Hart was growing up in Miami in the 1980s, he saw a specific government response to the crack-cocaine crisis—stereotyping, harsh policing, excessive prison sentences, and community disinvestment. This was an embodiment of othering. These are strategies that seek to abdicate responsibility for the shared work of building belonging. They promise easy solutions to difficult challenges through the force of control or domination.

We can see echoes of the same tendencies in the social exclusion that both Weeda and Sabrina describe. By pointing fingers at the supposed moral failings of a marginalized group of people, punishing them, and pinning fault for society's wrongs on their behavior, powerful players in society are engaging in the same fallacies.

From violent extremism to sexism to xenophobic nationalism to economic exclusion, so many of the headline challenges facing humanity are about people desperately grasping for some sense of belonging by dehumanizing or oppressing those they perceive as "the other." It's the fomentation of false belonging through ideas of "us versus them."

One of the most clearly pernicious examples of othering that we see today is racism. "Racist dehumanization is not merely symbolic," writes author and social critic Ta-Nehisi Coates, "it delineates the borders of power." Speaking about victims of police brutality, Coates says, "part of the idea of race is that whiteness automatically confers a decreased chance of dying like Michael Brown, or Walter Scott, or Eric Garner. And death is but the superlative example of what it means to live as an 'Other,' to exist beyond the borders of a great 'belonging.'"[19] Of course, in just a few years since Coates's writing, we must tragically acknowledge Breonna Taylor, George Floyd, Ahmaud Arbery, and the many more whose names are not widely known.

Toni Morrison was a powerful voice on the destructive impact of racism and the consequences of racist othering. She often spoke on the impulse "to own, govern, and administrate," an impulse that fuels the ugly flames of colonialism, perpetuates myths of the noble and brutal savage, and enables slavery, genocide, apartheid, political demagoguery, wage discrimination, and militarized policing.[20]

In contrast to this desire to "own, govern, and administrate," we also see "othering" manifest as what appears to be passive, systemic indifference. Strategies of control. Refusal to listen. Policies that don't purport to be discriminatory but, in reality, result in perpetuation of multigenerational inequities.

As just one example, consider racialized immigration and naturalization rules that prevent members of specific groups from becoming citizens of certain countries. In 2019, Indian lawmakers passed an amendment to the 1955 Citizenship Act, offering amnesty and citizenship eligibility to Hindu, Sikh, Buddhist, Jain, Parsi, and Christian refugees and migrants. The exclusion of Muslims from this amendment is a glaring example of pernicious othering. It means that, based on religious affiliation and belief alone, Muslim newcomers will have more difficulty finding a home and security in India. It's a direct question of who belongs and who does not.

The United States is still grappling with the legacies of racist Jim Crow segregation laws that were in place from the end of the Civil War until the second half of the twentieth century. While the formal laws are no longer on the books, their impacts still often manifest in unequal access to education, housing, healthcare, nutrition, and other basic necessities.[21]

On one hand, the question is: Shouldn't we know better than to fall into the shadow side of belonging? On the other hand, how could we not fall into these fallacies, given the separations that have been with humanity for untold millennia?

Father Richard Rohr, whom we met earlier, has published more than a dozen books exploring vital questions at the nexus of spirituality and social action. I asked him why, in a world that's ultimately defined by wholeness, we see so much polarization, violence, and hatred. He spoke of the origins of the human addiction to othering at both the personal and systemic levels. "The universal answer of the great spiritual masters, whether it's the Buddha or Jesus, is that simple word: *egocentricity*." He told me that it's "the problem of seeing the self as an enclosed and even all-important reference point, as long as you don't break out of that shell, you'll be threatened by all otherness, you'll be a fear-based person, because all of life is threatened."[22]

It's the same dynamic described to me by Albert Marshall—the Mi'kmaqp Elder we met earlier. It's forgetting that we're part of the pattern. It's the fallacy that we can find our wholeness by imagining that we're above or greater than the web of life, rather than a strand in it. "Egocentricity" doesn't just mean selfishness. It means the error of thinking we're alone or above in a world of "others." It can also mean the mistaken belief that one's own race or nation or socioeconomic clique is the central protagonist of history, destined to bend others to its worldview and will. It's an unwillingness to tend to the tapestry of belonging. It's the fallacy of believing that we'll find wholeness through the denigration or manipulation of those outside our own exclusive circle of connection.

When people with power engage in othering, the result is structures of oppression that may drive those forced to the margins to seek belonging in misguided ways, whether it's the escapism of drugs or extremist ideology or even violence. These misguided strategies then result in more harsh responses that perpetuate a vicious cycle of division. The way to break the cyclical feedback loop of denied belonging and growing inequality is to restore appreciation of the fact that we're all part of the pattern—of the interconnected whole—and act in accordance with that understanding.

As we look to the most pressing challenges of the twenty-first century—things like rising inequality and the systemic pillaging of our planet for profit—we are witnessing the consequences of intensified othering and denied belonging on an increasingly global scale.

Social isolation has always existed, but the feeling of loneliness as we currently understand it is a relatively new phenomenon. In a time characterized by rapid globalization and unparalleled interconnectedness, why are so many of us lonely? Why are we isolated? I would argue it's because the systems that our predecessors designed never considered belonging during the creation stage, focusing instead on metrics like efficiency, order, and bottom-line economic outputs. I'll speak more about systems change later, but in the current context, I will offer that in the absence of people, place, power, and purpose, individuals have become desperate for belonging, and too many bad actors are happy to step in, fill that void, and exploit the isolation and loneliness that has our global community in crisis.

STRUCTURES OF EXCLUSION

THE SHADOW SIDE OF BELONGING is ultimately most dangerous when it manifests in dominant systems of power in our societies—when entire social, political, and economic structures are built on the objective of actualizing belonging for some at the expense of belonging for others. It's when we deflect responsibility for addressing complex challenges together and instead retreat to exclusionary identities, blaming those who are not like us, and employing strategies of control, coercion, and punishment against the imagined "other."

This probably sounds familiar.

Whether it's backlash against migrants and minorities, or the dehumanization of ideological opponents and nonbelievers, there's a tremendous appetite for populism and exclusionary politics right now. It's usually predicated on the imagined ideal of some homogenous "whole" that once existed—a belief that it's possible to reawaken progress, greatness, morality, or prosperity by returning to "the way it was," perhaps before some "other" arrived. This kind of populist rhetoric sometimes wins in the media and at the ballot box because it speaks to the need for wholeness.

Our nostalgic impulse to return to "the good old days" is, in many ways, a façade, a Potemkin village, that allows us to justify denial of our responsibility to one another. If we reflect critically, the good old days were not so good after all, with intolerance, and the more insidious indifference, running rampant in many places around the world. Disease, poverty, racism, sexism, religious persecution, violence, homophobia, ableism, lack of equitable housing, healthcare, and education—all these things are not only some of the characteristics of "the good old days," but more importantly, they are the products of societal systems that have historically neglected belonging. Moreover, the illusory "simple life" is more complex than ever before as planet and people are navigating greater complexities, as we seek belonging amid structures of exclusion both visible and invisible.

Sadly, too few take the time to look past the illusion, ultimately allowing the domination of narratives that romanticize both the past and the practice of othering. Worse still, for those who recognize these narratives for what they really are, the acknowledgment of the problem confers responsibility to solve it, and for many of us with our busy lives, that's just too much work. And so, we turn a blind eye to what's right in front of us. These convenient narratives serve to infiltrate politics, further entrench long-held divisions that have precipitated violence for centuries, and continue to shape our systems in the name of oppression. They set the stage for law, policy, and the contours of human behavior. These are societal perceptions of who constitutes the in-group and out-group, who is righteous, trustworthy, and hardworking. These are foundational questions of who belongs.

Ta-Nehisi Coates describes how narratives of "othering" are often weaponized in laws and policies that build belonging for some at the expense of others. While slavery in the US ended with the Civil War and legal segregation largely ended with the civil rights movement, Black Americans continued to be systematically denied belonging through laws that enforced de facto segregation, all under the guise of protecting whites' traditional sense of "home."

Coates looks at historical records to see how, with the supposed transition to integrated housing, Black families were offered substandard mortgage and financing options that "combined all the responsibilities of homeownership with all the disadvantages of renting—while offering the benefits of neither."[23] The system rested on the assumption that people of color couldn't be trusted with normal financial terms, irrespective of their underlying economic conditions. Official agencies perpetuated policies of othering by rating the value of neighborhoods according to their "perceived stability" and offering high-quality mortgages accordingly.

This, as Coates describes, resulted in "self-fulfilling prophecies" in which poorly rated areas in "red zones" only continued to decline in value and "stability." The policies of delineating neighborhoods based on race, or "redlining" as it was called, "destroyed the possibility of investment wherever Black people lived," creating State-supported conditions for ghettos and intergenerational poverty.[24]

Through housing policy, we see here the attempted preservation of some perverse imagined "whole"—preservation of the sense of "home" as had been defined by white Americans for many, many years. The majority group largely assumed that the "other" would threaten their sense of shared culture, their safety, and, in turn, their property values, if they moved into majority-white neighborhoods. And the result was painful and enduring: an economic and legal regime that perpetuated de facto segregation and placed Black people at a systemic disadvantage over generations.

We see othering weaponized in yet another malicious way. The shadow side of belonging can manifest, for instance, in the control and oppression of the identities of others, forcing them to conform to an imagined, uniform "whole." Often, powerful systems make a demand of outsiders: abandon your own belonging in order to experience belonging as someone else defines it for you. This, in practice, is assimilation.

Dr. Kenneth Deer is a Mohawk Elder and secretary of the Mohawk Nation in Kahnawake in the province of Québec, Canada. Kenneth participated in drafting the original text of the UN Declaration on the Rights of Indigenous Peoples. He is a powerful advocate for peoples' belonging—notably in contrast to the painful history of forced assimilation. Speaking from his experience working in collaboration with Indigenous representatives from around the world, Kenneth emphasized to me that Indigenous Nations "want to belong to the world community"; however, "we don't want to assimilate, we don't want to disappear."[25] To Kenneth, belonging means "respecting others' right to belong to whatever society they belong to."[26]

Colonial nation-building harnessed, and continues to rely on, the shadow side of belonging. By creating imagined, homogenous national identities and superimposing them onto Indigenous Nations, violent assimilationist laws were an attempt to erase Indigenous Nations and histories from their own lands.

In Canada, the 1876 Indian Act—which remains in effect in amended form—explicitly aimed to set the parameters of who could be called Indigenous and who could claim membership to an Indigenous Nation. The goal was to assimilate Indigenous peoples—first categorizing them as the "other," and then attempting to force conformity to a nascent Canadian national identity. Among many genocidal and assimilationist measures—the banning of traditional ceremonies, laws and governance, and the theft and abuse of children over generations through the Residential School system—the Indian Act included "compulsory enfranchisement" provisions that required Indigenous peoples to relinquish their status if they were to earn a university degree or become a professional.

Kenneth tells me that when he was born in 1948, "you couldn't be a Mohawk and a doctor at the same time."[27] The doctors who delivered him were Mohawk by blood and culture, but he recalls that they weren't even allowed to live in the community. As Mi'kmaq legal scholar Pamela Palmater has argued, the objective of these identity laws was to ensure the eventual disappearance of Indigenous peoples. As she has written, the law and its successor policies have resulted in "the erosion of Indigenous identity, culture, and communal connection."[28]

Reflecting on these policies of assimilation and manipulation, Kenneth told me, "We're talking about belonging: it's about identity, and how our identity was stripped from our People." The Sovereign Mohawk Nation, one of the six Nations of the Haudenosaunee, and Indigenous communities in Canada and globally, have fought for generations to maintain their true belonging. Over and over again, federal authorities have sought to replace inherent belonging with a shadow side of belonging—the imposition of another identity and forced conformity to an imagined, homogenous whole. Despite continued attempts of erasure, Kenneth remains a member of his Nation. He is a powerful example of resilience.

The challenges of assimilation continue to this day. Throughout the world, we see related efforts to manipulate group membership and enforce control, aggrandizing the dominant groups at the expense of the "other." Assimilation means belonging on someone else's terms. It's about being forced to leave pieces of your whole self behind in order to experience some semblance of belonging.

In some instances, structures of exclusion that foment false belonging manipulate our sense of community and heritage, like our "traditional values." Though tradition can be a vital aspect of true belonging—creating a sense of meaning and connectedness with the past, to something bigger and more enduring than the individual—it can also be a means to enforce difference, to discourage dissent, to keep outsiders in line. I think, for example, of how claims of "tradition" are still used to justify forced marriage, virginity testing, so-called honor crimes, family violence, and marital rape.

"Othering," under the banner of "traditional" or "family" values, is also used to justify discrimination against—and even the imprisonment of—members of the LGBTQIA+ community. This oppression directly contradicts the founding principles of universality and indivisibility enshrined in the Universal Declaration of Human Rights. Most often, these types of discriminatory approaches are put forward as a means of affirming the belonging of an in-group relative to an out-group. For example, through a populist political campaign in 2013, Russia passed a law banning anyone from passing information about LGBTQIA+ relationships to young people.

Whether the focus is the LGBTQIA+ community or religious minorities, nations have drafted and passed laws like these through rhetoric of collective patriotic and communal identity. Such campaigns are often explicitly about belonging—about bolstering a powerful group identity and forcing minorities, to paraphrase Coates, "to exist beyond the borders of a great 'belonging.'" Ultimately, these aren't just jingoistic campaigns. Often, they result in the rise of extremist groups and settler-colonial projects that curtail the fundamental human rights of those who don't fit in the majority or privileged group.

Yet, hidden in the challenges—in the cycles of violence, division, domination, and greed—there is still a glimmer of hope: Whether or not we choose to acknowledge it, we are deeply and inextricably connected. That which we give, we will receive. The vision of wholeness—our true belonging—ultimately connects us all in a cycle of reciprocity. We can start working toward a shared future where everyone belongs when we find recognition of a simple fact:

There is no other. The other is only ever us.

The only way to stop these ideological conflagrations is to deal with the tinder from which they burn. We need to address the fundamental human yearning for wholeness. We need to realize our unfulfilled right of belonging. The question is: Where to begin?

CHAPTER FOUR

THE QUEST
FOR BELONGING

HOW CAN WE ILLUMINATE the pathway back to belonging?

People have been thinking about this question for centuries, if not millennia.

It's the question that underlies decisions about who can live in a city's walls, and it underlies documents like the Magna Carta and the US Constitution, which determine who has a say in the structure of governance. It underlies the choices we make that balance the individual and the collective, freedom and social order, independence and interconnectivity.

We can find explorations of this question in myth—and the living examples of mythic journeys toward belonging our modern heroes have made. We find these modern heroes in the athletes of Special Olympics International (SOI)—we'll explore this program later in the chapter.

For millennia, myth has been one of humankind's most important vehicles for communicating norms and values—and it continues to be, through the arts, books, movies, and modern entertainment. It's how humanity imagines and invokes our deepest purpose.

I see one myth in particular that has great relevance to the question of how we overcome the forces of separation in today's world: the Grail Quest. This myth has distinct significance in this day and age, given our current challenges and deficit in belonging.

MOST OF US HAVE HEARD of the Grail Quest, though we might not be able to place the story itself. Yet it's the subject of epic poems, operas, books, comic book series, video games and movies to this day. The story of the Grail Quest has been transmitted, reinterpreted, and revived over and over again by many cultures in different forms, even before medieval tales of King Arthur and the Knights of the Round Table were told.[1] It's the timeless and archetypal form of the hero's journey—the journey that each one of us makes in our own unique ways.

The hero of the Grail Quest is Parzival, a knight in the time of King Arthur and the Round Table. Parzival's story represents a new understanding of the individual's relationship with the collective—one based on compassion and reciprocity. Seen through the lens of belonging, the Grail Quest has the potential to open our eyes to the healing power of seeing the other as ourselves, worthy of our compassion and our care. It points to urgent lessons about the nature of, and causes behind, the deterioration of societies into "wastelands" that result from the misdirection of belonging, and how we can heal these wastelands by acknowledging the wound and asking the "healing question." It has immensely important, and radical, things to say about belonging, not only for its time, but also in the context of our own contemporary lives.

THE GRAIL OF COMPASSION

Compassion is the love that recognizes and goes forth to identify with the preciousness of all that is lost and broken within ourselves and others.

—JAMES FINLEY[2]

IN WOLFRAM VON ESCHENBACH'S well-known thirteenth-century version of the Grail Quest, Parzival is the only child of the widowed Queen

Herzeloyde, who raises her son in nature, outside of the order of knights. But he cannot ignore the deeper callings inside him. Enchanted by an encounter with a group of knights from King Arthur's Round Table in the forest one day, Parzival leaves home to become a knight.[3]

After some time, Parzival reaches the Grail Castle for the first time, and encounters the ailing Grail King, Anfortas, who floats along in his boat on a lake, suffering from a terrible lancet wound to the groin that won't heal. His bodily wound is mirrored in the Wasteland his kingdom has become. Parzival wants to ask the king what's wrong—he wants to know the nature of his wound. But he knows that knights are not supposed to ask unnecessary questions, and so he suppresses the urge to open his heart to the king.[4]

Yet it's this question that he doesn't ask—the question of compassion—that is the very one that would have healed the king, the land, the people. As acclaimed scholar and author Joseph Campbell remarks, "The social ideal interfered with his nature, and the result is desolation."[5] Indeed, Parzival failed to respond to the compassion in his heart, and so the Wasteland and the wound remained.

Parzival's story is about one person who finds success through the help of others—that's why I love it. I've often wondered why every knight in every grail quest must begin his journey alone in the deepest, darkest part of the forest. In myth and folklore, why is the hero so often an individual rather than a collective, why is stoicism so often seen as a virtue, and why don't we encounter more narratives rooted in the importance of human connection and the extension of compassion?

Parzival's quest has relevance for us all. It's about the power of belonging to drive reciprocity within a community, and heal the individual and the collective. Even on a solitary journey, Parzival teaches us that we need not walk the road of compassion alone. Indeed, it's entirely better to walk it together. Over years of teaching and writing on this subject, I've come to imagine this quest as a grail of another sort—what I call the Grail of Compassion. In my mind, there are three core principles essential to achieving this Grail—the end result being compassion and, more broadly, belonging:

1. Accepting and nurturing ourselves as we are, and accepting and nurturing those who are different from us.
2. Connectedness with everyone in the community and knowing that everyone in the community has a purpose and unique gifts to share.
3. Respecting that as members of a community, we have a sacred responsibility to hold everyone's life in high regard.[6]

I see the Grail of Compassion as the ultimate journey, to heal, enlighten, and illuminate our connection to everything around us. The three core principles are rooted in notions of reciprocity and rounding the circle—both ideas that we explore in this book. In pursuing this Grail of Compassion, which can present itself in our lives in myriad ways, and in choosing to accept the responsibility to then share that gift with others, I know we can build belonging for everyone.

THE GIFTS OF THE HEALER

WHEN PARZIVAL LEAVES the Grail King, he's told that he hasn't asked the healing question, and that the king and the earth will remain barren. The mysterious Grail Castle has disappeared, and Parzival wanders for five years in search of the Grail, undergoing great tests of heart and will, gradually becoming more humble and compassionate for others.[7] Famed psychiatrist Carl Jung's archetype of the wounded healer—in which the healer endures great hardships and suffering and, because of that, is able to bring healing to others[8]—can orient us here.

On his journey, Parzival encounters and jousts with another knight in the forest. Unknown to them both, they are actually brothers. His brother, Feirefiz, is a Muslim, while Parzival is a Christian—one from the East, one from the West. The story describes their fight in the forest:

It is easy for anyone to say: "thus they fought," if he wants to call them two, but they were both but one person. My brother and I are but one.[9]

This is a profound statement of common humanity that boldly challenges the instinct to cast the unfamiliar and the different as *Other*. It's also a call for equality.

The story here evokes the third principle of the Grail of Compassion— the knowledge that, as members of a community, we have a sacred responsibility to hold everyone's life in high regard.

The two are locked in battle with one another for a long time. After much exhaustive maneuvering, Parzival strikes Feirefiz's helmet, shattering his sword. Feirefiz, who could have killed Parzival in this moment, shows great honor by calling a truce, flinging his own sword out of reach, and asking Parzival who he is. They bare their heads and find that they are brothers.

As the late philosopher Roger Scruton argues of Wagner's late nineteenth-century operatic retelling of the story of Parzival, which he called *Parsifal*, "redemption comes from the other, who suffers as we suffer, and who, through compassion, offers to share our burdens and to retrieve what we have lost."[10] It's only when Parzival comes to see "the other" as his brother that the way opens for him to return to the Grail Castle to heal the king. Without his encounter with another, the truth of Parzival's deepest self would never have been revealed.

As Wolfram's poem reiterates, Parzival doesn't return to the Grail Castle as a solitary hero, though. When Cundrie, a female oracle of the forest, comes that night to tell Parzival he's finally ready to enter the Grail Castle again, he chooses his brother to accompany him. So Parzival rides into the elusive kingdom with his companions—a Christian, a Muslim, and a female oracle—entering the most holy of visions in all of Christendom, not for a first time but, indeed, for a second time, where even the most pious of Christians could not themselves hope to enter. Parzival was given a second chance.

On finally passing through the Wasteland and gaining entry to the Grail Castle, Parzival weeps, falls to his knees, and seeks in his heart to cure the king's sorrows. Rising to his feet again, he calls out to the Grail King:

What ails thee?

The question is love and compassion itself, and in asking the healing question, Parzival receives love and compassion in return. Compassion is expressed not through sword and armor, not through skill and ambition, but instead through heart and hand.

When Parzival shares in the Grail King's suffering, he and the king become one and the same. The fusion of the healer and the healed is the essence of belonging, of compassion, and of reciprocity—the Grail consciousness—the principle there is no other but ourselves.

As soon as Parzival asks the healing question, he realizes the Grail. The king's wound is healed, his skin glows again, the waters become abundant, and the soils become fertile. The individual restores the community. The community restores the individual. And the Wasteland is restored to life. As Scruton concludes, "Parsifal's compassion, which leads him to take on burden after burden, and to venture into the world of sin and despair, is clearly a way of engaging with life rather than a way of avoiding it, and engaging at the deepest level."[11]

As the author, mythologist, and Jungian analyst Jules Cashford claims of Parzival's journey of compassion, Parzival is now able to "heal the king and transform the Wasteland—in himself *and* in the world—because he has learned the primary virtue of compassion, which is simply to respond to the other as though that other were himself."[12]

The Grail Quest challenges conventional understandings of individual bravery and what a hero looks like and does. This isn't the stereotypical fairy tale that features a valiant knight rescuing a fair maiden from a tower, then living happily ever after. Parzival is held up by many figures in the story, each of whom helps him realize the Grail within himself, and guides him to a relationship of reciprocity with the community of beings who live in symbiotic relationship to him.

ROUNDING THE CIRCLE

THE GRAIL QUEST is a remarkable story of compassion and redemption, one that has gems of wisdom hidden in its arc. Yet what happens after the hero realizes the Grail—in Parzival's story, and in our own?

In the most well-known version of the Grail Quest, Parzival becomes the Grail King. He's joined by his beloved wife, Condwiramurs, and their two young children, whom Parzival hasn't seen in five years. They rule the Kingdom of the Grail in peace and compassion, and their son eventually inherits the responsibility and honor of tending to the Grail.

In many of our fairy tales and myths, the emphasis is not often what happens after the hero has slayed the proverbial dragon, realized the Grail, or otherwise emerges from the trials and tests victorious. We are often content to leave our heroes at the top of the mountain. Yet this stage of the journey, after the quest, is just as crucial as the realization of the Grail or the retrievals obtained in prior stages of the journey.

The journey undertaken by the hero must ultimately be for the benefit of the community. If the community is able to receive the seeker's gifts and the new form of the individual with open hearts and minds, those gifts will take root and grow.

In his book *The Gift*, the poet and essayist Lewis Hyde writes about the nature of gifts. "A gift must always move," he writes.[13] If we think of the gift as a constantly flowing river, the giver of a gift allows themselves to become a channel for its current. They become a conduit for the regenerative bonds of reciprocity among givers and receivers.

Parzival isn't perfect. He struggles and stumbles. His journey is marked by folly and error. But he perseveres. In his quest—from the sheltered child unaware of his mission to the ambitious young knight to the realized avatar of empathy—Parzival finds his place, purpose, and power. It's within the bigger archetype of the hero's journey.

Drawing on Campbell's scholarship, Jules Cashford explains that all heroes follow the same underlying pattern of transformation: "Separation-Initiation-Return." The first phase sees the hero turning away from society, its conventions and restrictions; in the second phase, the hero ventures out alone into an unknown realm; and in the third and final phase, the hero returns, "to the society he had originally to leave behind, bearing now his gift of a vision transformed."[14]

"A gift that cannot move loses its gift properties," Hyde writes, describing the paradox of gift exchange. "The gift that is not used will be lost, while the one that is passed along remains abundant."[15] Indeed, as Cashford explains of the final stage of the quest, "Return is realizing that in one sense you have never been away. What you bring back, or rather discover that you now have, is a change of vision—and that change of vision changes the world."[16]

Hyde writes that the most expansive form of reciprocal gift exchange is not a linear back-and-forth exchange between two points, but rather moves in a circle. Not only does this act of giving become an act of social faith that the gift will return in another form, but as gifts are given more and more broadly, the circle of reciprocity expands outward. For Parzival, this gift is compassion, which must be received in order to be given in turn. This act of giving and receiving must continue; he receives compassion, and then shows this compassion to the king.

We can think of the hero's journey as a circle, in which we set out into the unknown, often journeying away from society—society's rules and expectations, or literally into the wilderness or places different from what we're used to—and encounter trials and transformations within ourselves, emerging again to be reborn into our true nature.

I suggest that it's in the rounding of the circle—the integration of this new embodiment in the life of the individual within the community—that channels a previously unrealized life force in both and brings to fruition the wisdom and compassion gained during the journey. Without the rounding of the circle—without the integration—the gifts are lost, the union unconsummated, the insights called out but not heard. The next cycle unable to begin again. Both the individual and the community that holds them must attend to the reciprocity at the heart of their deepest bonds of belonging for each to know their true form more completely.

SPECIAL OLYMPICS: EVERYONE HAS A PURPOSE

Don't call us people with disabilities . . . we have DIFFabilities!

—EDDIE BARBANELL[17]

AS NELSON MANDELA SAID during his opening speech at the Special Olympics World Summer Games in 2003 in Dublin, Ireland, "Special Olympics is a telling testimony to the indestructibility of the human spirit."

He considered these athletes as "the greatness of humankind."[18] I couldn't agree more.

Eunice Kennedy Shriver, the sister of US president John F. Kennedy, founded Special Olympics in 1968 as a way to give people with intellectual disabilities "the chance to play, the chance to compete, and the chance to grow."[19]

Intellectual disability is a term used "when a person has certain limitations in cognitive functioning and skills, possibly including communication, social, and self-care skills. These kinds of limitations can cause a child to develop and learn differently than a typically developing child. Intellectual disability can happen any time before a child turns eighteen years old, including before birth."[20] Between 1 and 3 percent—as many as 200 million people worldwide—have an intellectual disability.[21] The unemployment rate for adults with ID is twice as high as those without ID.[22] Children with ID in particular experience higher levels of stigma—higher than those with physical disabilities alone—and are more likely to be bullied than children with typical cognitive development.[23] While the term "ID" is used refer to intellectual disabilities, the term "IDD" is often used in a more contemporary context, as it includes both intellectual and development disabilities.

For too many decades, and still, to this day, people with intellectual and developmental disabilities have too often been forced out of the public eye. Yet the stigma, shame, bullying, isolation, humiliation, and inequality faced by people with IDD are slowly being replaced with respect and recognition, on the playing fields and off, in part because of the work of organizations like Special Olympics.

In an era when people with intellectual disabilities were viciously mocked, constantly ridiculed, and routinely subject to hateful slurs, Eunice Kennedy Shriver was determined to change hearts and minds. While her own sister Rosemary, who had an intellectual disability, was well-supported in childhood and into her adult years, Eunice saw the lack of resources, respect, and support that were given to other children with ID and their families. Driven by an innate sense of justice, Eunice asked the healing question—she wanted to know how people with intellectual disabilities could be included as full participants in communities, in education programs, and in broader society.

Indeed, Mrs. Shriver exemplified all three principles of the Grail of Compassion: accepting and nurturing those who are different from us, knowing that everyone has unique gifts to share, and respecting that we have a responsibility to hold everyone's life in high regard.

One of the foundational steps on her quest was the creation of what became known as Camp Shriver—a place of genuine compassion, and ultimately, belonging.

Camp Shriver originated in Mrs. Shriver's backyard in the summer of 1962 at her family home in Potomac, Maryland. It was a place of enthusiastic welcome, where scores of children with intellectual disabilities splashed in the pool with the Shriver clan and played games in the yard with volunteer counselors. Amid the laughter, joy, and fun, it turned out the young campers were capable of far more than the prevailing "wisdom" had ever imagined. The camp started with just thirty-four children and twenty-six counselors, but over the years Camp Shriver models grew across the country, reaching more than 7,000 people with intellectual disabilities.[24] In 1968, six years after starting Camp Shriver, Eunice founded Special Olympics so that people with intellectual disabilities could train, play, and compete in sports year-round.

Today, Special Olympics movement provides free year-round training and competition in thirty-two Olympic-style summer and winter sports for five million participants in 172 countries. The Special Olympics World Games is a major international event hosted every two years, alternating between summer and winter games. It has provided place, purpose, and belonging for countless athletes, their families, and the wider community of people who have IDD, as well as those who do not; for those like me, who can experience a world of inclusion and understanding, a world of hope, whether participating in a Unified sports event, by being an active participant in the stands, or by helping to carry the message home.

Like Parzival redefines what it means to be a hero by leading with empathy and compassion, SOI re-envisions what is meant to compete, to win, and to succeed. As the Special Olympics Athletes' Oath declares, "Let me win. But if I cannot win, let me be brave in the attempt." Indeed, I have seldom seen at any other world-class sporting event athletes turn back to help a fellow competitor who has fallen on the track, showing compassion before competition. But I have seen this at Special Olympics.

Mrs. Shriver envisioned Special Olympics as a safe place where those with disabilities could find courage, joy, and friendship with others. Still, it's always been bigger than the individual. Special Olympics provides space for families of people with IDD to come together to lean on and learn from one another, and it offers the wider world a window into their myriad gifts and abilities. During a time of ridicule, during a time when despairing parents felt pressure to hide their children away, during a time when the R-word was thrown about freely and maliciously, Mrs. Shriver was breaking down barriers, leading with her heart, and doing the hard work to build belonging.

Eunice Kennedy Shriver was a persistent and inspiring woman. "My mother has always been about hope, love, and opportunity," says Dr. Timothy Shriver, her son and the chairman of the Special Olympics International Board of Directors. "Love being the most important. For what do we have if we do not have love? Hope for helping us through each day when life challenges us. An opportunity that each one of us is empowered to make the world a better place."[25]

While we have a long way to go, organizations like Special Olympics are not only creating and holding space for people with IDD; they are also promoting love, acceptance, and interdependence everywhere by demonstrating compassion and rounding the circle of belonging, endeavoring never to leave anyone behind, and to ensure that each person is respected and recognized in their entirety. As we'll see, however, the lessons from the Grail of Compassion are not realized solely through the intentional space that SOI fosters, but even more through the gifts that the athletes share with one another, with their loved ones, and with the communities in which they live, work, and contribute. These gifts, in turn, are recognized and nurtured by SOI; the gift moves on, and the circle rounds.

LORETTA'S JOURNEY TOWARD BELONGING

I am an expression of the divine. . . .
We will never have to be other than who we are in order to be successful. . . .
We realize that we are as ourselves unlimited and our experiences valid.
It is for the rest of the world to recognize this, if they choose.

—ALICE WALKER[26]

LORETTA CLAIBORNE—a storied multi-sport athlete, a decorated Special Olympian, and a captivating speaker—is one of the most incredible people I know. She found her pathway to the Grail of Compassion, and followed it, resolutely. She creates unity through the example of her life and the courage to be herself, building bridges through compassion and lifting up entire communities in the process.

As a Black woman, Loretta knows what it's like to grow up in a place where people struggle to belong, where compassion sometimes wasn't present. She grew up in York, Pennsylvania, in the 1950s and '60s, amid the racial unrest that was spreading across her country. "We had a horrible time in 1969 in York," she remembers. "You couldn't go nowhere. You had to be in at eight P.M. The National Guard would make an announcement. They would come through on bullhorns: *We're shooting to kill, eight o'clock.* They would throw off the horn. Everybody knew to turn out your lights, hunker down, because there was going to be the riots coming through. You could hear the tanks and the shooting, and you'd see the lights flash."[27]

The inner cities were experiencing the disproportionate burden of racial, economic, environmental, and political marginalization of people of color. Belonging was scarce. Loretta is also one of many people with an intellectual disability—as such, her challenges growing up were even starker than many others in her community because of the stigma and discrimination against people with ID.

Loretta dreamed of being a nurse, a veterinarian, or an athlete. Yet these dreams seemed outlandish to many. She once told me about her struggle to remain in the school system against all odds: "I was going to school and they knew I wasn't gonna make it into this school 'cause I was supposed to be institutionalized, and the school system was pushing against the grain to tell my mother, 'You know, Miss Claiborne, you really need to institutional-ize her. This is the third strike. She's done.'" Loretta continued, "My mom, being the big woman she is, she says, 'Don't tell me what you're gonna do. You got a school, you're gonna educate my child.'"[28]

Loretta grew up at a time when children with ID were often insti-tutionalized, living separate from their families and society. "My mother wanted to keep her seven children together," Loretta recalls. "But society was telling her, 'No, Loretta can't be educated, you must put her away.'"[29] Yet her mother prevailed. She refused to bow to societal pressure.

At first, it was a mixed blessing. "Most of my friends were hidden away in institutions," Loretta says. "I also wanted to go to an institution because I got bullied so much." The bullying she speaks of wasn't just from her classmates. Because of her ID, she says, "I was held back in kindergarten, first grade and second grade. I actually had the teacher tell me, when I was in her class: 'You! To the closet! I don't have time for dummies anymore.'"

If she didn't end up in an institution, she remembers thinking, she would soon be in one of two places: "six feet under, or in some prison."[30] Here, there was a breakdown between the individual and the community—a breakdown of reciprocity, trust, and compassion.

Still, a few people in her life found it in their hearts to extend their compassion to Loretta, asking if she was OK and trying to help. They asked the right questions of themselves, of their community, and of Loretta.

Bobby Simpson, for example, noticed Loretta's challenging circum-stances and asked if she would consider signing up for karate. She agreed. She learned to channel her frustration into martial arts, where she could transform the power and direction of energy.

A few years later, a social worker also showed great compassion. At a school-to-work program one day, Loretta was feeling increasingly unhappy and had a violent outburst. She was sent to the social worker, whom she assumed would send her off to an institution. Instead, the social worker handed her a slip of paper with some logistical details and two words in bold: Special Olympics.

These individuals were willing to go against the grain of society to help Loretta. It's these choices to extend compassion to another, even when society doesn't require or expect it—sometimes when it cautions against it—that buoyed Loretta's inner transformation.

Indeed, both Simpson and the social worker saw Loretta's difference as an asset, not something to hide, and they set her up to be nurtured because of it. They realized that Loretta had unique gifts to share, and they accepted their responsibility to hold everyone's life in high regard.

"It was the first time in my life I didn't get teased, I didn't get poked at," Loretta recalls of her time with Special Olympics. "I came home one day and I looked at my mom, and she asked me how was it, and I said: 'Man, nobody called me names.'"[31]

Loretta and Eunice became close friends—the two would talk every Monday night at nine P.M. Loretta remembers one night after she had taken the bus from York, Pennsylvania, to Washington, DC, to attend a meeting at Eunice's suggestion. On her way to the bus to return home, Eunice called out to her and asked where she was going. She wanted Loretta to stay on to help her with the program she was working on.

Loretta hesitated. "Oh, well . . .'"

"Before I could get the words out my mouth," Loretta recalls, "she lit into me. And I'll never forget it." "'Don't tell me what you can't do,' Eunice said, 'You show me what you *can* do.'"[32]

Loretta followed her mentor's instructions to show the world exactly what she can do. She's became a world-class runner, completing twenty-six marathons and landing among the top one hundred women in the Boston Marathon on two occasions. She's won six gold medals at the Special Olympics World Games and currently holds the women's record in her age group for the 5,000 meters with a time of seventeen minutes. She's a gifted motivational speaker, having spoken at the United Nations, at some of the world's leading universities, and at hundreds of student events in the US and across multiple continents. She is the recipient of three honorary doctorates. Even more heroic than her athletic accomplishments, however, are her grace, her humility, and her powerful voice, which leads others to greater compassion for themselves and others.

The Special Olympics movement created the space for Loretta to love and respect herself. "I was always told I couldn't be this, I couldn't be that, couldn't do this, couldn't do that," she said. "I could watch my sisters and brothers in drum corps, but I couldn't be a part of it. Special Olympics is where I started to change."[33] Through the actions of her mother, her mentors, and the Special Olympics family, Loretta was given the incredible gift of compassion. Rather than letting that gift sit idle and letting the muscle of compassion weaken or even atrophy, Loretta made sure to round the circle and pass those gifts forward.

At the end of her mother's life, Loretta went the extra mile, quite literally, to show her that her life was valued. She received the compassion that her mother had shown her, and gave it right back when she needed it the most.

"She fought tooth and nail for me," Loretta says, speaking of her mother. "So, it was my job to fight tooth and nail that she had the best care that she could get, the last couple years that she was on this earth."[34]

Loretta remembers showing up the first day at the care facility where her mother had moved. A worker at the center told her to try to show up as often as possible, telling her that the people who had relatives show up were much more likely to be treated much better.

This felt unfair. Given this advice, however, Loretta doubled her determination to be as constant a presence for her mother as possible—even though she didn't have a car. Loretta rode her bicycle for miles along busy routes to be with her on a regular basis. The staff at the care facility in time became like family.

When her mother passed on, Loretta remembers that her siblings were shocked at the number of people who showed up in support of her for the funeral. "Who are all these people?" her sister asked, in disbelief. Loretta felt a wave of gratitude for the wealth of love in her life. "They're from Special Olympics," she told her.[35]

If you look at Loretta today, you'll see a person who unquestionably belongs—both within her community and within her own consciousness. "When I walk out my door, I'm Loretta," she tells me. "I'm a child of God. And God's children, He's intended us on this Earth to take care."[36]

Loretta's work in her hometown and around the world is rounding the circle, passing forward the gifts of compassion and self-respect she's cultivated over years of inner and outer journeys. She's lighting the fires of alchemy in her community, turning lead into gold by sharing her story, and offering counsel and encouragement to young people who aren't yet able to see hope, to feel self-respect, or to imagine having the strength to weather today's daunting challenges.

"Young people, you as an individual have a voice," she says to a group of high school students in one of her hundreds of talks all over the world. "Please use that voice. To make this world better. By doing just one thing for somebody else. It's worth it."[37]

Loretta knows what a profound gift and responsibility it is to use her voice. "I have this joy that I share with others," she says. "If you can talk to one person, and change that one person's mind, then that'll spread to two, or three, or four, or a hundred, or thousands. So if I could just change one or two minds, hopefully it'll spread on to more."

MATTHEW AND CRYSTAL'S GIFTS

MATTHEW WILLIAMS is another champion for inclusion in Special Olympics and beyond. Matthew has epilepsy and an intellectual disability. Throughout childhood and adolescence, he struggled to fit in and keep up with his peers. When he joined Special Olympics in eighth grade, it had a profound impact on his life, helping him make friends, providing him with self-confidence, and giving him an opportunity to participate in sports. He told me, "When I got into Special Olympics, I found an environment that really accepted me for who I am, and really gave me that opportunity to demonstrate that even though I have a disability, there are those abilities and gifts that I can maybe offer, and hopefully inspire people and get people to think differently about individuals with disabilities."[38]

Matthew has achieved a great deal in his time with Special Olympics, participating in basketball, track and field, swimming, floor hockey, and curling. He's fallen in love with the message of the movement. It's been over fifteen years since his first practice, and since then, Matthew has become another powerful voice of compassion. He became a Global Messenger for Special Olympics, won two medals at the Canada Summer Games, and chaired the Third Athlete Congress. He's become a leader with vision and insight, serving on the British Columbia Leadership Council in his home province. I've been privileged to see him in action, both on the field as I cheered him on, and while we served together on the Special Olympics International Board of Directors. His leadership was recognized even further when he was named the 2021 Canadian Male Special Olympics Athlete of the Year.

Matthew has also taken on a leadership role in the Spread the Word to End the Word campaign—a movement launched by SOI in 2009 to end the use of the word "retard(ed)," and to foster greater respect toward those with intellectual and developmental disabilities. Matthew says, "People still use the r-word not really understanding the effects and how much it hurts people with intellectual disabilities." He continued, "I just really hope people will identify me as an equal. I understand there are challenges and that I am different. I just want people to see me as me."[39]

Fifty years ago, he says, few people imagined individuals with intellectual disabilities could be heroes. "Sixty thousand spectators filled the famous LA Memorial Coliseum to watch the opening ceremonies of World Games and cheer athletes from one hundred and sixty-five countries around the world. Far from being hidden away, we were cheered and celebrated. Special Olympics teaches athletes to be confident and proud of themselves. Special Olympics teaches the world that people with intellectual disabilities deserve respect and inclusion."[40]

For Matthew, Special Olympics is about countering the ignorance, fear, and misunderstanding that people hold toward those who are different from them. It's a place where it's not only safe to be different—it's embraced.

"Special Olympics really did change my life," Matthew tells me. "I was born with a disability, and for many years growing up, I was ashamed about it. I thought being different was negative. I hadn't learned that being different can be a positive, and being different, you can change the world."[41]

Matthew understands the importance of rounding the circle, telling me, "I think you get what you give. And it might not come back right at that moment, but at some time in your life when you need it most, the compassion and the caring that you've given to others, you're going to get that back in return."[42]

It's no surprise that Matthew is adamant that the values of compassion and inclusion can be taught. "If we can teach people to learn acceptance, respect, and inclusion, they're not only going to be learners. They go on to be lifelong teachers of those values."[43]

Matthew highlights Unified Sports as a program that teaches these values. Unified Sports is a program that brings together people of all abilities, with and without intellectual disabilities, to come together and play. As of writing, 1.4 million people worldwide take part in Unified teams, playing soccer in Romania, basketball in Egypt, and floor hockey in China.[44] Playing Unified helps break down the walls of preconception that prevent people from truly seeing one another. It fosters genuine respect among players, teachers, and coaches, and creates a space for the discovery of one's own gifts, as well as those of others. We see here the second principle of the Grail of Compassion in practice—*connectedness with everyone in the community and knowing that everyone in the community has a purpose and unique gifts to share.*

Research backs this up. A 2016 survey of schools across the United States implementing Unified Sports showed that 97 percent of students participating in the program reported feeling greater unity, inclusion, and respect for people with ID.[45] "Someone with an intellectual disability is able to learn from someone with ID and vice versa," Matthew says. "I think that's going to build inclusive environments and lead to inclusive communities around the world."[46]

Crystal Williams is a writer and an equally gifted advocate in the movement to educate and transform society's beliefs about people with disabilities. A writer and a dedicated equestrian, Crystal used to compete in Special Olympics, and has overcome enormous challenges in her life. She has a rare disorder called Kabuki syndrome, "a multisystem disorder characterized by multiple abnormalities including distinctive facial features, growth delays, varying degrees of intellectual disability, skeletal abnormalities, and short stature."[47] Crystal has been open about her mental health struggles—including severe depression—over the course of her life.

In school, she felt like she was not understood, and recalls not having her boundaries respected, especially by teachers.[48] Still, Crystal sees these challenges as an illuminating force at the heart of her life's purpose.

In September 2019, I got to see two of my best friends get married in their hometown of Langley, British Columbia. Matt, who cried at the sight of Crystal in her wedding dress, didn't take his eyes off her as she walked down the aisle, nor during the ceremony itself. The joy and depth in their union was and remains profound. Their wedding would not have been possible in other places in the world because of discrimination and misinformed ideas about people with IDD and their ability to be partners and parents to children, if they choose.

"Everybody deserves to find love, feel included, and to show compassion for everyone else," Crystal says. "Having a disability made me a strong and better person. Something that really shaped me was to realize I need to not only be an advocate for myself, but also, I need to stand up and help other individuals that are special needs, and also people that have an invisible disability."[49]

"What I've realized over the past ten years," Crystal says, "is that, for me, I have to share my story with other people, because I know there are other people out there that are going through the same situation. But also, getting to see other people that have shared their stories makes me feel better too."

FAMILY SUPPORT

IN THE SPRING OF 1997, I traveled to Washington, DC, to meet with Tim Shriver. I had actually made the trip with the hope of receiving support, not looking for ways to give it: My family had recently brought my dad home from the rehabilitation hospital, and the adjustment turned out to be much harder than we thought for him and for my mom. Suffice to say, I didn't have Special Olympics on my mind, though that was all about to change. Little did I know that I would soon become part of a community that would nourish my being, where I could contribute my whole self, where everyone belongs.

Later that spring, Tim introduced me to his mother, as he sensed that her passion for families and the unstoppable power of mothers might resonate with me, which it did, though it was her spirit that touched me the most. Within a year, together with Tim and many Special Olympics athletes, family members, and other colleagues, we launched the Family Support Network (FSN). Mrs. Shriver was not one to let any grass grow under her feet.

To this day, the FSN works at the grassroots level all around the world to connect Special Olympics families with new families of children with intellectual disabilities and provides supportive links and information, as well as camaraderie among families of people with ID. This is an example of a program whose structure helps round the circle—to create reciprocal networks of belonging. As of 2019, there were nearly one million families worldwide who had found greater belonging through the program.

Through several conversations, it became clear to me that the relationship between herself and her sister Rosemary was as its core, a big part of the "Why?" of Special Olympics, growing out of the compassion and wisdom they developed through their love as sisters, and the deep reciprocal bond they shared.

Over time, the research that stemmed from the FSN program revealed that siblings of family members with ID can face a unique isolation—disability by association, reduced parental attention, and other isolating experiences within their schools or communities. My Special Olympics colleagues and I saw that by supporting siblings of family members with ID in their own journeys would help them to become powerful advocates in the "Inclusion Revolution."

BEYOND THE FIELD OF PLAY

SPECIAL OLYMPICS doesn't leave its athletes on the playing field. In fact, SOI is asking the healing question all over the world, ensuring that the circle is rounded well beyond the presentation of medals and the close of competition.

Amid the COVID-19 pandemic, Special Olympics served as a lifeline for both athletes and their families, creating digital communities for those who would otherwise face profound isolation during a global crisis.[50]

Indeed, a recent internal survey from Special Olympics found that while 70 percent of SOI athletes felt more isolated and alone during the pandemic, the athletes that were connected through SOI's programs felt less isolated, and were more likely to use preventive measures, like wearing masks, washing their hands, and practicing social distancing.[51]

The support and connection provided through the Family Support Network has been an especially important resource during the challenges and uncertainty presented by the pandemic. Ben Haack is a Special Olympics leader from Australia, a gifted football and cricket player, and a member of the SOI International board of directors, where he serves as Athlete Representative on the International Advisory Committee. He recently shared that at this time, what families desperately need are "local events where they can come to a safe place. They can come to a place to vent, to talk to like-minded people that understand. They need to go to an event where their child can go and compete, to have fun, to feel safe and feel connected."[52]

AS PABLO NERUDA SAID in his lecture upon receiving the Nobel Prize in Literature: "All paths lead to the same goal: to convey to others what we are. And we must pass through solitude and difficulty, isolation and silence in order to reach forth to the enchanted place where we can dance our clumsy dance and sing our sorrowful song—but in this dance or in this song there are fulfilled the most ancient rites of our conscience in the awareness of being human and of believing in a common destiny."[53]

Parzival shows us that the Grail of Compassion is both about finding ourselves, and about understanding that we are part of something bigger.

Parzival; Loretta; Matthew and Crystal—all overcame hardship on their quest for belonging. All succeeded, thanks in large part, to the support of their community. And all rounded the circle long after realizing their "Grail," doing the hard work of building belonging with the people around them, and empowering new champions to carry on their important work. The Quest for Belonging is difficult but necessary. If we lead with compassion, and remember to ask the healing question, we can realize our Grail and, in the process, change the world.

CHAPTER FIVE

AT HOME WITHIN OURSELVES

THE NGUNI BANTU TRADITIONS of South Africa have a word that illuminates the meaning of belonging in these cultures and societies—*ubuntu*, a term whose most well-known translation, from Liberian peace activist and Nobel laureate Leymah Gbowee, is "I am what I am because of who we all are."[1]

The full phrase in Zulu is *umuntu ngumuntu ngabantu*, meaning "A person is a person through other people," a phrase theologian and anti-apartheid leader, the late Archbishop Desmond Tutu, shared often, including in relation to the process of rebuilding post-apartheid South Africa.

The term "*ubuntu*" has a rich history. In South Africa in particular, where the concept has in recent decades emerged in anti-apartheid dialogues, *ubuntu* has come to have multiple meanings and resonances.

Archbishop Tutu was one of the concept's most powerful messengers. He once remarked on the difficulty of conveying *ubuntu*'s full meaning in Western languages, which are often person-centric in grammar and syntax. Its nucleus is deep. "[*Ubuntu*] speaks of the very essence of being human. It is to say, my humanity is caught up, is inextricably bound up, in yours. We belong in a bundle of life."[2]

The principle of *ubuntu* can be heard in the words of Martin Luther King Jr. in his final Christmas Eve sermon, delivered at the Ebenezer

Baptist Church in Atlanta in 1967. "We are all caught in an inescapable network of mutuality, tied into a single garment of destiny," King said to the congregation, and to the world. "Whatever affects one directly affects all indirectly. We are made to live together because of the interrelated structure of reality."[3]

Ubuntu speaks to the values of group solidarity, compassion, human dignity, and collective unity. These principles are the heart of the concept. Yet, while these values of common humanity are often most celebrated about *ubuntu*, there is also an important emphasis on the relationship between belonging within the individual and belonging in community.

Within *ubuntu*, individuals in a community are not meant only to serve the collective and a monolithic idea of collective mission. Rather, they serve the community by embodying their truest, most authentic selves. "I need you, in order for me to be me," Archbishop Tutu observes of this aspect of *ubuntu*. "I need you to be you to the fullest."[4]

Former US president Barack Obama spoke to this dialectic between individual and community in his remarks at Nelson Mandela's memorial service, describing Mandela's extraordinary embodiment and transmission of the values of *ubuntu*:

> Mandela understood the ties that bind the human spirit. There is a word in South Africa—*ubuntu*—a word that captures Mandela's greatest gift: his recognition that we are all bound together in ways that are invisible to the eye; that there is a oneness to humanity; that we achieve ourselves by sharing ourselves with others, and caring for those around us.
>
> We can never know how much of this sense was innate in him, or how much was shaped in a dark and solitary cell. But we remember the gestures, large and small—introducing his jailers as honored guests at his inauguration; taking a pitch in a Springbok uniform; turning his family's heartbreak into a call to confront HIV/AIDS—that revealed the depth of his empathy and his understanding. He not only embodied *ubuntu*, he taught millions to find that truth within themselves."[5]

Obama suggests here that Mandela's moral integrity and fierce cultivation of inner respect and wholeness were an important source from which his unifying powers sprang.

Trappist monk, writer, and social activist Thomas Merton also speaks to the relationship between the individual and the community in a way that echoes that of *ubuntu*. "We cannot find ourselves within ourselves, but only in others," he writes in *No Man Is an Island*. "Yet at the same time, before we can go out to others, we must first find ourselves."[6]

The journey to becoming whole within ourselves—in many cases, regaining our wholeness—is part of the ground from which the individual can know and then share their gifts with the community. In a similar way, the community must also make its own collective evolution toward wholeness so that it is able to receive the gifts of individuals—especially those who fall outside what the collective considers "normal."

This is challenging work for both. In fact, it is often the work of a lifetime for an individual, and the work of generations for communities.

Ubuntu asks us to consider questions that have often eluded us in today's world.

What does it mean to belong to one's own self? What is the relationship between belonging within and belonging in community?

As the concept suggests, one of the ways forward is to journey into a deeper relationship between self and community, between internal and external. This journey allows us to cultivate love within, and then bring it boldly forth into the world.

Over the years, I've had the good fortune to be able to walk with many people who have shown me what belonging within means as a matter of real-world practice. We'll meet some of those people in this chapter.

The work of belonging to one's own self is challenging at every level. We're living in an age in which systemic barriers—both subtle and overt—keep us from knowing and respecting ourselves. In a global society that often confines definitions of interconnectedness to technology, it can be difficult to recognize our human gifts and find the power to share them in healthy ways.

Along our journeys, we find that inner belonging is inextricably linked to belonging with others. Our ability to see the other as ourselves is deepened as we uncover within ourselves the illusion of separateness, the fundamental unity at the core of our being. Our capacity for healing others, sometimes just through our presence, expands as we heal ourselves.

JOE'S JOURNEY TO BELONGING THROUGH MINDFULNESS

JOE CRAMER FOUND that fundamental unity inside himself in one of the places one might not expect to find it. An actor and an aspiring musician, Joe has been on a journey that has taken him from stardom as a childhood actor to the winding road of drug addiction, and finally to finding peace inside himself and coming into abundance in the world again.[7]

Joe had a successful career as an actor early in his life, starring in television shows and, most prominently, in the film *Flight of the Navigator*, for which he received a 1987 Saturn Award nomination for Best Performance by a Young Actor from the Academy of Science Fiction, Fantasy and Horror Films.

In his thirties, Joe struggled with addiction to narcotics and alcohol, receiving short prison sentences related to both. He grappled with shame and self-doubt that became amplified in the prison culture that treats inmates as numbers and as people who need to be punished, beyond having their freedom taken away.

The psychological burden of a prison system that dehumanized inmates took a toll on Joe and those incarcerated with him. Rather than serving to rehabilitate or deter him, he notes, many of the incentives he found there only deepened his embeddedness in negative influences and addiction.

Upon his release from prison, Joe was unable to kick his addictions. He was desperate to get help. He decided to take a massive risk: He would commit a crime and return to jail—specifically with the intention of seeking treatment. "My intention when I committed my crime was to get caught, which is crazy," Joe tells me. "Because I needed serious help from my addiction. I wanted to go to the Guthrie Program. I knew I couldn't get any funding for long-term treatment. So I was like, 'I just need to put myself away,'" Joe says.

Guthrie House was established in 2007 by the Nanaimo Region John Howard Society in the Nanaimo Correctional Centre, British Columbia, to support residents of prisons in overcoming life challenges. Guthrie's approach to addiction treatment sees the community as a healer and the method of change, helping participants to recognize negative beliefs and thought patterns through positive behavioral modeling and mindfulness techniques for relating to themselves and others more compassionately. These changes happen in a social setting, within a community, under the philosophy that negative patterns, attitudes, and roles are not acquired in isolation, and cannot therefore be altered in isolation.[8] Participants are called "residents" rather than "inmates," and guards receive special training meant to take the staff and the residents out of the dehumanization that often occurs in jailhouse mentality and hierarchical structures.

The program consists of four phases, which address the root causes of addiction, help residents develop recovery skills, and prevent relapse. It also prepares them for reentry in the outside world in meaningful ways, building their access to support networks in the community before they are released. The program has transformed prison culture by developing a safe community within which to catalyze change. It's also reduced the rate of individuals who reoffend by 44 percent.[9]

Internalizing the shift in values the program instills in participants is a process that recasts the lens through which residents view themselves and their lives. "What's amazing about Guthrie is that you're a person. You're treated like a person, you have stuff to offer, you have things to give. It takes a while for us inside to actually trust that that's ok," Joe says, referring to those "inside" prison.[10]

Joe found the mindfulness aspects of the program transformative.

Mindfulness is a practice of conscious and open attention to the present moment, where thoughts, emotions, or sensations are observed without judgment. Mindfulness techniques originated in Buddhist and yogic traditions, and have also been applied in a wide range of secular formats and modalities outside of religious practice to bring greater peace within oneself and in relation to others. The techniques are used in a range of mindfulness-based therapies used in Guthrie House—therapies that address stress, anxiety, and pain, and that retrain the brain to mitigate negative emotions before they spiral into more extensive negative states like depression or panic attacks.

Joe describes how he started his journey in prison using mindfulness to learn simply how to be present in his own body, whether it was brushing his teeth and feeling fully the sensations inside his mouth, or feeling the water on his skin when he washed his hands. Gaining greater awareness of his physical body and the thought patterns and self-narrative he had constructed about himself over the course of his life allowed him to regain control over the forces driving his psyche and his consciousness.

Joe learned through the mindfulness concepts and techniques in the program about the nature of emotions within the mind and how to understand their signals more skillfully. "I learn[ed] that emotions come. To be able to just feel them out and let them happen instead of avoiding them or trying to sweep them under the rug. It takes their power away. Saying, *I'm sad, I'm angry, I feel guilty.* It's ok, just let it happen. Because the more we reject something, the bigger it gets," he says.

The more Joe observed his thoughts and emotions consciously, the more he understood about the roots of his addictions. "Mindfulness was really instrumental in helping to change the self-narrative. And a self-narrative was such a huge piece for my recovery from addiction," he says. "It's that self-talk that keeps us in these negative patterns, in addiction or alcoholism or stress. Because you don't want to think, you don't want to feel these things."

Gradually, he was able to train his mind to shift the negative beliefs into positive affirmations. "For so many years, I would say horrible things to myself in the mirror," he says. "Now I wake up and the first thing that happens is, 'I'm joy, I'm love, I'm happiness, I'm health, I'm wealth, I'm disciplined, I am dedication. I'm pure spirit, love, and joy.'"

This was a conscious, challenging practice that Joe worked at every day in prison. He would take a dry erase marker and write on the mirror—*I am health, I am wealth, I am joy, I am love, I am happiness*—so that even if he didn't want to read it that day, his subconscious would pick it up. "I would see it in the mirror and instantly it would say it back. Even if it's just a flash, right? And that's how I started to instill this new self-talk."

The new narrative began to change his relationship with himself and those around him. It gave him belief in himself as a worthy human being, capable of helping others and of realizing his dreams.

The Inside-Out program that took place at Guthrie House was also foundational to Joe's journey to reclaim belonging within himself, and within a community. Founded in 1997 by Lori Pompa, a professor in criminal justice at Temple University in Philadelphia, Pennsylvania, the Inside-Out Prison Exchange Program, known as "Inside-Out," creates a forum for dialogue and education across social differences, bringing traditional college students together with incarcerated students in prisons for semester-long classes. The program now operates in the US, Canada, and several other countries, and has created spaces for more than 40,000 "inside" and "outside" students to "move beyond the walls that separate them."[11] Joe's Inside-Out experience was in partnership with Vancouver Island University (VIU), a school that we'll learn more about later in the book.

Joe was initially hesitant to take part in the course, and almost quit when he saw the curriculum, which was based on fourth-year university-level criminology coursework. Receiving encouragement from the facilitators of the program, Joe persisted, and quickly became one of the students whom others turned to for help in the class. He felt a swell of inspiration and meaningfulness as those people, too, saw that they were worthy, that they could speak from their heart, and that just the way they were was enough.

"Inside-Out was such a huge foundation. I'd been doing the mindfulness work, but it solidified all the work I'd done, and brought out these things in me, this confidence and this assurity that I could do something and that I was part of society and that I had things to offer. That was my first step to belonging somewhere."[12]

Part of the transformative power of the class was its creation of spaces where belonging opened up between the "inside" and "outside" students. "I get goosebumps because I love it," Joe says of the icebreaking and privilege exercises that happen at the beginning of each class. "You look at someone in fourth-year criminology class in university, in this completely different scope of living or humanity. And then you see that you're not so different at all."

Natasha Karod, one of the "outside" students in the Nanaimo Inside-Out program in 2019 and 2020 and a criminology major at Vancouver Island University, describes the spaces of belonging that are cultivated in the program as crucial and unique elements that make it an agent of change in the world in a way that transcends received definitions of inside and outside, healers and healed, imprisoned and free. "Inside-Out brings out the vulnerability in you," she tells me. "You want to build these connections. We were all gaining and receiving stuff, and you're all giving at the same time. It was like a circle. It was a big circle of care. It was an equal amount of taking and giving."[13]

On graduating from Inside-Out and finishing his time at Guthrie House and the Nanaimo Correctional Centre, Joe continued to work with the facilitators of Nanaimo's Inside-Out program, Joanne Falvai and Beth McLin, and taking advantage of the post-release support network that Guthrie had linked him to over the course of that program. He has returned to Guthrie to share his experiences and successes in the outside world. He's also involved in Inside-Out teacher training, helping to educate more teachers so that the program can continue to evolve and expand. Joe is doing the hard work of "rounding the circle," and has found meaning and confidence in being a resource for those communities.

"I feel like I belong in my community. I feel like I belong in the world. I feel like I belong in my own skin. All of those things came from the work that I was doing in mindfulness and Inside-Out," he says. "We're starting to learn more and more that when we actually follow our hearts, our dreams, our imagination, and our natural energy, that we can achieve wealth and success and joy."[14]

(I am large, I contain multitudes)

—WALT WHITMAN, "SONG OF MYSELF"[15]

Celebrated actress, producer, director, and author, Goldie Hawn also knows the power of mindfulness and the human mind. Early on in her career, Goldie found herself seeking out ways to quell the anxiety brought on by demands of the acting profession.

"In 1972, I started meditating. Meditation became such a great joy to me because I was revisiting what I felt was a place in me that I had abandoned somehow, that deep-seated joy that I felt I had lost. And when I started meditating, I realized that I was revisiting my core."[16]

In 2003, after years of researching and practicing mindfulness meditation, combined with her search for a deeper understanding of happiness, Goldie created the MindUP program in partnership with the Goldie Hawn Foundation, to help children understand their emotions and minds. Working in collaboration with educators, neuroscientists, and educators, MindUP created a classroom curriculum for students and teachers in grades K–7, focusing on developing emotional and cognitive tools.

Mindfulness-based interventions draw from Buddhist teachings with the goal of promoting holistic development and well-being. MindUP's ethos is largely grounded in the educational philosophy of social and emotional learning (SEL),[17] which teaches children critical emotional and social skills through five core components often absent from standard school curricula: self-awareness, social awareness, self-management, responsible decision-making, and relationship skills.[18]

Goldie explains that MindUP also teaches children about their amygdala and their prefrontal cortex. "The amygdala of course is their barking dog that helps us and saves us, but also can become extremely reactive. And it also mitigates learning."[19] In this way, the children are taught about the neurological pathways that affect their emotional states, and are reminded of the importance of breathing deeply and taking "brain breaks" so that they can think, analyze, listen, and communicate more effectively. As Goldie explains, "Breath changes the brain. Focus changes the brain."

Not only does mindfulness training like that carried out through MindUP benefit the children and teachers in the program, it also creates positive spillovers. Families benefit from children who are now able to use mindfulness techniques at home, creating a greater sense of well-being for their parents and siblings. So, while programs like MindUP focus on children, they also catalyze an environment of compassion and happiness for increasingly expansive circles of care around children's lives. In other words, the work of creating greater awareness and belonging within oneself through mindfulness is also, by extension, part of the work of creating belonging in families and the wider community. Thinking differently and critically about the formative role of education in creating caring, empathetic, thoughtful young citizens—this is essential to broad-based, far-reaching systems change, which we'll discuss in greater detail later in the book.

For Goldie, mindfulness has meant a unification of separate pieces of herself into a greater whole that she's radiated outward into the world, through her acting of course, but also through the MindUP program, which has benefited over six million children in schools around the world.

The effect of mindfulness and meditation on Goldie's sense of belonging within herself has been profound. "Now I am not two people; I am one. I don't leave myself anywhere. I take myself wherever I go. I like who I am. I have nothing to hide. There's no pretense about the work that I do. I don't hold myself [in] any higher esteem than anybody else I talk to in the street. It's just the authenticity of knowing enough about yourself to carry it with you."

CAROLINE'S JOURNEY TO BELONGING WITHIN

CAROLINE CASEY has a similar kind of presence. It's a presence that begins with an innate understanding of her own journey, which she then radiates outward to help heal those around her.

Caroline's journey came to a crossroads when she was seventeen. She was getting an eye exam and she told the doctor, excitedly, that she was about to learn how to drive. Caroline, a teenager in Ireland, dreamed of racing motorcycles and loved blasting loud country music. Her father called her his rebel-hearted wild child.[20]

Yet for all the excitement in her voice when she told the doctor about driving, all she got in response was an eerie silence. It was the kind of quiet that meant something was wrong.

And then:

"You haven't told her yet?" said the doctor to her mother.[21]

It was the moment she finally realized what her family was trying to hide from her for her entire life. She was legally blind.

I first met Caroline in 2019. She was giving a talk at the World Economic Forum Annual Meeting in Davos, Switzerland. Running late, I walked into the panel after everyone was already seated and Caroline had begun to speak.

I saw her and I remember thinking, *Who's this woman with wild blonde rocker hair, funky glasses, wearing bold pink among all of these dark suits and snow boots?*

FINDING INNER BELONGING TO TRANSMIT OUTER HEALING

CAROLINE'S PARENTS never wanted her to be defined by a medical condition. While she could only see a few feet in front of her, they decided she shouldn't receive special treatment in school. They knew she was a hard worker who could always find ways to adapt.

She knew this strategy so well that she carried it forward with renewed ardor in the years following that eye exam. Caroline spent the next decade succeeding in university, earning outstanding marks in business school, and landing a prime position with a global management consulting firm. Yet she continued to hide this basic reality about her life.

"I always knew I was different for sure. But I could play the game," Caroline told me. She just wanted to have the same choices and the same chances, and so she didn't tell anyone about her eyesight. While she excelled in the business world, she recalls, there was something going on in the back of her mind. "It was like there was a restlessness. A little rebel restlessness in me," she says.[22]

While she would face comparatively minor mishaps like walking into doors or into the men's restroom, the most significant challenge, she says, wasn't being perceived as "clumsy." It was a feeling that she had to be strong and not ask for help. It was also seeing virtually no one with a disability represented in her company or industry, and realizing that she was falling into an unhealthy drive to "fit in."

Hiding was taking its toll. Two and a half years into the job, she temporarily damaged the remaining vision she had and put herself under extraordinary stress, resulting in physical and emotional exhaustion.

She mustered the courage to walk into the office of the head of Human Resources and disclose the reality of her condition. The HR office sent her to an eye specialist for an exam.

And then something serendipitous happened. The exam was a counterpoint—almost a perfect antithesis—of the experience at the eye doctor when she was seventeen years old.

"I had no idea this man was going to change my life. But before I got to him, I was so lost. I had no idea who I was anymore," she says in her TEDWomen talk.[23] A decade later, she told me, "In this yearning to belong and to be part of the gang and to get all the same things, I actually started losing sight of who I was. And I really didn't like myself."[24]

The specialist didn't bother testing her eyes that day. Instead, he asked, "Why are you fighting so hard to not be yourself?"

Choking up, Caroline was unable to speak.

"Do you love what you do, Caroline?" he asked.

How do I tell him? she recalls thinking, searching for words.

He spoke after a few moments of silence. "What do you love to do? What did you want to be when you were little?"[25]

These were the healing questions—the questions of compassion that began to heal the wound.

As she made her way out of the office, he said, "I think it's time. I think it's time to stop fighting and do something different."[26]

The game was up, and she knew it. The paradigm of her life had shattered. She had lost her belief in the old lens through which she had seen the world, the one society had seemed to have given her, and now she found herself grieving where that belief had taken her. "And now I really couldn't see," she remarks. "I was crumpled."[27]

Yet this was the moment when her true self began to emerge. She kept thinking about the questions the eye specialist had asked her. *What do you want to be? Do you love what you do? Do something different.*

Nine months later, Caroline was in India, riding an elephant named Kanchi on a thousand-kilometer trek, raising funds for the Irish National Council for the Blind and Sightsavers International. She raised enough money to fund six thousand cataract operations After returning home, she quit her job and launched a social enterprise focused on reframing issues of disability, particularly in the workplace. She called the initiative *Kanchi*. "My organization was always going to be named after my elephant, because disability is like the elephant in the room," she says. "I wanted to make you see it in a positive way—no charity, no pity."[28] She wanted to help transform the narratives of victimhood into visions of possibility and belonging.

Today, Caroline is a leading global social entrepreneur. She's worked to integrate diverse elements of herself—from childhood to her business career to activism—into a unified whole.

Caroline notes that, on paper, the world has made strides in terms of disability rights. Yet she's cognizant that many of the underlying issues are not yet resolved.

People with disabilities are still systematically underrepresented in the workplace, the media, and advertising. Today, an estimated 15 percent of the global population lives with some form of disability.[29] The prevalence of disability generally is on the rise, due to aging populations and the global increase in long-term health conditions like diabetes, cancer, and mental health disorders.[30] Most of this population is largely invisible and ignored. The forces of shame and stigma that prevented Caroline from being her full self for more than a decade still loom over the world for many other people with disabilities.

With most of her career having been in the private sector, Caroline identified a major lack of attention within the business community to foster inclusion. She realized this was one of the places where she could make a strong impact on inclusion. Caroline told me, "What business includes and values, society includes and values."

"We have to find a new language," she concludes. "We have to find a new way."[31]

In 2017, Caroline embarked on another trek, this time across Colombia on a horse. She set out after the sudden passing of her father in October 2016, who, pulling her into his chest four days before he died, urged her not to wait to follow her emerging dream of initiating a global campaign to reframe issues of disability. She called this journey the "Blaze a Trail" campaign, and it ended with her riding onto the main stage of the One Young World Opening Ceremony in Bogotá.

The longer-term vision behind the trek, which she hoped would kick off a global conversation, was to recruit a "catalytic" group of leading CEOs who would commit to shifting the paradigm of inclusion and respect for people with disabilities. She was adamant that the movement had to focus on business leaders. "Leaders make choices. Choices create cultures. I fundamentally believe inclusive business creates inclusive societies," she says.

In 2019, Caroline worked to foster partnerships with high-level businesses within the private sector, culminating in the launch of the organization the Valuable 500—a play on Fortune 500—at the World Economic Forum's Annual Meeting in Davos, Switzerland.

The disability inclusion movement seeks to meaningfully recognize and act on the truth that the 1.3 billion people living with disabilities are inherently valuable. These firms commit to working to "unlock the social and economic value of people living with disabilities across the world."[32] She has approached 3,000 companies to make her case. By May 2021, she had 500 CEOs from national and multinational companies pledge to address disability inclusion in their leadership agendas and commit to action in their companies, which in total comprise twenty million employees across thirty-six countries and a variety of sectors, including hospitality, finance, and big tech.[33]

Intel is committed to increasing the percentage of employees who self-identify as having a disability to 10 percent of its workforce. British Airways now has a specialized Accessibility Customer Service team who can better assist customers with a range of disabilities. Adobe has committed not only to actively recruit employees from the disability community, but also to build more accessible controls into their products. These are the kinds of real, tangible changes being driven by Caroline Casey and the disability inclusion movement.

One of the things that's so powerful about Caroline's work with the Valuable 500 is how she's able to go beyond addressing disability as a limitation and instead focus on opportunities for human thriving and societal advancement. "I think some of the greatest innovations that are going to come for our society's physical design and digital design, or communication design, are going to come from people who live on the extremes, which is often people with disabilities who have a very different way of living."[31] She points out as an example that text messages were originally designed for deaf people. Television's remote control was initially developed for blind people. "I think there's some absolutely extraordinary innovation that the disability community has to offer," she says.

Still, Caroline contends we must go deeper than business. In her work today, she objects to the notion that "diversity and inclusion" must always have an economic justification. "I get so disillusioned when we talk about the business case for racial equality, the business case for LGBTQ, the business case for women," she tells me. "Since when did we have to have a business case about human beings? Business does not exist without humans. Business leaders are human beings first."

Caroline's journey to inner authenticity and bold outward vision for healing has led her to speak from a place of experience that's been hard-won around what it means to belong to oneself. She understands that a human being is going to be most powerful—and empowering—to their community if they are given the space to embody their true nature and purpose, not the purpose society seems to assign them.

"I have had an extraordinary two decades of my life, but it wasn't easy, and it wasn't a straight journey. If you're hiding who you are, you can never hope to belong. And you can never have the life that you might want, if you're pretending to be somebody else."

In our recent conversation, Caroline and I spoke extensively about power and purpose. She is often described in the media as a disability activist. "I'm not," she tells me. "I often think I'm a belonging activist. I don't want anybody to be defined by one part of themselves. I want us to be free to be who we are, whatever way that that comes out. The activism I do is to try and create systems where people can flourish as who they need to be." That's how she sees her own mission, and it's woven into a broader vision that reaches out to millions of others around the world.

REBIRTH

JOSINA MACHEL is another hero whose journey to inner belonging has been one of rebirth and renewal. I see her as a true warrior for women, fighting tirelessly against the scourge of gender-based violence (GBV). The daughter of Graça Machel and Samora Machel—the first president of an independent Mozambique—Josina has fought with fierceness and grace to claim her survival, and to help others claim theirs. She's helped to create inner and outer refuge for women all over Mozambique, working to transform what it means to be a woman—and a human—for generations of Mozambicans across the country.

"I grew up in one of the most interesting family settings on earth," Josina writes. "Samora and Graça's daughter—one of a few people born in a presidential palace." She was raised with some of the most prominent liberation activists and freedom fighters across Africa as family friends and colleagues, aunties, uncles, and grandparents.[35]

Josina's life was turned upside down when, on October 19, 1986, her father died in a plane crash in South Africa. "I cried and cry for my dad. My dad who smiled whenever I came into a room."[36]

Her mother, Graça, whom she describes as a "phoenix" during this time, surrounded her and her siblings with love and loyal friends after her father's death, and raised her to know she had the same value and rights as men.[37]

The work of addressing systemic injustice is deeply ingrained in her family. "I started fighting for the rights of women when I was very young," Josina says. "I always wanted to be in the space of healing. I worked to open up the opportunities for women to heal in different ways. Throughout my university years, that is what I worked towards."

In 1998, Graça married Nelson Mandela. He, too, became a guiding light in Josina's life's work of empowering women.

"Life gave me one of my best rewards when I had the unique honor of calling Nelson Rolihlahla Mandela *Papa.* Papa brought me back the blessing of being a daughter again. Because of his presence in my life, I learnt what being a mother, a wife, a valued-female woman of society is like."[38]

Josina channeled her energy into a far-ranging work in sociology, child development, modern dance, and advocacy for women's rights. She was involved in this work when her life shifted course again in October 2015, when she was brutally assaulted by her then partner.

"On the day that happened, I was savagely beaten, and as a consequence, I lost my right eye," she says.[39] "I guess the universe wanted something different from me. Although I had worked and studied and had spoken to women who have been survivors of violence for ten or fifteen years, I never imagined that one day I would be put in that position."

Following the assault, Josina encountered a justice system that did not protect her or her rights. She was denied a protection order despite being subject to a campaign of intimidation and harassment.[40] Two years after the assault, after the courts granted the defendant multiple delays to the trial, her attacker was finally tried and found guilty of assault and of domestic and psychological violence. He was given a suspended prison sentence of three years and four months, and ordered to pay Josina damages.

In June 2020, however, Mozambique's Higher Appeal Court overturned the conviction, citing "no proof that the accused injured the victim because the event allegedly occurred when the accused and the victim were alone and there were no witnesses to this crime"—this despite a confession from the attacker himself.[41]

In the wake of the decision, nongovernmental organizations (NGOs), women's organizations, and civil society all over the continent came to Josina's defense. Amnesty International called on the courts to reconsider the decision. "This case illustrates quite clearly that even the most powerful women are not protected against violence. Instead, the criminal justice system further perpetuates the abuse and suffering of victims and survivors of GBV."[42]

Josina and her family met the ruling with renewed determination. "This struggle chose me, and I will continue using my voice and my face to advocate and fight for the eradication of gender-based violence till my last breath," Josina says in her TEDx talk. "Together, and only together, we will challenge and dismantle this system of oppression."[43]

I met Josina in New York City in 2018. Graça had invited me to an event hosted by the Kuhluka Movement, the organization Josina founded within the Graça Machel Trust dedicated in part to addressing GBV. Around twenty of us were sitting around the table, including some professional basketball players from all over Africa. Josina's piercing sense of dignity and strength was moving as she was telling her story—qualities she shares with her mother. She stood just as tall as the basketball players in her persona, and commanded the room. In the years since, Josina and I have supported each other's organizations and missions, and have collaborated across continents.

Gender-based violence is present all over the world. An estimated 87,000 women were intentionally killed in 2017 globally—137 women a day—and more than half of them were killed by intimate partners or a family member.[44] Violence against women is pervasive but also widely underreported. Less than 40 percent of women who experience violence will report these crimes or seek help.[45] The global cost of violence against women is estimated at US$1.5 trillion.[46]

In Mozambique, 37 percent of women have experienced some form of gender-based violence, and 45 percent of women who have been married have experienced violence committed by their husbands.[47] While progress has been made in legal frameworks in the country, patriarchal values and beliefs, among other barriers, prevent these laws from being fully implemented, as is evident in Josina's case.

In the years since the assault, Josina's journey for justice and healing has become a deeper summons for her. In 2017, she founded the Kuhluka Movement. The word *kuhluka* means "rebirth" in Tchopi, a language of the

Vatsonga of southern Mozambique. The movement seeks to change gender norms and create safe spaces where those who have survived domestic violence can be validated, taken care of, and regenerated.[48]

Kuhluka has established shelters in Maputo city and province for women who have experienced domestic violence, free psychological counseling, therapy, medical services, and police protection. They also give "dignity packs" for women who have been abused, to be distributed at police stations and medical centers in the first twenty-four hours. The dignity packs have served women all over Mozambique.

"Some of us reach these places in a very undignified way," explains Josina. "Many of us go to these places without clothes, without shoes, or our clothes have been torn apart. We are bleeding, and we have to stay in those places and make a criminal report, in some of the most undignified conditions."[49]

The pack is intended to give comfort and dignity in a very difficult time, and includes a *capulana* (a long cloth worn in Mozambique that can be wrapped around the body as a dress or skirt), essential items like flip-flops, undergarments in case women need to leave forensic evidence with investigators, and sanitary pads if women are bleeding from wounds or menstruating.

The dignity packs also include a small booklet that explains the journey the survivors are about to begin. It explains their rights, how they should be treated by the police, and what they should demand. The booklet also speaks to some of the possible emotions the survivors may experience, and where they can seek help for processing their experience, including through Kuhluka. "The feedback is amazing," Josina says. "There are many women that have cried when they received the packs."[50]

Josina has also expanded the work of Kuhluka into communities and the workplace through the creation of Circles of Support. The Circles of Support are comprised of around twenty people, including family members of survivors, who share their stories and receive counseling in order to be better equipped to deal with the repercussions of violence.

Because the fabric of a family will never be the same after GBV has been experienced, Josina says, these groups help empower everyone in the family and the community to deal with survivor violence, because all people in a collective are affected by an act of domestic violence. The concept behind Circles of Support is one that we can and should export to jurisdictions around the world. Think of the immense benefit that could be brought to your own neighborhood through a group like this. Coming together in support of one another—this is what happens when we keep the focus on people, and offer support, love, and resources to facilitate the long but necessary journey toward healing.

By focusing on healing within the collective, Josina envisions the creation of positive cycles of belonging: "Part of the work that we do is to build up this sense of belonging. Knowing that you are fine, you are who you are, and you don't need to justify your existence. Belonging is not just the physical space that we talk about," she says, such as the shelters the organization has created. "Belonging is actually the wellbeing within us, it is knowing that we are because we are."

"We just need to be able to give ourselves the space to meet ourselves, to allow us to crack," Josina continues. "Allow us to crack and get familiar with who we are when we crack. And in that moment, we get the strength to build. Find a reason to stand up. Every single human being has that ability, given the opportunity to do so. We all have it. It's in us. It's in here," she says, pointing to her heart.[51]

For Josina, creating inner and outer spaces of belonging extends into the intergenerational vision to transform gender norms into forces that nurture dignified lives. "All of us as human beings recognize that we have the privilege of life, and it is a privilege both for men and women. We need to respect ourselves and respect others, which means allowing us to belong, and share the sacred space that is our life," she says. "We need to do that both for girls and for boys, so that all of them grow with that same sense."[52]

Josina's journey toward her life's purpose, which is fully emerging out of great hardship, embodies the heart of what being human means in a world that is often messy and complex, and where our humanity is indeed, as Archbishop Tutu told us, inextricably bound up in that of others.

"My ultimate purpose on earth is really empowering women," Josina says. "And I call myself my spiritual name. I call myself a service. That's ultimately who I am. And when we meet, when it's my time to meet the gods and all the beings, the wise beings, and they look at me, I hope I'll be able to stand tall and say I did my journey. And in it, I was able to share my peace with other women I love in order to do their own journeys, whatever they were."[53]

The women and men we've walked with in this chapter have built belonging for others by first finding belonging in themselves. Their paths in life have been vastly different, yet together, they share a common thread of seeking to expand upon their innate internal selves. This deep understanding of the self has, in turn, built the foundation for greater community resonance. In recognizing their truest selves, these changemakers have gone on to share their innate gifts with the world, and have created spaces within which others can flourish.

CHAPTER SIX

THE TRUE VALUE OF PLACE

AS I SAT WITH WENDELL BERRY, surrounded by hundreds of books, sipping iced tea and listening to bird songs coming from the front yard of Lanes Landing, the home he shares with Tanya, his wife of more than sixty years, it occurred to me that *this* is how I would like to spend my first morning in heaven.

The Berrys live amid oak, walnut, and maple trees in the green rolling hills close to where the Kentucky and Ohio Rivers meet. Their home is delightfully liberated from the tethers of computers and smartphones and, accordingly, liberated from many of the tensions of the modern world. It's filled with an extraordinary number of books on topics from Renaissance literature to modern ecology. From the moment I arrived, I thought back to memories on my family's farm. I felt time begin to slow down a little bit. I felt grounded. I felt peace. I've never been one to wax nostalgic about some glorified imagined past, but I felt a sense of wholeness that's hard to find these days.

He and Tanya met in 1955 when they were both students at the University of Kentucky in nearby Lexington. They married in 1957. In the fall of 1964, after some years of "wandering about"—including prestigious stints in academic life in the US and Europe, they bought a twelve-acre property called Lanes Landing, near Port Royal, where Wendell's family had lived and farmed for generations. They first intended it as a place to spend summers. But it wasn't long until they started feeling like something was missing. He recalls Tanya saying on a visit there in the spring of 1965, "You don't want to spend weekends here. You want to live here, and so do I." That was that. They packed up their big-city lives for good, got in the car with their two young children, and set off to live on and with the land.

For more than half a century, The Berrys have been fully immersed in this place—cherishing their family, caring for their home, tilling the soil, tending to a flock of sheep, and some cropping too. And all the while, with Tanya's editing and advice, Wendell has been writing poems, essays, and novels, inspired by his family and his connection to the earth, his faith, and a tight-knit local community. He's published more than fifty books. He's won the National Humanities Medal, among a long list of other honors. Yet, talking with Wendell Berry, I get the sense that he doesn't care all that much about the acclaim.

Most of Berry's work feels like a prayer of gratitude to his home. "When we bought this place and realized it should be our home," he told me, "we made a submission to this place's claim on us. That kind of thing changes you. I came to see that this place is not ours, but we are its."

Berry has a specific vocabulary for talking about these matters. In our conversation that day, I noticed he didn't speak about his farm. He called it his *homeplace*.

"Prepositions have always meant a lot to me," he said. "The homeplace is where you're *from*." He went on: "Part of manners used to be you met a stranger, and, among the first questions would be: 'Where are you from?'"

Berry observed that we rarely ask the question with meaningful interest in the age of global culture, rapid transit, integrated markets, and instant communications. He finds that most people, when asked these days, will demur: "'I was an army brat, or a university brat . . .' or, 'Oh, I'm just from a little "no place" in Kansas.'" Some might even say: "I'm not from any place, no place."

The place we call "home" says less about who we are these days than it might have even a few decades ago. Yet our sense of home is essential to our experience of belonging. When we lose our rootedness in what's specific, we lose more than we think.

RESPONSIBLE DEPENDENCE

ONE SOLUTION for building belonging is, according to Berry, the recognition that *we come to depend upon the places where we live and so far as possible live from.* We depend upon the places we call home—in terms of household economy, and help from neighbors. "There is no such thing as autonomy," he's written. "Practically, there is only a distinction between responsible and irresponsible dependence."[2] When I asked him to clarify this point, he smiled and put it in the most straightforward and personal terms possible: "I am dependent upon Tanya. And because I am dependent upon her, I want her to last! That means I must do the best I can to care for her and make sure that she remains." He went on: "It's the same with our place here. I want it to last."[3]

"Responsible dependence" is about reciprocity. Just as we depend on our home, we fulfill responsibilities to it.

For more than fifty years, Wendell Berry has been foretelling the crises of disconnection that humanity is confronting today. He foresaw the modern challenges of environmental degradation and extreme social and political division. He identified some of the root causes of these afflictions: our loss of direct connection to place, including our sources of food, our local community cultures, and our networks of reciprocal care and support. As he underscores, we've built a global system that prioritizes values like the mobility of labor over the sustenance of places and communities. We put values like efficiency above the value of home.

Growing up in the town of New Castle and the Port Royal community, Berry remembers most people worked where they lived, whether on farms or in locally-owned small businesses. He showed me photos of Port Royal in the old days and reminisced about how people genuinely relied on one another within a radius of a few dozen miles for their survival—whether for food or a paycheck or essential services, or the help of family and neighbors. People needed the community, so they wanted the community to last. Now, he explained, it's different. Most people either commute or telecommute, typically serving distant bosses in increasingly global corporations. "Community is not just about a feeling. 'Community spirit' is worthless unless there is a practical interdependence that's worked out and economic."

He then summed up one of the core attributes of the homeplace. "People have to need each other," he said. And they must be aware of it, too.

We also spoke about resilience. In his view, resilience depends upon our humility. When we're grounded in the reality of a specific location—our own particular homeplace—we don't presume to know universal answers to all the challenges facing the world. "If your work is on the right scale," he told me, "then you can take responsibility for it without fear."

Berry admits this is an increasingly uncommon viewpoint for our globalized age. It's the opposite of the *bigger, faster, cheaper* mindset. It's different from the dogma of measuring progress through gross domestic product. Yet this rustic and seemingly traditional approach may be one of the most important aspects of rebuilding belonging—as well as safer and more nourishing food systems, more sustainable and equitable economies, and more compassionate, connected communities. It's a paradigm that honors the power of place, that has the potential to reclaim wild locales and family farms and resilient local economies—even if it's at the expense of some economic efficiency.

In *The Home We Build Together*, the late Lord Rabbi Jonathan Sacks, a celebrated moral thinker, explains, "'Home' means that we care about belonging. . . . 'Build' means that we focus on responsibilities, not just rights."[4] As with Berry's notion of "responsible dependence," belonging to a homeplace means we have to actively serve our home in order to help sustain it.

"My work has been motivated," Wendell Berry writes, "by a desire to make myself responsibly at home in this world and in my native and chosen place." In this way, resilience and responsibility are at one, serving as an anchor of belonging.[5]

Homeplace is also an anchor of belonging. It's essential to our experience of, and provides steadfast and meaningful connections to, the four dimensions of belonging. As an anchor, homeplace connects to belonging through relationships with our communities as well as knowledge of and care for our lands. It serves as a locus for our ability to enact our values and contribute meaningfully to decisions about ourselves and our communities. And it can serve as a connection point for leading a purposeful life.

Homeplace is rooted in "where you're from." For Berry, this is where there's an intricate connection between the land itself and the stories we tell about the place and its people. Its foundation is a physical setting, a geographic location where we're grounded and secure.

Yet all over the world, long-held connections to homeplace are eroding or increasingly coming under threat. What, then, happens to belonging?

THE DAM

IF YOU TRAVEL 260 MILES north from the Canadian city of Winnipeg, Manitoba, up a highway lined with silver birch and tall pines, you'll come to a land of abundant waters—a place that is home to wolf and lynx, deer and moose. The Misipawistik Cree people, who have called these lands home for many generations, have long-standing traditions as hunters and fishers—traditions that include pulling fish from the lakes in depths of winter, when the surface of the water is three feet of solid ice.

The Saskatchewan River, which runs through this place, gets its name from the Cree word *kisiskāciwani-sīpiy*, meaning "swift flowing river." Here, where the river meets the northwestern shore of Lake Winnipeg, the water falls more than seventy-five feet in the course of just three miles. As the river hurtles down at this incline, the waters crash and bubble with a great roar.

"Misipawistik" means "rushing rapids." The municipality is known as Grand Rapids, Manitoba. But the waters are now silent. They don't flow as they once did.

I traveled to Grand Rapids once with my friend Ovide Mercredi— statesman, legal scholar, artist, and poet from the Misipawistik Cree Nation. Grand Rapids is Ovide's home. He grew up with his nine brothers and sisters, hearing stories about previous generations from elders, and learning how to be a good steward of the forests, plains, lakes, and streams. "As a child, I spoke my language. I didn't learn English until I went to public school. So I had a sense of identity that was not Canadian, which I still retain, and a sense of identity that was based on a people that made their livelihood from the Earth."[6]

Ovide was born immersed in the traditions and livelihoods of his people, and he recognized that these were intertwined with his home. "We were fishermen, and trappers, and hunters," he says. "And our People have lived that lifestyle for centuries. So I didn't feel the isolation as a child because I didn't understand the colonial impact until later on in my life."

These livelihoods and hunting and cultivation practices are relationships of respect and "responsible dependence," where communities have invested care for and knowledge about their lands for generations, understanding their responsibility to them as a part of receiving its offerings as a homeplace.

In his poem "Being Human," Ovide writes about what home means to him—what it means to be in relationship with the land and community in a specific place, and recognizing a reciprocity between those elements.

We are like the forest,
not just a single tree,
not just a solitary being.
To be human,
we have to be complete like the forest, whole.
Not a single tree, alone.[7]

As he grew older, however, the forces of colonialism, government, and industry threatened this experience of home and his relationships of belonging with the land and his community. The impact of colonial intrusion brought devastation to both human and environmental systems.

THE RIVER HALTED ITS FLOW

IN THE 1950S, the government of Manitoba approved construction of a dam on the Saskatchewan River. The government's intentions were based on measures of economic productivity: Its stated aim was to provide affordable electricity to the people of the rural area, create jobs, and strengthen the regional economy.

However, the process was implemented in a careless manner. Provincial government officials failed to consult the people who lived on the land around the river, and forced thousands to relocate. When the dam construction was finished, parts of the singing waters of the Grand Rapids—a unique feature of the ancestral home of the Misipawistik Cree—became parched riverbed. With the shifting waters, much of the area's sacred burial grounds was flooded. Many in the local community fled. "Collective experience is personal," Ovide said.[8] The pain of losing so many aspects of home—pain that was both collective and personal—was immense.

It was during this time of mourning and doubt that Ovide looked inward and found his innate gifts to bring forward. He recognized that his people and their homeplace needed organized defense in the corridors of power. It was through this conviction that he discovered what would become a lifelong purpose: the defense of homeplace.

After attending law school, practicing criminal law, and serving as a constitutional advisor to Manitoba chiefs, he was elected Regional Chief of the Assembly of First Nations of Manitoba in 1988 and became a rising star in national politics—taking on important roles in legal negotiations around the country. He played a role in the defeat of the Meech Lake Accord, a set of proposed constitutional reforms to provide greater governance power to Québec and other provinces that failed to address the right to self-governance and sovereignty of First Nations. He also helped to resolve the 1990 Oka Crisis (also known as the Kanehsatà:ke Resistance), a high-profile standoff between the Mohawk people and Québec officials over a controversial land development that threatened the Mohawk territory of Kanehsatà:ke.

In 1991, Ovide was elected as the National Chief of the Assembly of First Nations, the organizing body of the more than 600 First Nations across Canada. Through two terms over the course of six years, he led the push for expansion of First Nations' sovereignty through the Charlottetown Accords, a set of amendments to Canada's Constitution, as well as a series of individual battles over questions of land use and legal autonomy with provincial and federal authorities. He raised the global profile of Indigenous issues—particularly on issues of environment and sovereignty—speaking to international media and before the United Nations in New York and Geneva.

Ovide returned home in 2005. He turned to the administration of his own community, becoming Chief of Misipawistik Cree Nation. Over the course of his tenure in Manitoba, he made progress toward reparations for colonial-era injustice during his youth, winning agreement from the regional hydropower authority to provide a major multi-decade settlement of community development funds to help address the destructive legacies of the dam project. Throughout his career, Ovide has entered the halls of power to defend the rights of people to connect to nature and community.

While the political and legal work remains essential, Ovide knows this is just one part of the work. Preserving and restoring the foundations of homeplace is a mission that ultimately runs deeper than politics or law. It's about renewing personal connection to the land and community and restoring knowledge of the culture and the specific place as well—honoring the knowledge of responsible dependence, the spirit of reciprocity, on multiple levels between community and homeplace.

"The Indigenous community in Canada is attempting to reclaim what they've lost," he told me in a 2014 interview. "We're trying to reclaim even the spirituality that was taken from us. Our own traditional beliefs about Creator, and our own beliefs about creation itself. We're trying to rediscover what our ancestors had, and then also our land has been taken from us. We're trying to reclaim our land as well. We're involved in trying to reclaim back our languages. We're trying to reclaim ourselves."[9]

Let me find my talk
So I can teach you about me

—RITA JOE, *I LOST MY TALK*[10]

Today, Ovide has turned his focus toward the promise of reconnecting youth and elders with land and tradition in the community.

One of the people working alongside Ovide is Becky Cook. Becky grew up on the land surrounding Misipawistik and Lake Winnipeg. She studied the traditions of her people with elders from her community, and also earned a PhD in marine geophysics from the University of Southampton.

Today, Becky is a key organizer and educator with the Misipawistik Pimatisiméskanaw land-based learning program and the Misipawistik kanawenihcikew Guardians program. Through these initiatives, local young people are taught fishing, trapping, and the use of plants for medicine, and they're given the opportunity to serve as ambassadors for Misipawistik Cree Nation at various events and gatherings. These important programs provide a holistic approach to teaching connection to nature, traditional knowledge and histories, and the sense of homeplace—ultimately supplementing a governmental education system that has largely ignored these things.

The initiatives are ways in which connection to homeplace is reclaimed and regenerated. It's also intergenerational, with elders and youth working with each other on multiple levels: through education in Cree language, laws, and storytelling.

Reclamation of language is a critical part of reclaiming homeplace. Through the Residential School system, which lasted until 1996, education was used as a weapon for assimilation and the erasure of Indigenous identities. The number of Indigenous people who spoke an Indigenous language as their mother tongue dropped from 87 percent in the 1960s to 15 percent by 2011.[11] Today, there are fewer than 500 fluent speakers of twenty-five Indigenous languages across Canada.[12] The US is also suffering a similar decline in Indigenous language use. A 2011 report showed that among those who identified as American Indian or Alaska Native, 20 percent of those over age sixty-five spoke an Indigenous language at home—compare this to just 10 percent of Indigenous youth between the ages of five and seventeen.[13]

The Pimatisiméskanaw programs Becky leads, as well as the Guardians program, which is coordinated by other community members, also focus on practices and ceremonies, including the Sundance—celebrations of life, community, and nature through prayer, dancing, and feasting. Many such practices and teachings were banned under the Indian Act, leading to a breakdown in families as well as a challenge to identity, culture, and belonging for many Indigenous communities. The program has begun to bring these traditions back into the community, facilitating their transmission from elders to youth.

The youth also gain essential survival skills, carrying out activities such as fishing, working with rawhide, local archaeology, and medicine picking and preparation. They also receive the opportunity to sit in circles with elders who share stories and transmit knowledge.

In 2015, the Truth and Reconciliation Commission (TRC), which documented the atrocities of Canada's colonial policies on Indigenous communities, especially Residential Schools, released ninety-four "Calls to Action." The calls for education reform emphasized reinforcing Indigenous language rights and providing culturally relevant curricula to Indigenous youth. This is the essence of the programming in Misipawistik—restoring connection to homeplace through reframing histories and language in a way that honors its importance in identity and sense of purpose in people's lives.

"Home," Becky underscores, "is the land." She tells me, "For Indigenous peoples, it's not just relationships with other people that you learn from. Indigenous people recognize that you can learn from animals, you can learn from the land. Having that relationship is important for that kind of learning."[14]

Becky describes the approach of the land-based learning education as different from the curriculum taught in Canadian schools. Fundamentally, it's about establishing identity and responsibility to one another in ways that deepen awareness of reciprocity in those relationships. "Your contributions are alive," Becky says of the participants in the program. "You're contributing something to a larger good."

While the work is about a deep kind of reorientation and reclamation, it's also highly practical. Young people are learning how to live off the land and how to navigate change. "I think wisdom is learning and knowing how to use that knowledge in a good way," Becky says. There is also an opportunity for deep listening and learning by others. As noted by Celine Thomas, who leads SCSC's collaboration with the Misipawistik Cree Nation and other knowledge holders and educators from across Manitoba, this has been an incredible journey towards understanding what it truly means to be involved in an Indigenous-led and Indigenous-serving project, and how important it is to cultivate belonging thorugh culturally relevant education over one's lifespan.

By empowering youth in the community to become stewards of land and community, the new initiatives seek to transform these circumstances: to find renewal collectively. Indeed, Indigenous teachers and scholars have recognized that academic performance is "inextricably tied to an education that is firmly grounded in the context of culture and language and founded on history, spiritual beliefs, songs, ceremonies, the land or place of origin, art, music, oratory, contemporary community customs and Nation building for First Nations citizenship."[15]

I spoke with two young people from the program, Evan Constant and Tyrell Ballantyne—at the time both eleventh-grade students from the Grand Rapids School. They emphasized to me how it's been the norm for people their age to feel disconnected. There hadn't been many opportunities to get to know the culture and land. Just look at the school system, they say.

"They don't teach us about our ancestors. Or even our culture," Evan comments.[16]

"We learn stuff about the pyramids and Mount Rushmore. And we could be learning about our story," Tyrell adds.[17]

The Guardians program has addressed some of those gaps. "It's a special connection," Evan says of the program. "Not many of us could experience that, sitting around elders every day, seeing them and them telling us stories of what they did when they were young. Or how it all happened, how they were schooled, too."[18]

Tyrell emphasizes that the more people know and care about their land, the more they will want to defend it: responsible dependence. That's the power of a land-based learning curriculum.

"I think I have a really good connection to the lake," he says. "I care for the fish—my dad's a fisherman, and both my grandpas were fishermen, and my great grandparents. So I definitely have a bloodline of fishermen. And I want to protect the lake. I don't want it to be that my kids, and maybe my grandkids, won't be able to eat fish because it was overfished. That's why I'm doing the Guardians' program."[19]

"We don't have to be afraid of the bush," Becky points out, reflecting the realizations she sees in so many participants in the program.[20] This land is interwoven with culture—with home.

Ovide's poem "Dene Drums" references what unconditional belonging looks like for his people: a renewal of prayer, song, and dance; a place where no one is scolded or rebuked; where the natural order of the earth and sky prevail; where life runs its course in harmony and celebration.[21]

Today, the struggle continues for legal and political rights—for a transformation of the cruel logic that resulted in that hydroelectric project flooding sacred lands. Yet so much of the work is also personal: It's how we cultivate knowledge of and affection for our lands, our waters, and the histories that they represent.

With Ovide's support and encouragement, Becky is now working on something larger: building traditional education programs that promote lifelong learning. For many Indigenous communities, education is seen as a lifelong pursuit. Each stage of life, from infancy to adulthood to old age, offers new opportunities for learning and reflection. Pimatisiméskanaw, which roughly translates to "life road," is one of many important aspects of traditional learning. Becky is working alongside elders and knowledge holders from Cree, Ojibway, and Anishinaabe Nations in Manitoba to understand what traditional education might look like specifically from a Cree/Nehinaw and Ojibway/Anishinaabe perspective, a mandate that deepens their connection to homeplace. They hope to build a framework that can offer traditional education—ranging from land-based programming to history workshops and traditional ceremonies—to people in their respective nations and in the province of Manitoba.

"The ultimate goal of a traditional education is for each person to be strong (ta-sokikapawi-t) and know who they are, to understand their strengths, weaknesses and responsibilities in life," Becky writes. "That is, to find their calling, to understand how they can use the skills they have been gifted with to contribute to the community/society. To truly know who we are as indigenous people we must also understand our language, history, ways of life, laws and relationships to the land water and animals on which we depend. When we know who we are and have a strong connection to our ancestors we gain a sense of community and greater purpose in life."[22]

RECOGNITION OF HOMEPLACE IN OTHERS

OVIDE MERCREDI JOINED us in Montreal and Toronto for both the 2014 and 2016 Global Symposia on "Overcoming Social Isolation and Deepening Social Connectedness. In 2016, he sat on a panel with Meitamei Olol Dapash, an Elder from the Maasai of Tanzania and founder of the Maasai Environmental Resource Coalition. Meitamei spoke about the "right of a people to their own destiny" and the necessity of overcoming challenges like land dispossession, cultural destruction, forced assimilation, underdevelopment, stereotyping, and national and global isolation.

After Meitamei spoke, Ovide paused for a moment and looked at him. "You could have been the voice of every Indigenous person in Canada,"[23] Ovide said. It was a moment of recognition.

They saw one another as Elders of their respective communities and also as keepers of traditions based on underlying worldviews that speak to principles of social and ecological interconnectedness, and, above all, rootedness in place and tradition. "When it comes to other people from other countries, like Indigenous societies in places like Australia or New Zealand, or South Africa or, for that matter, in Peru, or Central America, or the United States," Ovide says, "we have a common bond. That bond is twofold. Firstly, we have a common experience with a colonizer who has come and taken over everything in our traditional lands. The second is that we had societies and cultures. And we still have them, with their own values about humanity, how you raise children, how you educate them, how you make your livelihood and how you create wealth."

Ovide speaks of the right to connect to tradition, nature, the means to share and communicate, and a sense of shared values. He speaks of the responsibility to act as stewards of the places we live—the homeplaces where we find belonging.

There's a certain vulnerability in recognizing that we are inherently dependent on the places where we live. Yet in accepting this reality of dependence, in taking on the attitude of responsible dependence, we can find a key to belonging.

Think of where you were born, and the natural world that nurtured you throughout your childhood and adolescence. You may feel affection for the neighborhood park where you played with friends, the woods where you walked with your family, or the lake that kept you cool in the hot haze of summer. Maintaining and protecting that park or that woods or that lake means more to you when you feel connected to it, when it forms a foundational part of your sense of home. When we get to know our homeplace more intimately, we take a greater stake in its success. We feel rooted, and we want to preserve those roots.

Still, despite the crucial importance of homeplace to belonging, finding connection to a geographic home can be fraught in today's world—when so many people are denied the experience of home, when so many can't access the land they hold sacred or aren't secure in their own dwelling places.

The challenge still remains for those who don't have a home or cannot return to it. We don't always grow up in one place or have a community that has a deep sense of homeplace that can support us. Given the trends we are seeing today in migration and forced migration, how do we create a connection to place and a sense of home for all?

Indeed, underlying the notion of homeplace is a collective responsibility to cultivate home not only for ourselves but for our neighbors, for those who have been forcibly displaced, for those without adequate shelter, for those who don't feel safe in their current environments.

This responsibility can manifest in many ways. First, we might understand and look deeper at the lands we live on. We can ask ourselves: How did my community come to be? Who lived on this land before? How can I build a personal connection to this place that honors its history and biodiversity?

Then we might turn outward and look at our collective responsibility to those without a home or connection to place. And it must be bold. It can be political, like defending land rights or housing rights, or advocating for the preservation of a place that isn't recognized yet as a heritage site. It can be connecting with newcomers or refugees to build a sense of community and connection to their new home.

We also have a growing range of tools and roadmaps to help reverse these trends. The people of the Misipawistik Cree Nation show us one way it's possible to recover land-based traditions and knowledge that a dam's floodwater could not erase.

Part of the solution is political: defending people's rights to their lands and supporting the preservation of ecosystems. Part of the solution is personal: asking deep questions about the meaning of home, what it means to share a home, and who is permitted to call a place home.

To reverse so many modern injustices and structural inequities, restoring a sense of respect for the lands on which we live is crucial. As Wendell, Ovide, Becky, Tyrell, and Evan show us, this often stands in contrast to powerful political and economic forces in our world.

HOME IS WHERE YOU DREAM

WHILE HOMEPLACE CAN BE an anchor of belonging, belonging is also becoming an increasingly important aspect of homeplace, one that can emerge as a lifeline when a geographic one doesn't exist. This is more and more the case in our globalized world. This requires an even more intentional focus on cultivating relationships within our communities, however we come to define those across time and space.

Amid a warming climate, widespread discrimination and violence, inequalities that threaten access to shelter, and the continuing legacies of colonialism, the global community will continue to be faced with the ever-increasing reality of displacement, transiency, and uprootedness from physical place.

Nujeen Mustafa's story offers valuable lessons in finding oneself. "Belonging is a sense of relief when you arrive at *the place*," she told me in a recent conversation.

Nujeen has arrived over and over at "the place" in her life, both within herself and geographically. To Nujeen, this idea of belonging is inextricably linked to her idea of home. Home for her is an inner reality as much as it might be a physical place. "I think home is when you are yourself, when you do not need to pretend, when you do not need to put on a poker face. Home is where you fight for your future. Home is where you dream."[24]

Nujeen has an effervescent positivity about her, with an optimism and strength grounded in experience. At twenty-three years old, she has lectured at dozens of universities and conferences around the world, and has helped support refugees, migrants, and other marginalized peoples navigate politically, economically, and emotionally complex situations. She's overcome as much in her lifetime as many people several times her age.

Much of Nujeen's early life was spent in a fifth-floor apartment in Aleppo, Syria. She was born with cerebral palsy and has spent her life using a wheelchair, although as Nujeen recently recounted, to her family, "I'm just Nujeen. I'm not the girl in the wheelchair."[25] Her apartment in Aleppo had no elevator and did not facilitate access to life outside its walls. Television, books, and the fictional characters that lived within them became her companions and her school. She learned polished English mostly from watching English-language television, and came to know other parts of the world through music, traversing genres and cultures.

In 2011, Syria was swept up in protests that quickly escalated into war. Aleppo was a key battleground between government forces and rebels. Three years later, when Nujeen was just sixteen years old, the family fled. They didn't have enough money for the entire family to make it to Germany, where Nujeen's brother already lived, so Nujeen's parents stayed in Turkey. Nujeen and her older sister Nasrine continued the journey north, persevering against seemingly insurmountable odds. Nasrine pushed Nujeen on for most of the way, their efforts fixed on moving forward safely together.

Nujeen describes this journey as "an adventure," the two sisters facing many hardships together. They were once among eleven young migrants waiting on the docks to board a small, barely seaworthy dinghy. This was, as Nujeen recounts, "the fine line between death and a new life." After uncertainty as to whether they would be able to take Nujeen's wheelchair, without recourse and hoping for the best, they loaded the wheelchair onto the boat and set off into the expanse. "It was terrifying," she said, "but also my first time seeing the sea. It was just a yearning for experience that I had. For someone like me who had been locked up her whole life, doing a journey across Europe is like a dream."[26]

In December 2017, Nujeen and Nasrine were granted asylum in Germany. They're now settled in Cologne, where both sisters attend university. Nujeen is currently finishing up studies in business management, and she plans to continue her education by pursuing a degree in social psychology next.

"What belonging means to me is feeling at peace with myself and what I am in the world," Nujeen says. "Feeling safe and secure, and being myself around the people surrounding me. And not having to explain the way I am to anybody, and having the freedom to express every part of my identity the way that I wish to."[27] "Belonging is a place and a feeling I get, where my rights are accepted, my differences and my identity is also appreciated and treasured, instead of being scorned," she adds.

This ideal "place" that Nujeen speaks of is a state of connection—to one's internal purpose and power, to one's community and geography, to the larger communion of being alive as a human being. This is connection to homeplace on a level that transcends geographic place. But it's not an easy internal journey to this depth of belonging. Nujeen has had to work hard for the wisdom required to recognize "the place" within herself and in her new communities.

The reality of arriving in Europe after such a harrowing journey was complex. Although Nujeen describes the thrill of her adventure, she also seeks to advocate against the mistreatment, detention, and interrogation she and so many others face on their journeys to safety. "When you arrive in Europe, you realize that everything you do, everything you are, *everything* is strange, foreign, and unfamiliar."[28]

Throughout their journey, Nujeen and her sister were repeatedly denied border entries and struggled to find food and shelter. The word "refugee" for her became the antithesis of belonging or of homeplace. Recently, Nujeen shared that she finds it difficult to see other children and children with disabilities endure what she experienced as a refugee on her long journey north. That's why, along with other activists and advocates, she runs an organization called Empowerment Now, which raises awareness about the needs of refugees with disabilities.

Nujeen's story isn't about a linear path to belonging, however. She speaks of how today, part of herself is in Germany, part in Turkey, part in Syria. "I have three places or four places I could call home," she says, "and the sense of belonging is split between different places."[29] This is a fracture that she's working to heal—for example, finding ways to reconnect with family from whom she's been separated, and working to establish deeper roots in Germany.

In spite of these challenges, it's clear that Nujeen's belonging is also grounded in a resilience within herself that has been borne both out of her own nature and out of the challenges she has overcome. Nujeen recently shared that, growing up in Syria, without the necessary infrastructure in place to allow her to access a formal education, she had always feared she would not be able to contribute to society.[30] Today, however, she is finding belonging and homeplace through a sense of mission and purpose. She sees pathways to build more inclusive, accepting, participatory societies through the education system and better modes of refugee resettlement. Through a fierce perseverance and the love and support of her family, Nujeen has forged a homeplace and a space for wholeness. She is now fighting for the same for others.

In 2019, Nujeen became the first person with a disability to brief the United Nations Security Council. "Behind all these figures and reports" Nujeen told the UN, "are humans who are suffering."[31] Drawing on knowledge gained through personal experience, she petitioned the Council for greater recognition of the realities of disconnection and inequality faced by those in conflict zones.

"This is not a favor," she urged the Council. "This is not a charity. This is our right." Nujeen's work is the work of realizing that each and every one of us, by virtue of the fact that we were born into the same state of wholeness, has the right to belong, despite the persistence of systemic divisions in our world.

As Nujeen contends, "Different is not dangerous."[32] When we spoke, she emphasized to me the need to create spaces in which people of different backgrounds—particularly young people—get to know each other, so that "the unfamiliar becomes familiar, and therefore accepted." She applies this approach not only to the work of improving outcomes for refugees, but also for persons with disabilities.

"Educating people on other cultures and bringing them up, especially from a young age, to have compassion and curiosity about other cultures, would be of great help," Nujeen says.[33] "To me, belonging is losing that label of *refugee*." She clarifies that she doesn't mean this in the literal sense of losing a legal designation or a fact about one's personal history, but rather shedding the societal perception that a person is defined by victimhood or a sense of lack. "I would like people to look at me . . . without going back to that first oppression or label."

Nujeen gives me hope that we really can cultivate, in her words, more "respect for what makes us different but equally beautiful."

"We are born in belonging."[34]

Satish Kumar is the founder of the Schumacher College international center for ecological studies and the editor emeritus of *Resurgence & Ecologist* magazine. The Indian-British philosopher, environmental activist, and former Jain monk recently shared with me this fundamental belief about our shared belonging. Satish has spent more than half a century envisioning a positive vision for global society and contemplating questions about the true meaning of human progress.

Satish tells me, "When you put a seed in the soil, the seed and the soil belong to each other. And the seed becomes the soil. . . . With the seed, soil transforms itself into a tree." So, he says: "Belonging is the origin. The fundamental. The basis out of which everything grows."

It can be hard to stay connected to this truth. Our global environment is in an unprecedented state of precarity. Social contracts and communities in many places are struggling; disrespect across racial, ethnic, gender, and age lines remains endemic; and there are major crises of mental illness and addiction brewing.

The simple proposition that "there's no place like home" can be fraught in today's world—when so many people are denied the experience of home, when so many people can't access the lands they hold sacred, when so many people don't feel safe or secure in their own dwelling places.

Stories of forced displacement like Nujeen's are not new, and will only become more familiar in the years ahead. For many, even with a roof over their heads, a home isn't a place of belonging. It can be a place of isolation, of fear of abuse, where home is one of the most difficult places to belong.

It can be a place where water is unavailable, on lands that have become unsafe due to environmental pollutants and toxicity, often in communities that don't have a say over where or how governments or businesses decide to deposit waste.

The right to shelter is one of the basic human requirements set out in the Sustainable Development Goals, and is a foundation for the ability to uphold other rights. Yet a physical structure of shelter alone does not ensure the experience of "home" as the anchor of belonging. Plenty of prisons, care homes, and residential schools, for that matter, provide shelter, but erode or eliminate conditions of belonging.

A real homeplace must allow for or create acceptance and an absence of shame, connection with others, capacity to affect change in one's life, and a sense of meaning and purpose. We must feel we have a say in the decisions that affect us, that we are being listened to, and that we have the space and context in which we can listen to others, too. We must feel a connection to the world and our larger human family.

As I think about that day with Wendell Berry amid the oak trees in Port Royal, Kentucky, I come back to the feeling I knew as a child, spending time in nature. I feel what I felt then: grounded, peaceful, time slowing down just a little bit. I'm reminded of the preciousness of connection to a place. I'm reminded of how essential it is—for our individual and collective resilience, for our personal and global belonging—to restore our reverence for homeplace.

I find hope by looking to examples of individuals and communities who have faced the destruction of their homes due to forces beyond their control, and who have then taken creative and courageous action toward restoration and renewal. Such examples exist everywhere, from Indigenous communities in New Zealand seeking to reconnect to their heritage, to those creating new communities entirely in the wake of forced migration.

In the wake of environmental degradation due to coal mining, as well as pervasive regional stereotypes, Appalachia is yet another example of resilience, coupled with a sense of renewal, that exists amid destruction. As scholar Samuel McQuillen writes, "Rather than being alone at the bottom of a well, Appalachians may instead be understood as collectively stuck at the bottom of a coal shaft, deeply connected to one another but none-theless profoundly cut off from the surface. Despite being metaphorically far underground, Appalachians have successfully raised their voices to col-lectively advocate for their own rights; if we want to simultaneously fight Appalachian poverty and foster national connectedness, all we have to do is listen."[35] Even in an age of so much displacement, people are recognizing and affirming the value of home.

It's both in our best interest, as well as our responsibility, as individu-als and as collectives, to extend the belonging of homeplace to all people in our societies, as well as to the lands and waters, animals and other beings in the environment. This is the heart of responsible dependence. It's also one of the keys to our future survival.

Dr. Vandana Shiva, a prolific Indian author, environmental activist, food sovereignty advocate, and leading voice for ecofeminism, has been thinking deeply about these questions for decades. "Belonging means being deeply aware of all relationships," she recently shared with me. "Belonging for me means being deeply grateful to those who have gone before and have shaped your being and belonging. It also means your responsibility to those who have to come."

Vandana speaks to our responsibility to place as a "law of gratitude," explaining. "You cannot belong if you don't give. You don't belong to a fam-ily if you don't have reciprocal relationships. Then you'll fight and tear each other apart. You can't belong to a community if you don't have mutuality. You can't belong to the Earth if you don't give back. [When] you belong to that place, you love it, you care for it."[36]

We humans are but one part of a larger, holistic ecosystem. We must nurture the ecology that surrounds us so that we can be nurtured in turn. This kind of responsible dependence and reciprocal giving and receiving—the heart of belonging—is something we find on all levels of the natural world. As Vandana puts it, "The seed gives rise to roots. Roots root where they find their belonging. And they find belonging where they find the welcoming. They find the welcoming where there is fertility in the soil. And then all the organisms at work say, 'Welcome home.'"

CHAPTER SEVEN

DESIGNING THE CITY
OF IMAGINATION

IF HOME IS FOUND EASILY in nature, as we saw in chapter 6, it can be more elusive when built with human hands. How do we design our human-made spaces for belonging?

The spaces we live, work, and gather in—the natural and built environments around us—impact us on all levels: our psychologies and emotional states, our sense of physical and emotional safety and well-being, our sense of connection to each other and something greater than ourselves. Whether it's a place of worship, a home, a hospital, a long-term care facility, or a prison, the design of these spaces matters to our ability to find connection.

Richard Sennett, notable urban connection and development scholar and Centennial Professor of Sociology at the London School of Economics, describes a city as "a milieu in which strangers are likely to meet."[1] Indeed, our cities are places where principles of design affect the possibilities for belonging in populations on large scales. Unlike the designs of nature, which are inherently interconnected, cities are human constructs. This means that the values on which municipalities and governments, businesses, architects, and economists base urban planning decisions have the potential to create societies of belonging or societies of isolation.

William Blake—"the supreme poet of the City," according to Kathleen Raine—envisioned the city as a "living organism."[2] The city is for Blake "the inner lives of its inhabitants as these act and interact upon one another"; it is, above all, human.[3]

Blake envisioned a "City of Imagination," a utopian vision of London that represented the pinnacle of human design and gathering. "My Streets are my Ideas of Imagination," he wrote of this vision.[4] Raine goes on to explain, "Its regions extend with the number of those who participate—all belong, not in part, but whole, to all, like the light of the sun itself."[5]

For Blake, the City of Imagination exists in order to embody the highest human values, reflecting back to humanity a vision of the eternal. "It takes the form of a mandala," Raine writes. "The gates are the four channels through which knowledge reaches us: reason, intuition, the senses, and feeling. And these gates are the gates of each individual and the gates of the city as collectivity."[6] As Raine suggests, we should ask ourselves: "Are we being nourished by our cities in all these four areas? Or does the city exist in only one dimension or two?"

With the City of Imagination as our reference point, we might also consider how designing for belonging refers not only to buildings, streets, and green patches—but also to the interplay between structural spaces and the social, spiritual connections that bring them to life.

The potential for urban design to create and stimulate spaces of belonging is significant. Yet many of our societies have not placed attention on designing for belonging. Human settlements all over the world have caused adverse impacts on ecological processes and human health, and the burden of these impacts is often disproportionately placed on people of color and the poor.

Medieval towns were traditionally centered around a religious place of worship, a confluence of people joined by economic cooperation and friendly interaction through festivals, markets, and cultural activities.[7] As time went on, urban planning became more oriented toward fixed grid layouts as developed historically in pre-Classical and Classical Minoan, Mesopotamian, Egyptian, and Central American systems.[8]

At the beginning of the twentieth century, urban design was oriented largely around the automobile, catering urban spaces around roads and traffic patterns. Many policies implemented in the 1980s refocused urban planning principles to shift away from public commons and toward commercial profits and privatization of public spaces and resources.[9] Some of these policies resulted not in trickle-down benefits to all, but in unequal and discriminatory access to urban spaces and services. More recently, many groups in society are calling for the urgent need to address the injustices and inequities encountered by people of color in city spaces. Disability rights movements across the world have also called for awareness of inclusive design to create urban environments that enable people with disabilities equal access to services, transportation, and participation in urban life.

In 2014, journalist Amy Bernstein wrote that many of the world's great cities are founded as "ideas." Whether we are walking in New York, London, Rio, or Shanghai, the distinctive patterns in design and commerce, in the parks and public art, in the form and tenor of discourse and debate can feel like the impression of an idea, a reflection on the purpose of our lives.

Still, as Bernstein concludes, the ideas behind cities are always evolving. "Cities founded on ideas can suddenly, sometimes violently, come to represent entirely different ones," she says.[10] We are continually making these choices as we go.

What does it mean to build and maintain a city on the idea of belonging, and what happens if we don't? These questions are intersectional. They have implications for urban planning, architecture, ecology, arts, economic policy, and human rights. They are questions of both how to respond to crises like climate change in urban spaces, and how to proactively support sustainability and inclusive prosperity. They also enter a field of inquiry into how urban design can make connections between nature and society, people and spaces, histories and purpose.

Dominic Richards, a visionary architect and founder of Our Place, a UK-based holistic property development firm, is perhaps best described as a "placemaker," one who utilizes human-centered design elements to cultivate connection. Dominic once said to me, in a way that almost took me aback for being so simple and yet so powerful, "Either you design for belonging, or you end up with isolation."[11]

More than half a century ago, scholar and activist Jane Jacobs foresaw this challenge. She pinned many such problems on choices that public authorities made with respect to design, participation, and investment. Back then, she posed a poignant question: Are our cities for cars or for people?

Of course, the car is a proxy for more than the automobile. It's symbolic of a set of values: industrial efficiency, aggregate economic growth, an atomized vision of society. It's distinct from a people-centered vision of the city: rich social connection, uniqueness of place, empowerment of marginalized communities, and social solidarity.

For Jacobs, there was a seemingly mundane facet of the urban landscape that symbolized something extraordinary: sidewalks.

She once wrote that "sidewalks" are the site of an "intricate ballet in which the individual dancers and ensembles all have distinctive parts that miraculously reinforce each other and compose an orderly whole." She saw the sidewalk as a jumping-off point for community life: where people stop to ask directions, pet a dog, or simply say hello. "Most of it is ostensibly trivial but the sum is not trivial at all."[12] This sum, she said, is "a web of public respect and trust," a kind of everyday guarantee of contact that's just not found in an anonymous exurban housing block or low-density suburbs.

"Sidewalk contacts," Jacobs concluded, "are the small change from which a city's wealth of public life may grow."

Behind this simple idea is an important ethos that appreciates that power of diversity. It's about trusting and respecting people, underlining the logic of moving from "top-down" to "bottom-up" solutions.

Jane Jacobs offers the example of a sidewalk as a space that's emblematic of this kind of connection. Still, what she's describing isn't exclusive to the sidewalk itself. It's any space that brings people together in this spirit.

This is what it means to *design for belonging*.

As the author and urban planner Jonathan Rose puts it: "The quality and character of our cities will determine the temperament of human civilization."[13]

With more than 80 percent of North America and 70 percent of Europe urbanized, and countries in the global south rapidly urbanizing as well,[14] we must intentionally design cities for belonging or risk the vast majority of the world's population experiencing isolation where they live.

"Community is created when individuals find something around which they coalesce," Dominic Richards told me. "That is the difference between an apartment block where nobody knows each other and a community."[15]

As Richards sees it, there is a risk in modern cities of ghettoization not only of the poor, but of everyone. In separating people's living areas from one another, each group gets shut in as much as others are kept out. That naturally impacts social solidarity. It breeds multiple kinds of inequality. "Who wants to live in a world where only the wealthy can have a particular city," he asks, "and the people that might be your children's teachers, or your doctor, or your nurse, or your police person, or your fire person, or any of these people, can't afford to live there?"

I believe Suzanne Lennard, the late architect and the director of the International Making Cities Livable movement, would have concurred with Richards. "If we had deliberately aimed to make cities that create loneliness," she wrote, "we could hardly have been more successful."[16]

If cities are "Ideas," then urban design must actively reconceptualize the way we see our social, economic, political, and spatial configurations as maps for creating a more equitable, environmentally sustainable, and compassionate vision for human gathering—gathering in which strangers encountering each other encourages a sense of inclusion and belonging in a diverse human family.

We must attend not only to the structure of our cities, but to the spirit of them as well. We cannot design for one and hope for the other: Only both of these, together, can catalyze true belonging.

AS I CONTEMPLATE the work of building belonging in our contemporary world, I've been thinking a lot about the history of human belonging. In a world of growing population and shrinking arable land, in the age of so much political and economic inequality and so little trust in our shared institutions, it's understandable to think that the pressing challenge of isolation is specific to the times in which we're living. Yet this is not solely a twenty-first-century problem. The quest to meet our unfulfilled belonging did not start with the Industrial Revolution or the rise of the Internet. If we look deeply into our history, we can trace how shifts in values have altered the structures of belonging for many societies over thousands of years.

The celebrated Ghanaian philosopher Kwame Anthony Appiah has written, "For most of human history, we were born into small societies of a few score people, bands of hunters and gatherers, and would see, on a typical day, only people we had known most of our lives."[17] As the British social theorist Robin Dunbar and other scholars have argued, human beings likely lived primarily in groups of about 150 people. Dunbar based this finding on cognitive research on the number of stable relationships that an individual can maintain over time, as well as surveys of the Neolithic village and tribal group sizes.[18] These and other research findings have important implications for our understanding of the arc of human belonging over thousands of years.

Today, more than half of the world's population are living in urban areas—roughly 4.2 billion people. By 2045, this number is expected to reach more than six billion. Today's most populous cities are Tokyo (37.4 million inhabitants), New Delhi (28.5 million), and Shanghai (25.6 million). By 2030, the number of "mega-cities"—cities with more than ten million inhabitants—is expected to increase from thirty-three to forty-three, with the fastest growing in Asia and Africa.[19]

SOCIAL ISOLATION AND ENVIRONMENTAL BURDENS IN DESIGN

AS CLIMATE CHANGE INTENSIFIES, the values that are embedded and expressed in our urban designs will be amplified and have significant implications for billions of people. This is a reason for reflection as we head into the coming decades. Climate change is already presenting urban areas all over the world with unprecedented challenges of flooding, temperature changes, and storm impacts. Our urban planning must design for environmental and ecological resilience—and do so for the benefit and protection for all. It must also design for inclusive relationships.

I've been contemplating the relationship between environmental challenges and social isolation for some time. Angel Hsu has been an important partner in this work. She is the founder and director of Data-Driven EnviroLab, an interdisciplinary team based out of the University of North Carolina Chapel Hill that works to distill signals from large-scale and unconventional datasets and develop policy solutions to contemporary environmental problems.

As an academic, her job, as she describes it, is to connect the dots between climate science, policy, and sustainability. In the decade that I've known her, she's helped me connect the dots in my own thinking, pointing to the ways in which urban areas all around the world are facing interwoven issues of environmental change and inequalities of political and economic power.

Angel offers a shorthand for what keeps many cities in ruts of "designing for isolation:" top-down. "Governments implement policies," she told me, "and they often go unchecked. People frequently don't have any idea of whether or not those policies are actually being implemented, and whether or not they're effective in meeting goals."[20] Nor do they have clarity on the values and the "spirit" that underpin those goals.

While there are no easy answers for managing urban environmental challenges in inclusive and participatory ways, Angel believes there's one vital starting point: information. She believes that democratizing data can democratize action. It's this kind of data that allows urban communities, governments, and businesses to understand the requirements for designing for inclusivity. This isn't just about making statistics available, but also about collecting the right kinds of data, and telling the stories of what's really happening in terms of climate trends, economic needs, and policy responses in urban centers. As Angel has said, "data makes the invisible visible."[21]

To spur action, she says, "we have to be thinking more locally—that's really where the impact of climate change, a global problem, is being felt. We need to be thinking about how every community is facing a different set of vulnerabilities, how we solve those problems and reduce the vulnerability."

IN 2018, Data-Driven EnviroLab, in partnership with the Samuel Centre for Social Connectedness (SCSC), developed the Urban Environment and Social Inclusion Index (UESI). Tying the data to where people live, the UESI is the first spatially-explicit assessment of how cities are sharing environmental benefits and burdens among residents. It is also the first indicator system of its kind to place a social inclusion and equity lens on urban sustainability measurement by including neighborhood-level indicators of household income and population size within cities.

The major findings from the UESI reveal some troubling trends. Across the 162 cities included in the index, 95 were shown to burden lower-income populations with poor air quality, exposure to urban heat, and lack of access to tree cover and public transport.[22] Many of these cities perform strongly in the index across all indicators, yet this research has shown that the distributional equity of environmental benefits—such as green spaces and clean air—is weak, and this is one of the things cities need to improve upon.

Through the work of our teams, we uncovered new insights about the intersection of social isolation, environmental burdens, and inequality in urban design.

The UESI includes a measure of the phenomenon called the urban heat island (UHI) effect—the temperature differential between dense urban environments and more suburban or rural areas. The main finding of the UESI data is made most clear when looking at the urban heat island effect: Socioeconomically marginalized parts of cities are hotter.[23]

For example, in the US, UESI found that people of color in lower-income urban areas experience significantly higher UHI effects than white counterparts. Black residents, on average, encounter 2.67°C (36.8°F) higher temperatures, while Hispanic residents encounter 2.64°C (36.7°F) higher temperatures. Though an average difference of one or two degrees

Celsius might not seem like much in everyday life, a small increase in average temperatures means much larger increases on single days, which often lead to sudden increases in adverse health effects, including heatstroke and other serious causes of death.[24] In the city of Montreal, Québec, a 2021 Data-Driven EnviroLab study revealed that lower-income neighborhoods experienced nighttime temperatures 1°C to 3°C (33.8°F to 37.4°F) hotter than neighborhoods with higher average incomes, indicating that heat disparities within urban settings are a problem that transcends any one nation.[25]

Why does urban poverty correlate with increased heat? In part, lower-income areas have fewer trees, exposing one of the effects of designs that aren't oriented toward belonging and equity. The UESI, which also tracks urban green space, shows that poorer and predominantly minority neighborhoods generally have less shade cover and more heat absorption in asphalt. Green space in a city—whether it's parks, forested areas, or manicured tree-lined boulevards—generally indicates higher levels of investment, attention from municipal government, and the relative quality of land.

Not only are green spaces important for clean air and healthy ecosystems, they also amplify social connection for all residents through accessible common space. Access to green spaces also has a restorative effect on mental health and increased social cohesion within the community.[26] This is especially important in low-income neighborhoods with access to fewer social services and resources.

With all the benefits made widely known through research, the UESI reveals the inequalities within cities. Green space is a powerful proxy for socioeconomic power in an urban area. The absence of green space— and the lack of investment and influence that it signifies—means more deadly heat waves and more vulnerability to climate change. If people have few resources to address or combat heat (e.g., the ability to afford air-conditioning), lack of green space can further isolate them, making it difficult to find feasible solutions to cope with heat escalations.

When conducting this research, Angel was shocked to see the extent of the urban heat island effect in her hometown of Greenville, South Carolina.

Neighborhoods with higher urban heat island effects were particularly associated with Black and lower-income communities.[27]

The aim of the UESI is to reveal important information like this, particularly at the local level, so communities can be empowered to move from top-down to bottom-up solutions and reorient urban design toward equity and a more inclusive vision for human gathering and living structures. Rather than relying on outside authorities or technical planners to mandate strategies that might not be responsive to the needs of people in a given area, this kind of equity-focused and intersectional data can help communities take action: for example, by planting trees, creating urban farms, or advocating for more parks or other green spaces. This is timely, essential work, and SCSC's research partnership with Data-Driven EnviroLab continues to this day.

IN AUGUST 2017, Category-5 Hurricane Harvey tore through the city of Houston, Texas. Engineering experts agree that the damage was increased exponentially by lax zoning laws that were designed to maximize profit at the expense of ecologically sound construction and neighborhood resilience.[28] This is, sadly, not a surprise.

Too often, the primary value underlying the planning and governance of our urban centers is quick expansion and efficiency—constructing the most units for the least cost, developing every square inch of real estate to its maximum, bypassing meaningful community consultation and participation to act with expediency. Questions of long-term vision and planning for climate-driven disasters take a backseat to short-term interests. When we fail to plan thoughtfully, we suffer the consequences.

On June 14, 2017, Grenfell Tower—a 24-story public housing complex in North Kensington, just blocks away from my home in London—went up in flames. Seventy-two people died. The survivors lost their home. As the world now knows, the apartment building was encased in highly flammable cladding—material banned for use in tall buildings in the United States and most of Europe. The building lacked working fire alarms or sprinklers, and there was just one narrow staircase through which residents could escape.

An independent public inquiry launched a few months later revealed a deeper layer to the tragedy: It was easily preventable. For years, residents lobbied the Kensington and Chelsea Councils, warning officials that the state of the building was a disaster waiting to happen. Reports show that it wouldn't have cost much to do the right thing. For an extra £5,000—roughly US$6,500—the building's dangerous exterior cladding could have been upgraded with fire-resistant materials.[29] Seventy-two people could have been saved, and many more could have been spared from injury and devastating trauma. Yet no one acted.

To me, this wasn't just a failure of building design, public planning, or even income disparity. It was an instance of social isolation. The authorities, the neighborhood, the broader London community—of which I'm a part—simply failed to *see* and *hear* the people who lived at Grenfell.

In the decades ahead, we will face urban design choices about whether to respond to environmental shifts with the value of belonging or not. Will we compound inequalities, walling off wealthier communities and leaving lower-income people to bear the brunt of climate impacts and poor infrastructure, or will we invest in shared solutions that prioritize participatory decision-making and solidarity? These questions are not just distant scenarios. We are beginning to face them now.

Jakarta, Indonesia, provides us with a clear picture of the intersectionality between climate change, inequality, municipal policy, and urban design. Jakarta—with a population nearing eleven million—is the fastest-sinking city in the world, with half of the city limits below sea level. This sinking phenomenon is known as land subsidence—groundwater extraction due in large part to insufficient potable water, accelerated by the weight of rapid urbanization and construction, has caused the land beneath Jakarta to deflate, sucking the city downward. Climate change, with its rising tides and more intense storms, has brought the issue to a breaking point.

As Jakarta sinks, the natural flow of water from rivers into the sea is slowed or disrupted. This means that during flooding events, instead of clearing into the sea, floodwater remains in the inundated areas. The communities most affected are those living next to the rivers, which, in Jakarta, happen to be among the poorest.

It might have once been possible to find a participatory approach to the problem—as Tokyo did for a similar issue many years ago by increasing regulations, building strong infrastructure to access potable water, and educating the public.[30] Yet, today, Jakarta is running out of clear options. It's now focused on reactionary infrastructure responses, like broadening canals, expanding flood reservoirs, and installing coastal protection walls.

Although these climate adaptation approaches could protect some communities against increased flooding, such projects are being implemented in ways that perpetuate inequality—defending belonging for some at the expense of belonging for others. For example, the canal and reservoir expansions are forcing the evictions of thousands of low-income households from informal riverside settlements.[31] While the government has made efforts to relocate these residents to low-cost apartments, few if any dislocated people have been consulted. No one has received compensation. Officials have rejected that any restitution is needed on the grounds that most riverside settlements were "illegal" anyhow.

Jakarta is emblematic of the challenge of finding belonging in a modern city, highlighting how poor urban design can exacerbate the intersectional issues of inequality and climate-driven displacement.

DESIGNING FOR INCLUSION

WHEN WE DON'T intentionally design for belonging, we end up valuing things that create isolation, disconnection, and inequity. For Dominic Richards, designing for belonging must be an intentional process, one that creates spaces of connection for all.

Among his many innovative projects, Richards has created an East London redevelopment project at Spitalfields, near Liverpool Street station. It's a mixed-use site that centers on affordable homes—catering to families who might not otherwise be able to get onto the housing ladder—while also focusing on amenities like farm shops and artisan pop-up stores that attract a diversity of socioeconomic profiles. For Richards, the focus is on the kind of mixed-use development that draws people together into a sense of shared community, inhabiting a space they'll care for together.

"The more you have a sense of 'belonging to somewhere,' the more you feel like you have a stake in the place that you're in," he told me. "If you look at when people feel that they have a sense of belonging somewhere, they take pride in the place and they have a different relationship to the place."[32]

Richards believes that there's magic in a well-designed urban space: the power to connect people not only to one another, but also to the natural environment and a sense of collective belonging. It's possible to awaken this, even in places that have been defined by disconnection or environmental degradation.

Many approaches to urban design hold promise for creating belonging in our cities. Designing and adapting cities to anticipate the changes awaiting us in the future requires fundamental shifts toward belonging in both the spirit and the structure of design.

Universal design (UD) is a design framework that guides urban planning to create more inclusive cities for those with disabilities—an important consideration for structures that hold the spirit of belonging within them. It allows for small adaptations that can be mobilized to create large impacts.

With more than one billion people—or 15 percent of the global population—estimated to live with some form of disability,[33] there's a growing recognition of the need to build accessibility into all forms of city planning and design. UD brings together city planners, engineers, environmental design researchers, and architects to create more equitable and participatory spaces that benefit everyone. Although it's not a one-size-fits-all doctrine for design and planning, UD seeks to create contexts that advance a series of principles that push the boundaries of "mainstream" products, services, and environments to include as many people as possible. It also includes an emphasis on customizable design of structures, facilities, and services that minimize the difficulties of adaptation for users with disabilities.[34]

In the Redhill neighborhood of central Singapore, amid brilliantly colored banyans and mahogany trees, and beneath modern apartment complexes, is a successful experiment in design for this kind of inclusiveness. The Enabling Village is a mixed-use development—including shops, offices, playgrounds, and meeting venues—that focuses on connecting, training, and employing people with disabilities.[35]

Building on global universal design principles in a way that's specific to local context, the village ensures accessibility and inclusion priorities, including "barrier-free movement" for people in wheelchairs, "hearing loops or audio induction loops," extensive braille signage, and tactile floor indicators with knobs and bars for blind and visually impaired people to find their way around. Most of all, it's dynamic and inviting—a haven of belonging in a dense urban setting.

Redhill sets an example for the rest of the city, demonstrating what's possible when we build for both structure and spirit. Inclusive, accessible design of neighborhoods should be our goal at all times, and Redhill, Singapore, shows us that it's not only possible—when done right, it's beautiful.

DESIGNING FOR REVITALIZATION

GOOD URBAN DESIGN can transform urban spaces to meet the needs of the population in sustainable, locally relevant, inclusive, and connected ways. Done well, it can resuscitate weathered economies, and bring new life and industry to the places we call home. On this, I'm reminded of two "Evergreens"—Evergreen Cooperatives in Cleveland, and Evergreen Brick Works in Toronto.

Cleveland, Ohio, is consistently ranked as one of the poorest cities in America.[36] But it wasn't always that way. In 1950, at the height of the country's industrial boom, Cleveland was home to a population of 915,000 people and some of the biggest steel producers and automakers.[37] World-class hospitals, universities, and philanthropies came with the prosperity. But, with the rise of outsourcing from the late 1960s onward, many companies moved overseas in search of lower-wage workers and fewer regulations. As opportunities declined, crime rates increased, and the city's wealthier residents largely departed, poorer Clevelanders, mostly African Americans, remained. Over recent decades, there have been few economic opportunities, and poverty has been rampant. Amid abandoned houses and shuttered factories, there's a pervasive sense of isolation. Most of the jobs that have stayed in Cleveland have been in low-skill, highly-repetitive roles like fast-food service that offer little sense of agency or chance of advancement. The city's declining population, around 385,000 at the last census, is less than half what it was in prosperous times, and Cleveland's poverty rate of 30.8 percent is more than double the country's average.[38]

In 2008, several of the local educational, medical, and philanthropic institutions that had been established during last century's boom times—including the Cleveland Clinic, University Hospitals, Case Western Reserve University, and the Cleveland Foundation, along with the municipal government—joined together to do something unprecedented. They formed a new initiative to pool their collective "purchasing power" to support the emergence of a consortium of employee-owned, locally-based cooperative businesses. The new effort was given a name to symbolize resilience: The Evergreen Cooperatives.[39]

Because the city's hospitals, schools, and government institutions together purchase billions of dollars of goods and services—from food catering to energy to cleaning services—they're capable of supporting thousands of jobs in the community. Typically, such big institutions contract out to major multinational firms or national chains to provide these kinds of services. With the new model, however, they commit to contract, when possible, with empowerment-focused, homegrown firms that invest profits locally.

All the firms work to hire people who have previously faced significant hurdles to employment—for example, due to old criminal convictions or the lack of a high school diploma. Many people who had not succeeded in traditional jobs in the mainstream economy are thriving in the Evergreen system. Claudia Oates, who works in marketing for the Evergreen laundry, has described how it's a radically different way of participating in the economy. As opposed to simply showing up and performing a task, "we are learning how to really be worker-owners, with quarterly statements, profit-sharing and looking at how to reinvest our money," she says.[40]

In Cleveland, Ohio, we see the notion of inclusive city-building on full display over the last decade and a half. And just north of the border, in my hometown of Toronto, we see another "evergreen" example of designing for revitalization.

A FIFTEEN-MINUTE WALK to the east of where I live, through a system of ravines, brimming with maple, cedar, and elm trees, stands a towering relic of a bygone industrial era—a century-old brick smokestack. Beginning in 1889, the Don Valley Brick Works manufactured many of the bricks that built the surrounding city. For a century, the site functioned as one of Canada's leading brick works factories, helping rebuild Toronto's key landmarks after the Great Fire of 1904, and contributing to many other nationally recognized buildings in other parts of the country.[41] When the quarry became almost fully depleted in the 1980s, the factory shut down, leaving behind a heavily polluted ecosystem, widespread unemployment, and abandoned facilities, replete with acres of debris and broken glass windows. It was a scene that's familiar to many big cities facing the decline of industry.

In 2002, the Evergreen Foundation, a Canadian nonprofit dedicated to improving interdependence between, people, the natural environment, and the built environment, began the multiyear process of revitalizing the Don Valley Brick Works. The enterprise worked with the broadest range of partners that it could assemble: park planners, architects, engineers, botanists, educators, farmers, chefs, healthcare companies, museums, and social services programs to imagine and design a hub for thriving community life. Rather than trying to build on their own idealistic vision of urban redevelopment, they listened. They investigated the needs of the community and what it would take to build a space that would meaningfully improve people's quality of life. By the end of the public consultation period, the revitalization had widespread public support.[42]

As I often stroll through the rows of vendors with their produce on a Saturday morning, now the largest market in the city, I feel a sense of a genuinely co-created place. And it is conveniently located a short ravine walk away from my home. Known as Evergreen Brick Works in its new era, the site is home to a forty-acre complex of marshlands, hiking trails, gardens, art galleries, markets, workshops, and conference spaces that seeks to provide young people in low-income areas the opportunity to get outdoors, to offer community groups access to affordable meeting space, and to give local farmers an open area to sell their produce. What was only recently a symbol of social and ecological decay is now a vibrant model of inclusion and sustainability. It's also reflective of the patterns of nature that are intricately connected, linking different kinds of patterns to each other in harmony.

Evergreen Brick Works likewise focuses on demonstrating the potential for environmental stewardship. Through a mix of innovative design elements, the site is approaching carbon neutrality. It's also revitalizing 200 hectares (approx. 494 acres) of surrounding parkland and connecting a broader network of trails for the community. As Angel Hsu's research with the UESI demonstrates, green spaces like these promote diverse benefits for people living in surrounding areas—including, for example, increased social connectedness through additional opportunity for face-to-face interactions. Environmental enrichment is also shown to contribute to other positive externalities, including reduced crime, and a "stronger sense of ownership, and agency amongst neighbors."[43]

Evergreen CEO Geoff Cape speaks of "the layers that build and evolve"[44] when a redevelopment honors place and history, while innovating toward greater inclusion, participation, and sustainability. In 2019, Evergreen launched a new consultative process with architects and residents to better understand how to adapt their spaces to the needs and wants of residents—enabling people of all backgrounds from the neighboring community to shape the future of the project.

This is a model of how to continuously engage with the community and cultivate urban spaces based on a positive vision—rather than simply following trends of the market or the requirements of roadway planning.

Diverse movements are advancing this kind of participatory planning in cities at scale. Increasingly, the local work of urban planning and redevelopment intersects with global social and economic policy. "An inclusive city," says Rhonda Douglas, program strategy advisor for Women in Informal Employment: Globalizing and Organizing (WIEGO), "is one that values all people and their needs equally. It is one in which all residents—including the most marginalized of poor workers—have a representative voice in governance, planning, and budgeting processes, and have access to sustainable livelihoods, legal housing and affordable basic services such as water and sanitation and an electricity supply."[45] These are the ways in which social and political infrastructures of belonging interact in reciprocal relationship with the built infrastructure of urban spaces.

Both Evergreens—Cooperatives in Cleveland and Brick Works in Toronto—show us what it means to build inclusive, people-centric cities. Indeed, when we design for revitalization, we so often end up with belonging.

DESIGNING FOR HARMONY

NEW URBANISM is one of the frameworks that seeks to reorient our cities and living spaces back to ancient design principles used in medieval and pre–modern era towns in order to recapture a sense of place, and to design the town and city as a unit in support of the community and the activities it carries out. At the same time, it aims to reestablish the connection between design and the community by drawing on historical architecture, materials, and ordering of environmental and pedestrian-centric spaces in ways that also support our increasingly flexible economies. This framework aims to address the figurative "erosion" between new residential buildings and the environment by drawing on locally-specific elements of space and character that have historically enabled people to feel more connected to place and each other. New Urbanism recognizes the reciprocal relationship between the structure and spirit of design to build belonging in our cities and foster connection to people, place, power, and purpose.

In his book, *Harmony: A New Way of Looking at Our World,* Charles, Prince of Wales, writes, "It seems that communities work best when the principles that Nature depends upon in order that she is self-sustaining are applied to urban planning and architecture. These principles bring together patterns of complexity and a sense of overall unity that, in turn, creates an order and a harmony that reflects Nature's own patterns of self-organization. Like Nature, communities thrive from the roots up, not the other way around."[46]

I have known Prince Charles since 2003, when we were introduced to one another by Kathleen Raine in what turned out to be the last months of her life. Our short conversation was poignant, not only for that reason, but also because when he spoke of sacred geometry deriving from Nature's ways of knowing, I saw community, and when he spoke of communities that "thrive from the roots up," I saw belonging. In a life filled with thousands of public engagements, people often clamoring for Prince Charles in circles crushing inward on themselves, I've often thought about what it must be like for him to maintain a sense of personal harmony, let alone personal space. So I was struck in a subsequent conversation when he spoke with empathy about the person, "at the back of the room," standing all alone. And it occurred to me that perhaps both of them feel isolated in their own way, one surrounded by many people, the other surrounded by none. And that perhaps the prince's ethos derives from empathy, much more than convention. Over many decades, he has put this ethos into practice in countless ways, notably in his work with young people, providing opportunities for education, job training, and entrepreneurship, his enduring leadership in the global fight against climate change, and in reimagining the built environment. I have also come to know him as an inspiring teacher, who, like other inspiring teachers, maintains the intuition and inquisitive energy of a student. It's a quality I've found in people who have inspired me throughout my life.

In 2017, I made my first visit to a place that beautifully encapsulates Prince Charles's vision of Harmony—a small English village called Poundbury in the Duchy of Cornwall.

IN 1989, Prince Charles and the West Dorset District Council set out to facilitate a multi-decade experiment that sought to imagine what it would look like to design an urban center based on this kind of design. They envisioned the development of an affordable, accessible, large-scale mixed-use housing initiative that would meaningfully reflect the priorities and preferences of the people who would come to live there, as well as the historical traditions and architecture styles and materials that had been present in past centuries. They also wanted to carve out green spaces that enabled connection to nature and the community.

The Poundbury Masterplan was initiated when local residents of the Dorset County town in Dorchester, England, came together to share their insights on what they would like to see in a future neighborhood, whose land was set aside for expansion in the coming decades. The community identified priorities including efficient land use, minimizing pollution, and enhancing biodiversity while meeting housing and employment needs and reducing the need for commuting.[47] The plan also paid particular attention to place-making, honoring local traditions in architecture as well as selection of local materials. Under the initial vision laid out by Prince Charles, the community united to clearly design a cutting-edge, inclusive space that would be conducive to not just living but, ultimately, connection and belonging as well.

The result of this community development process was Poundbury, an urban extension to Dorchester. The twenty-year plan set out development for five thousand residents at the city's western outskirts. Poundbury is an ode to urban design activist Jane Jacobs's vision of prioritizing "people over cars." The street designs are whimsically winding on purpose, bending to accommodate the shapes of parks and homes, rather than a rigid, auto-friendly grid pattern. It's walkable and forested. It's a place that puts a premium on sidewalks and the person-to-person interactions they foster, in addition to environmental and human health.

With a nod perhaps to Jane Jacobs's work, Prince Charles has written of architecture and urban design, " 'Putting the human being at the centre of the design process' goes beyond seeing people as pedestrians. As traditional thinking teaches, basing designs on the timeless universal principles expressed by Nature's order enables the full scope of our humanity to be fulfilled, on the physical, communal, cultural and spiritual levels."[48]

The town has four distinct quarters, each of which is mixed-use, providing local education, employment, commercial, and community opportunities. Communities in each quarter are given power to establish and define a character within each quarter, but the quarters reflect the principles and design elements of the town as a whole. Architecture is shaped by environmental surroundings. And the form, design, and materials of buildings reflect the local building traditions of the area in an effort to maintain the specificity of place and local identity.[49] This intentional design was firmly grounded in a spirit of design *with, not for*, an approach that placed significance on what goes into making a community.

This approach seeks a return to harmony between the places people live and work, rather than siloing a city's various functions into zones of industry, housing, shops, and amenities as separate spaces, which encourages urban flight. León Krier, the architect who designed Poundbury, designed this kind of polycentric settlement to "create a collection of somewheres instead of an ever-expanding nowhere" that typical urban zoning creates.[50] Krier notes that this design is intended to allow connectivity and proximity to community spaces and resources.

Krier's vision is directed at reflecting the deeper parts of the human psyche and ideas of home, much like Blake's idea of the City of Imagination. Krier says, "By creating our cities, we create ourselves. When we despoil our cities, we despoil ourselves. A beautiful village, a beautiful house, a beautiful city can become a home for all, a universal home."[51]

ON A SUNNY SPRING DAY in April 2021, Dr. Michael Dooley stands dignified, hands clasped in front, smiling on as a young trumpeter plays "God Save the Queen" and a chorus of local voices chimes in. Donning the ceremonial uniform of a blue velvet coat, breeches, and buckled shoes that have been worn since the seventeenth century by those holding his office, Dr. Dooley has just been royally-appointed to be the 2021–22 High Sheriff of Dorset. In this role, which has existed for over a millennium, he serves as the Queen's representative in his county for all matters relating to the judiciary and the maintenance of law and order, and is engaged with the nonprofit sector.

Dr. Dooley, an obstetrician and gynecologist, has been the medical director of the Poundbury Clinic, an integrated clinic that seeks to create harmony in women's health and well-being, for almost two decades. Dorset has long been his home, and Dr. Dooley speaks of Poundbury with joy and warmth.

In his role as high sheriff, Michael shared that "through my active role in supporting, encouraging and listening, I hope the eyes of Dorset will begin to shine a little brighter."[52] Indeed, the eyes of Dorset are luminous in Poundbury. When I asked Michael about what makes this developing arm of Dorchester so special, he beamed with pride. "I think when we all work together, we can make the place better and healthier," he said. "Health and care need to be at the center of society where everyone is equipped to stay well and thrive, where medicine is not just a pill. That's why we're looking within the community, and it's happening in Poundbury."[53]

This spirit of community is carried through the many structures that make up Poundbury's thoughtful design, bringing the village vibe to life.

Michael told me about Poundbury's butcher shop that not only provides health and nourishment for the community, but also donates ingredients to the local school every Friday to supply the students' cooking classes. He spoke of the local food bank, which uses food as a means to encourage community members to access support for a whole range of things like reducing debt, securing housing, and finding a job. Michael says that these services are "all in the food bank, but in the background. The food gets the person in."

Poundbury's design supports intersectionality and interconnectedness. Dr. Dooley explained how Poundbury's Pavilion in the Park holds a café, and an alcohol education trust, and provides meals to local students with lunch vouchers during school holidays. He described the central hub Queen Mother Square as the "heart" of Poundbury, and talked about the creation of community for marginalized populations: "The Dorset Council have bought a farm that is helping prisoners and helping the homeless and creating, within the farm, its own little community."

The same spirit of harmony that inspired the development of the town's infrastructure is carried through the spirit of its residents and what they choose to make of this developing community. The Damers First School, nestled in the northeast corner of Poundbury, has adopted Harmony Education, a values-based pedagogy developed by a passionate educator, Richard Dunne, as a way of embracing Harmony and interconnectedness in education. Harmony Education is about not only what we learn, but also how we learn.[54] The students of Damers First School are taught the seven principles of harmony: geometry, interdependence, circles and cycles, diversity, health, beauty, and oneness. Indeed, these same principles informed the design of their town—all through thoughtful and easy-to-understand engagement with literature, art, geometry, and nature.

The communal spirit of Poundbury is one that Michael Dooley hopes will grow for generations to come. He shared with me his vision for the future of this small but bustling branch of the larger Dorchester center, noting that its design has ensured that it has all the essential pieces that will work together as a whole. "Like any orchestra," he reflected, a town "always needs a conductor. I think one's got to now cultivate in the individuals and the community spirit, that this is a legacy, not only for us but for generations ahead."[55]

THE PEOPLE WE'VE MET in this chapter know what it takes to design and sustain cities of belonging—cities of imagination, where our highest human values can be embodied in the built fabric of urban spaces and the social and spiritual infrastructure that rise up within it. They show how we can be nourished by our cities in multiple dimensions, creating radical shifts in how we reconceptualize urban spaces, and also our relationship to others around us.

As placemaker Dominic Richards reminded us earlier, either we design for belonging or we end up with isolation. This is as true of our cities as it is of all systems we design, whether it be infrastructure, healthcare, education, or political governance systems. And as we do this important work, we must keep our political representatives focused on the task at hand.

Too often, governments around the world abdicate their responsibilities to their citizens, choosing instead to let charities or the private sector step in to deliver crucial programming and infrastructure. There are myriad examples of groups and organizations doing incredible work for people around the world, but we can't allow those who control the allocation of taxpayer dollars to simply rest on their laurels. Government investment, informed by and in partnership with charities, the private sector, and citizens themselves, is how we can build cities that truly support the people that live there.

Designing for belonging can, and will, change everything. If oriented toward values of inclusivity, equality, and reciprocity, purposeful design recognizes that everyone has a Right to Belong. Cities and systems that reflect and cultivate these values allow us to build societies that are resilient and compassionate.

Cities have been agents of change over time, since the beginning of time. As we look toward the future, our urban spaces must continue to innovate and capture the imagination of enormous populations, driving home the central point:

Our cities belong to all of us.

CHAPTER EIGHT

RECIPROCAL CAREGIVING

If they say why, why
Tell them that it's human nature

—MICHAEL JACKSON, "HUMAN NATURE"[1]

MY SISTER TAMMY exuded a gentle resilience and the warmth of home-place. She was a fighter, too. When she was diagnosed with terminal cancer in 2004, the doctors gave her six months. She lived for four years. She held on for her kids, striving to be their mom for as long as possible.

They say the bond between sisters is special, unlike any other sibling relationship. I know for a fact that's true. With Tammy, I always felt like I belonged. She was her, I was me, and together we were Kim and Tammy—unstoppable.

As she battled through what seems like unending rounds of chemotherapy, I supported her as best I could. I never asked her outright, "How do I do this? How do I support you?" Rather, I was, as I think she would attest to, quietly there. Not overbearing, not flitting in and out of her life on the worst of days, but present throughout. A sounding board, a reassuring hand on her back, a corny joke and a laugh.

Ours was a caregiving relationship built on reciprocity—giving and receiving, from the time we were little right up until the very end. I belonged with her, and she belonged with me. Throughout her struggles, and throughout mine, you couldn't quite tell who was giving care and who was receiving care. We were just existing, together, building that foundation onto which we'd routinely unburden ourselves of the weightier parts of life.

Now that she's gone, I often reminisce about the times we were lucky to share. I'll always remember one particular day on the steps of the Princess Margaret Cancer Centre in Toronto.

Tammy had just gone through a particularly rough session of chemo. Like always, she got through it like a champ. We were heading down the hospital steps, tired and happy to be going home. Suddenly, I was approached by a kindhearted man, a Good Samaritan with a caring look in his eyes. He reached out to steady me, and asked with such genuine concern: "Are you okay? You look so weak. You will get through this, I promise. Stay strong."

It took a second to realize that this very kind stranger thought, looking at the two of us, that I was the sick one.

As he walked out of earshot, I turned to Tammy who started to chuckle.

She deadpanned: "It's always about you, Sis."

We burst out laughing, and I reflected on the absurdity of the moment.

Here was my brave, beautiful sister going through hell, and I was the one who looked ill.

The funny thing is, the person who supported me most throughout Tammy's cancer experience was Tammy herself. She consoled me when I got emotional thinking about the inevitable conclusion of her journey, and she reassured me that the world would keep turning long after she was gone.

In her darkest hours, I gave of myself, and more importantly, she just as willingly gave of herself. But that was just in her nature—always giving, always caring for others, always making sure those she loved were doing OK even when she herself was in pain.

I'll never forget this one particular evening after our father died. We had just wrapped up the second of two services: first a funeral and then, later, a celebration of his life. Countless family, friends, and many others—some whom we'd never met or known—came by to extend their condolences and share fond memories of our dad.

I snuck upstairs for a moment of respite, seeking silence after an emotionally draining three months.

Within what felt like mere minutes, there was a gentle knock at the door. It was Tammy with a plate of toast, generously buttered.

"Hi, Sis. I thought this would be a good time for a cup of tea and some warm toast. You need to keep your strength up." And then she turned and was gone.

It was such a small interaction, but one that speaks volumes about who she was. Tammy was my anchor. We had both lost the same father, we both loved him enormously, but here she was, taking care of me on one of the toughest days of both of our lives.

When we think of caregiving, we often think of the classic examples of professional care—doctors, nurses, social workers, teachers, counselors, personal support workers. But caregiving can be found everywhere. And caregiving done well often doesn't feel like caregiving at all. It feels like two people interacting in a way that seems normal and natural.

My presence by Tammy's side throughout her cancer journey was caregiving, but so was her making sure I ate on the day of our dad's funeral. Caregiving for Tammy and me was in our all-night phone calls, our inside jokes, our impromptu therapy sessions.

The thing we often forget as a society is that we don't have to be sick to be worthy of care. It's not just when we're babies, or when we're injured, or when we're old that we need to be cared for. In a world where so much of our well-being is rooted in our sense of belonging, our sense of community, our sense of fulfillment, we should be giving and receiving care always. We need to normalize building and maintaining reciprocity in how we care for others, true reciprocity in which each person gives and receives. It demands effort that eventually—hopefully—transcends into the realm of ritual.

Reciprocal caregiving is a two-way street. It's not simply helper-helpless, but rather, being human and engaging in a way that values others' agency while offering support freely and often. Caregiving done well has the power to combat social isolation, engender a true sense of community, and, ultimately, gift us with the belonging that we all yearn for as human beings.

I sometimes think of caregiving like tending to a garden. Do we water our plants only when the leaves brown and droop, and the petals start to fall? Of course not. We know that in order for that garden to thrive and be beautiful, it requires regular maintenance. It requires nurturing. That's how we should think about our relationships to one another.

Building our social resilience requires enduring care and reciprocity, long before a crisis strikes.[2] Rather than swooping in only when things are bad, let's normalize constant caregiving, rooted in reciprocity, in acts big and small. That is when we show others that we love them, and that they belong. That is how we build social connectedness with the people around us, cultivate collective resilience, and grow our communities into holistic, dynamic, nurturing places within which we can all coexist and thrive together.

"CALLING PROFESSIONS"

THERE ARE PEOPLE for whom caring is their calling. People who turn their passion for care into their lifelong profession. They include doctors, nurses, social workers, first responders, personal support workers, teachers, education workers, and counselors.

We all know these heroes. We've heard them talk about how they felt a calling to teach, to help, to heal. For them, their job is more than just a job. It's a vocation, a mission, a purpose. It grounds their sense of belonging and their sense of community. It's in these individuals that we see compassion and humanity at work. And sadly, it's because of this deep sense of purpose that we see work-related stress and burnout take an outsized toll on professional caregivers.

Systemic challenges like inadequate pay, lack of recognition, and burdensome bureaucracy can all stand in the way of caregivers doing what they were born to do—give care. And it's these roadblocks within the professions themselves that can have serious mental health impacts on the people working the front lines.

We so often forget that our professional caregivers are human, choosing to see them instead as unbreakable. COVID-19 has only worsened the pressure facing those for whom their life's work is caring for others.

With at least 6.1 million dead and a minimum of 475 million infected as of March 2022, COVID has proven an unimaginable challenge for the global population, with an unparalleled impact on our collective mental health. António Guterres, UN Secretary General spoke of the impacts of COVID on mental health just a few months into the onslaught of the pandemic. In May 2020, he wrote, "The shocks associated with COVID-19 are now pushing many toward greater fragility and pain: grief at the loss of loved ones; anxiety at the loss of jobs; isolation and restrictions on movement; difficult family dynamics, uncertainty and fear of the future. Each of these on its own can trigger or deepen distress."[3] He noted that the pandemic was leading to devastating cuts in mental health services and the closure of vital facilities at a time when support was needed most. The numbers bear out that truth: In a September 2020 report, nearly 41 percent of American adults reported at least one adverse mental or behavioral condition stemming from COVID-19.[4]

To say that the virus and its many variants to date has caused harm to our overall well-being would be a gross understatement. This ongoing emergency can be understood as a prolonged crisis, in which physicians and nurses had little relief from what were unrelentingly high case numbers and overburdened healthcare facilities. And the impact on those tasked with working the front lines—notably our healthcare professionals—has been unfathomable for those of us not directly charged with solving this crisis.

A study out of Columbia University in June 2020 reported on the negative impacts of the pandemic on healthcare workers in New York City: Nearly half of the nurses and doctors surveyed showed depressive symptoms. More than half had high levels of acute stress. One-third had anxiety, and most were experiencing insomnia and loneliness—and that was only a few months into the pandemic.[5]

Indeed, COVID-19 only added to the stress and mental health challenges facing a group already predisposed to these types of work-related struggles. The American College of Emergency Physicians reports that the physician suicide rate has increased by 35 percent between 1999 and 2018. Male physicians are 1.4 times more likely than the general population to die by suicide. Female physicians are 2.3 times more likely. Of those physicians who died by suicide, half did not have a known mental health condition.[6]

CARING FOR CAREGIVERS, NYC

"BURNOUT IS A HUGE PROBLEM in medicine, and it's been a problem for a long time,"[7] explains Dr. Lori Plutchik, a psychiatrist in New York City. We connected recently to talk about mental health challenges during the pandemic, as well as an impressive new initiative she co-founded.

Physician burnout, Dr. Plutchik told me, is rarely a result of patient care. Rather, she said that the clinical care of patients is "usually the light in their day." She pointed to interactions with insurance companies, the process for medication approvals, and administrative work as incredibly time-consuming parts of the job. She also mentioned the typical grueling hours and low pay for residents, many of whom have just graduated medical school with hundreds of thousands of dollars in debt. During the COVID-19 pandemic, doctors were routinely working double and triple shifts, the hours were longer, the interactions more dire, and, in some circles, there existed a political climate that framed doctors as the enemy. The penchant for physician burnout only worsened. As a society that so often relies on our professional caregivers to support us in our times of need, we must ask ourselves: On their darkest days, while they work tirelessly to care for us, who cares for the caregivers?

It was exactly this question that led Dr. Plutchik to join forces with Dr. Marianna Strongin, a clinical psychologist in New York City, to create Caring for Caregivers NYC. Caring for Caregivers was created to provide psychotherapy support to frontline physicians working in NYC hospitals during COVID-19. Understanding full well the mental health challenges facing this group during non-pandemic times—and understanding that the virus would certainly exacerbate these challenges—Drs. Plutchik and Strongin recruited more than seventy-five experienced therapists and psychiatrists to volunteer their time to provide frontline physicians with up to three months of complimentary, individualized therapy. The sessions were tailored to the individual physician's needs, and the overall approach to the program was decidedly hands-on—physicians weren't simply given a number and left to their own devices. Knowing that this group would be hard-pressed to reach out and follow through with asking for help, Dr. Plutchik and Dr. Strongin ensured that physicians were guided through the process. The program operated from April 2020 to July 2021, and successfully provided care to nearly one hundred physicians, nurses, and physician assistants working hard in the fight against COVID-19.[8]

I spoke with the doctors after the program launched to better understand why this uncommon approach to caregiving proved so successful; it turned out that the answer lay in the idea of curated care, which started with acknowledging some tough truths about physician belonging.

As human beings, we all want to belong—physicians are no different. Dr. Plutchik agrees: "Most physicians tend to put a lot of pressure on themselves. They have a very perfectionist type of personality, and very much value independence, strength, and competency. Part of the sense of belonging in medicine also has to do with this feeling of being like a superhuman and that you should always be able to take care of anything that comes your way. If you can't do something, if you can't be on call for a thirty-six-hour shift, if you can't get in the arterial stick, whatever it is, it's really looked at as a sign of weakness." This stigma makes seeking outside help a significant challenge. "There's still a sense that if you go seek help outside the group—like to a therapist or a mental health provider—that is weakness."[9]

If admitting that you are struggling—and subsequently seeking help for mental health challenges—has the potential to jeopardize a physician's sense of belonging and lead to social isolation from one's peers, it's no wonder so many professionals avoid asking for help. Stigma is a powerful, limiting force—our brilliant doctors are not immune. It turns out that those who are used to giving care are less likely to ask for and receive it themselves.

So what does it mean, then, to successfully care for our caregivers in a crisis like the COVID-19 pandemic? What does it mean to foster and protect belonging in a physician community that is so traditionally averse to seeking outside help?

Dr. Plutchik tells me, "One of the most important things about the therapeutic relationship that we have with our patients is the personal connection." Dr. Strongin agrees: "Connection is the most vital piece."[10] The doctors tell me that caring for physicians in the time of COVID involves validating their feelings, allowing them a safe space to talk about those feelings, and reassuring them that their struggles are not a sign of weakness. Effective care, then, means allowing physicians to share openly and honestly without feeling like they have failed the group to which they belong.

Dr. Plutchik and Dr. Strongin credit the success of Caring for Caregivers with their hands-on approach to care. Dr. Strongin says, "What we're realizing is they're not going to find a therapist for themselves. They're not going to find the *right* therapist for themselves, and they might not even make the phone call after we'd made the introduction." Indeed, the program worked in helping so many frontline physicians because those providing care—Dr. Plutchik, Dr. Strongin, and the volunteers—took these physicians by the hand and guided them along the way. They weren't given information and then abandoned. Rather, they had someone walk with them on their journey and ensure that the necessary mental health support was being delivered.

There will no doubt be challenges in the physician community once this pandemic is over—challenges like PTSD, anxiety, depression, burnout. But what this program modeled extremely well was an effective path forward for holistic physician wellness. Caring for Caregivers has demonstrated how we as a society can provide effective care to those—physician and non-physician alike—who are hesitant to ask for help in the first place. I am grateful for leaders like Dr. Plutchik and Dr. Strongin doing this important work, figuring out how best to foster genuine social connection, preserve belonging, and, ultimately, care for the caregivers.

LIONEL AND JUNE

ON THE TOPIC OF CAREGIVING, I often think about what happens in our society when one partner in a couple dies, and the subsequent lack of support that is too often experienced by the surviving spouse. We all know people in our communities who have lost a partner. Many of us will have witnessed this tragedy up close in our own families—I saw my mother lose my father, and then I saw the corresponding toll it took on her.

Readers will recognize how it typically unfolds. The situation, as we know it, too often plays out like this:

A couple have been married for decades. For the sake of storytelling, let's call them Lionel and June—they could easily be your next-door neighbors, your parents, your best friends. Lionel's health has taken a turn for the worse. Maybe he suffered an injury, maybe it's cancer, maybe it's dementia. Whatever the cause, Lionel needs care in the later years of his life. June, ever the supportive wife and partner, wants to keep Lionel in their home. She decides that she will provide daily care for her husband.

At the outset of this decision, June gets supportive calls from her friends. They tell her that what she's doing is wonderful, and if anyone can help Lionel, it's her. They tell her that if she needs anything at all, don't hesitate to pick up the phone and ask. Then a few weeks go by, and people stop calling. No one checks in. June cares for Lionel, day in and day out. She receives no help. She is Lionel's caregiver—that has become her de facto role and the core of her identity. She does not have a network of peers to turn to for support or advice. June feels trapped at the bottom of the well—she is isolated, and she is alone.

Her adult kids who live in faraway cities call once a week to check in on their dad, and old friends she bumps into at the grocery store say things like "You're a rock, June. He's so lucky to have you." Prior to Lionel's injury, June benefited from reciprocal caregiving. Over the course of their life together, she cared for Lionel and Lionel cared for her—a true partnership. And now, June has lost that partner. She is giving care to Lionel, but she no longer has someone to care for her.

And then one day, Lionel dies. Friends and family tell June that they had no idea it had gotten so bad, and they wish she would have reached out sooner for help. There is a funeral, and half the town shows up to pay their respects. They come to the house for tea, they drop off casseroles, they fill the living room with flowers. And then, just like that, they're gone. Once again, June is alone.

What June doesn't say is that she struggled the whole time. It was hard, every single day. But June has been conditioned to believe that admitting you need help while caring for your sick partner isn't strength. It's weakness. And in a time when Lionel needed strength, she wasn't going to be weak. She was, after all, "a rock." And now that Lionel is gone, June, emotionally exhausted and without someone to care for her, slips further into loneliness and isolation.

This story belongs to the many people who have been tasked with caregiving and left without the support necessary to care for themselves. As a society, as people who want to belong and want others to feel like they belong, too, here's the bottom line: When things get hard, we need to show up *sooner*, we need to show up *more often*, and we need to stay for *longer*. When we prioritize reciprocity in caregiving, we directly counter social isolation and loneliness. We must care for the caregiver, and tend to our relationships constantly. Remember, we don't water a garden when the leaves droop and the petals fall—we maintain it and nurture it from the start.

A COMMUNITY CHORUS

ONCE UPON A TIME, I auditioned for the school choir. It seemed like everyone in my class was there to try out. I was nervous, but I loved singing. I wanted to be part of the group. I was prepared to sing "Morning Has Broken" by Cat Stevens, now known as Yusuf Islam, for my audition. Unfortunately, everyone was required to perform a verse from a particular hymn. I remember standing in front of the music teacher and starting to sing, only to be stopped after the first few lines. And then I waited. When auditions were over, the teacher told everyone to stick around to get sorted into the appropriate sections: "Except you, Kim. You can call your mom to come pick you up." That was it—I didn't make the cut. I was heartbroken. I wanted so desperately to sing, but more than that, I yearned so desperately to belong.

The singer, songwriter, and social activist Annie Lennox once told me: "Music is diverse and eclectic by its very nature, appealing to many cross sections of cultures and societies. It affirms our joy, our longing, our sense of self and . . . 'belonging.' "[11] I couldn't agree more. And singing with others toward the common goal of music-making is special in its own unique way.

I fundamentally see singing as an act of caregiving. There is incredible power in uniting the voices of many through song. Amazing things happen when people come together through art, when all are recognized for their diverse gifts, and when care is given freely and without prejudice in a safe space built by and for community—for a real-world example, look no further than the Thurrock Community Chorus. It was created out of an expressed need for greater community interaction—especially for older people and those with disabilities—but it quickly became so much more for so many. The Chorus is a lesson in reciprocal caregiving and a testament to the power of belonging.

It all started in 2010 when the Royal Opera House moved its production facilities from East London to Purfleet, Thurrock. There, the ROH developed the High House Production Park to create the stage scenery for the Opera. The site is shared between several arts organizations, including a production and rehearsal venue for hire, artists' studios, community space, and business and workshop space, and is home to the UK's first ever National Skills Academy for technical and stage crafts for the performing arts and live music industries.

Thurrock is historically an industrial town, replete with once-bustling docks and factories, but was hit hard by the deindustrialization of the 1970s and '80s.[12] Many of Thurrock's residents now commute to other parts of the UK to work,[13] and women in Thurrock experience higher rates of unemployment than the national average.[14] In 2012, Thurrock recorded levels of life satisfaction lower than any other place in the United Kingdom.[15]

The Thurrock Community Chorus (TCC) began in 2011. Operating under the wing of the Royal Opera House (ROH), the TCC emerged because community members were excited about the building of the new ROH facility in Thurrock, and they, too, wanted to sing. A collective of community members asked if the ROH could create and run a chorus for local folks (read: nonprofessional singers), and, not long after, the Thurrock Community Chorus (TCC) was born.

I had heard about this upstart group not long after its founding. No doubt colored by my unsuccessful attempt at joining the choir as an adolescent, I was very intrigued by the concept of a community chorus. Apparently in the TCC, anyone could join, and no training was necessary. The youngest member was eight years old, but the average age skewed decidedly older. About 10 percent of the members had mental health issues or physical or intellectual disabilities. It sounded, to me, like an initiative that placed great value on inclusion and care.

In January 2019, I decided to stop by and check it out for myself—maybe even sing a few bars if they'd have me. What I stumbled upon was, I realize now, belonging in the truest sense. The warmth and caring nature of this group reverberated off the walls. The safe space that was created, and the solidarity among members, inspired unfiltered and charming honesty. I asked one chorus member how she was doing, to which she responded, "Oh I'm feeling a bit bipolar today, dear!" I knew right away that I had found a place where everyone could really be themselves and be valued for their gifts—a place where reciprocity and connection were paramount. I was placed into a section based on my vocal range, and off we went. I went back a few more times, each time greeted by familiar faces and a warm welcome.

Alex Beard, CEO of the Royal Opera House, recently spoke with me about the power of the performing arts to bring people together. "For me, the heart of it is a collective of people, the community people coming together on stage and in the audience together in one space, sharing one breath, reflecting on what makes life worth living; the really, really important stuff." He went on, "Fundamentally, it is about the really, really big stuff in life. It's about love. It's about hate. It's about despair. It's about hope."[16]

This kind of connection to others and reciprocal caregiving should not be limited to an exceptional few, and the TCC is made stronger by bringing together the voices of many, regardless of ability. As one chorus member, Martin French, shared, "You don't need any previous experience. If you like singing, you're welcome. There's everyone here. We've got school children, students, nurses, teachers, and professionals alike."[17]

The Samuel Centre for Social Connectedness has interviewed a number of Chorus members over the years on the lasting impact that the TCC has had on their lives, their sense of belonging, and the broader community.

Sarah moved to Thurrock over a decade ago and joined the Chorus in search of community. "It could have been clique-like, I could have been judged not to be good enough. But these people are the most welcoming," she says. "This is what made me feel part of the community."[18]

Gary had been active in the community for years. He was terrified to join TCC, but decided to push himself out of his comfort zone one day and show up. His bravery paid off, and he speaks fondly of the Chorus now. "Singing and art bring people together," he says. In his mind, TCC is about "giving ordinary people an extraordinary chance."

Not only does singing provide an outlet for community building, but it has proven wellness benefits, too. Singing, especially in a group, improves one's mood, and helps reduce feelings of stress, depression, anxiety, and even fatigue.[19] Weekly participation in a choir can improve both mental and physical health.[20] And attending a choir regularly has positive effects on improving memory, even helping those suffering from dementia.[21]

David and Anne St. Pier have been together for fifty-four years and married for fifty-one. Anne is a retired nurse, and Dave used to work as an IT manager. They joined the chorus in 2012, soon after it was established. Though I had met them for tea years ago during a visit to Thurrock, we recently caught up to talk about what being a part of this chorus has meant for them. Sitting closely together, playfully nudging one another along, finishing each other's sentences, they joyfully told me how this community of choristers has been nothing short of life-changing.

"Singers are happy people," Dave told me that day.

Dave was diagnosed with Parkinson's disease in 2014. In 2017, he began participating in a speech language research project to improve some of his symptoms. "They were trying to improve the way people with Parkinson's speak," he shared. "We tend to talk very softly, and people can't hear you. And because people can't hear you, they ignore you. And in the end, you become an outcast."[22]

After joining the research project, Dave was delighted to discover that the voice exercises he was learning in therapy had already been put into practice by the chorus. "It just so happened that the choir that we were singing with were doing the very same exercises the therapist was showing me," he said. Dave shared with me that being a part of the chorus has actually helped with the symptoms of his Parkinson's disease.

For Anne, the welcoming spirit that permeated the chorus was immediately apparent. "It was all audition free. You felt accepted and embraced. You don't have to be a wonderful singer to be part of the chorus," she shared. "You were accepted, even if your voice wasn't that good. It was such a lovely, warm community feeling, people that I only met through the chorus that have now become lifelong friends."[23] For Dave, "the chorus promotes everything: friendship, collective participation, aiding one another."[24]

Anne and Dave shared that the care they receive from being a part of the chorus extends well beyond the physical health benefits; it supports their mental and emotional well-being, too. Anne told me that joining the chorus gave them both a sense of pride and improved their self-esteem, and that to this day walking into a chorus rehearsal "makes you happy, excited, fulfilled. Oh, so many feelings. It's just lovely to meet up with your friends."[25] Dave nodded in agreement, adding, "An activity just like singing in an opera group is good therapy. It's good therapy for meeting new people." He continued, "That's what you learn from this activity, you see. You support each other."[26]

Reciprocal caregiving can take place anywhere care is given and received. Sometimes, the best examples are outside the walls of a hospital or a school. Informal care happens every single day among people for whom "professional caregiver" is not in their job description. This too is valid, necessary, effective caregiving—by community, for community.

Madeline, another chorus member, can attest to the wellness benefits of singing, telling us: "Singing should be prescribed. Any group activity is brilliant, and worries fade into the distance." One anonymous interviewee was bullied in school and suffers from anxiety, but they found solace—and community—in the Chorus. "My friendship group is through the Chorus. We're involved in each other's lives," they said. "As long as the Chorus is here, I'm going to stay in the area. I have thought of moving, but no, these are my people."[27]

Mike, a longtime member of the group, perhaps summed it up best, saying simply, "The Chorus brings people together."[28] The data show this: A 2017 Royal Opera House report found that a full 75 percent of members said they would not be singing without the Chorus.[29]

The ROH has grown because of its relationship with the Chorus, too. "The work that we did with the community chorus was totally inspirational," shared CEO Alex Beard. The TCC and the many other programs the ROH began in Thurrock have sparked the development of other ROH programs in schools and with communities across the UK. "From that very first moment of being there in 2010 through to today," Alex continued, "developing a really strong sense of our relationship with that place, our relationship with that community enabled us to develop programs and approaches to community engagement in Thurrock that we're now taking way beyond."[30]

In its first year, the TCC had sixty members. By 2020, it had 140 members—and a waiting list. Despite this incredible success, in 2020, amid the challenges posed to the arts by the COVID-19 pandemic, the ROH announced that it couldn't continue funding the TCC, as did the Thurrock Borough Council.[31] Following this difficult decision, the Thurrock Community Chorus shut down. Though of course the members understood, it was a bitter pill to swallow. For Dave and Anne, this loss was devastating.

"When that was taken away," said Dave, "my Parkinson's took a nosedive. I would say it probably advanced about five years." He shared that having these vital connections to community severed resulted in lethargy, and a "downward spiral," explaining "you need to see people, you need to talk to them, and you need to share experiences with them."[32] For Anne, too, this was difficult, speaking not only of how her husband's health suffered as a result of the loss of the chorus and community, but of her own isolation as well. "Everything just disappears from your life," she told me. "We kept in touch with all our friends in the community chorus, but you couldn't see them. You just feel very, very isolated."[33]

Recognizing the significance, the members were determined that the Chorus will live on. In 2021, they formed the Thames Opera

Company (TOC), founded on the same values as the TCC: everyone welcome, no experience required. They realize the inherent value in keeping the chorus around—after all, it has become a crucial outlet for older people in the community to engage with others, and it democratizes access to the arts. Not only that, but the chorus allows those with disabilities an important forum in which they can participate as equals, and provides a lifesaving outlet for people who were previously isolated, allowing them to find community and come together with others to create something beautiful.

"Thankfully, since we've actually gone back to some of that activity, some of the energies I used to have, have now started to come back," Dave told me. "You know people say they have bucket lists of what they want to do? The chorus has actually given me a new bucket!" He continued, "I didn't even know what was in it. And now I've been given the opportunity to do things I never would've thought possible. You wouldn't even believe what we've done, what we've been involved in. Making a record, acting on the stage, being involved in the creation of new operas."[34]

Chorus members give and receive care in the act of singing as a collective, providing a network of support for many of life's challenges. By vowing to sing on, belonging triumphs, and social connectedness perseveres. With this community chorus, something created *for* the community became *of* the community.

THE FRIENDSHIP BENCH

A LARGE WOODEN BENCH sits underneath a tree in Harare, the capital city of Zimbabwe. It seems unassuming enough. Yet this park bench represents one of the country's most promising initiatives to create belonging. The "Friendship Bench" comes from the incredibly bright mind of a young psychiatrist named Dixon Chibanda.

I met Dixon sitting on a wooden Friendship Bench at the World Economic Forum in Davos, Switzerland, in 2018. I was inspired by his story and his work. He sat next to me, and we connected immediately. I knew I had met a kindred spirit. A working partnership and friendship quickly formed between us, and our work has been interwoven ever since. To hear Dixon speak about the Friendship Bench and the importance of community-driven solutions to combat social isolation is really incredible. Similar to the Thurrock Community Chorus, the Friendship Bench was created *for* the community and has quickly become *of* the community.

In the early 2000s, as one of only fifteen psychiatrists in a country of 16 million people, Dixon had seen firsthand the impact of inadequate mental health resources in Zimbabwe, especially for those living in rural and remote communities.

Dixon had been treating a young woman, who he'll call Erica, from a rural village 160 miles away. She had just passed her exams in school, but she was feeling pressure to find a job and start a family. She was worrying compulsively. She couldn't sense her place in the world, and she couldn't imagine a positive future.

Following a troubling episode when Erica took too many of her antidepressant pills, Dixon asked that she come back to Harare for treatment. Weeks passed, and he didn't hear from her. One day, he received a call from her mother delivering the grim news that she had died by suicide.

Dixon asked immediately: "Why didn't you come to Harare?"

Erica's mother responded that they didn't have the fifteen-dollar bus fare to make the trip.[35]

Dixon came to recognize that he couldn't count on someone in Erica's situation to come to him. Looking beyond his clinical training and the boundaries of psychology as a discipline, he started thinking about some of the structural factors at play in Zimbabwe. He decided to devote his career to public service—specifically, to the vexing challenge of how to help people in isolated, remote, or resource-poor situations overcome conditions of hopelessness.

Dixon worked with the Ministry of Health and Child Care and the University of Zimbabwe to develop an effective, affordable, viable means to help people experiencing social isolation and mental health challenges; in 2006, the Friendship Bench was born. The solution hinged on a group of people who already had empathetic communication skills, rich life experience, and respected status: grandmothers.

"Grandmothers really are a source of wisdom in our communities," Dixon says. "Not only in Africa, but in any community. Grandmothers are rooted in their communities, and they in essence are the custodians of local culture and wisdom. And they have this strong sense of belonging in their communities."[36]

The grandmothers in Dixon's program are trained in evidence-based talk therapy known as "problem-solving therapy," in which their innate abilities are reinforced to help people seeking support feel a sense of respect and belonging, and in which patients are guided toward their own solutions. Starting with fourteen grandmothers in Harare, Dixon and this inaugural group decided that, rather than seeing people in crowded and under-resourced clinics and hospitals, the grandmothers could provide their services somewhere simple, unpretentious, and accessible: a park bench. "When you ask the grandmothers what it is they do," Dixon tells me, "they say, 'We create space for healing on wooden park benches.' "[37]

From the beginning, the grandmothers led the way in advocating for transforming technical medical terms into concepts that made sense culturally. When Dixon initially proposed calling it the "Mental Health Bench," the grandmothers laughed at him. Who would want to sit on that kind of a bench? Instead, they suggested calling it the Friendship Bench, where there wouldn't be any shame or stigma when people sat down to seek counsel. They also explored the use of local idioms and language to describe mental health conditions. One of these terms is *kufungisisa*, which means "thinking too much" in Shona, and is commonly used by people to describe emotional distress.

"We don't use the same sort of terms that are used in the Western world," Dixon says. "We don't talk about depression, we don't talk about bipolar or schizophrenia. We use words that are accepted by the community in a way that shows respect and that shows that people are being understood when they present with certain challenges."[38] Instead of calling the people they serve "patients," the grandmothers refer to them as grandchildren: *muzukuru* when referring to one person, *vazukuru* when referring to many. These terms are used to reflect traditional structures of care and trust already built into local communities and language—the opposite of institutional settings.

This model works because the Friendship Bench approach prioritizes respect and understanding. Dixon tells me, "It seems when you have those two things, respect and understanding, a person feels they belong." *Muzukuru* Susan, who came to the bench with marital and financial problems, says, "With belonging, I believe that if I get into a community, I will be accepted."[39] Susan aspires to become a grandmother herself one day so that she can help people in the same way that she herself was helped.

And the bench doesn't just foster belonging for the *vazukuru*, who feel seen and heard within their community—it also fosters belonging for the grandmothers, too. Dixon had the opportunity to spend time with one of the very first grandmothers, Grandmother Rudo, in her last days before she passed away. "She said something that was profound and left me with a sense of gratitude," Dixon recalls. "She said, 'The Friendship Bench has given me a sense of purpose in my community.' "[40]

Other program elders agree. "I feel like I'm rooted in the program," says Grandmother and trainer Charmaine. "And I feel like I'm really part of it."[41] Grandmother Sabinah tells me, "When I'm working, I put all of my heart and all of my effort and energy into doing it, because I feel that it's *belonging part of who I am* and I need to work hard to make it successful. . . . It is important that it creates an identity for me. And wherever I go, I carry that identity with me."[42]

It's not just through anecdotal stories that we understand the impacts of the Bench. Research conducted on the Friendship Bench program found that *vazukuru* of the bench, for example, feel happier, valued, less stigmatized, and less lonely.[43]

This sense of belonging doesn't happen by accident. It is fostered through a deliberate focus on intergenerational reciprocal care—the grandmothers benefit from participating just as much as the *vazukuru*. The grandmothers bring their wisdom, and the *vazukuru* bring their trust. Grandmothers are shown that they are valued, they are needed, and they are integral to their community's success. "I learned that I am important to other people," says Grandmother Sabinah. "People keep coming to me and . . . it makes me see that I am doing a good job. . . . I am someone who is respectable in the community and if someone has a problem, or [even] without a problem, they can still come to me anytime to talk to me."[44] This intergenerational approach respects and recognizes the inherent value of older people in the community and helps the *vazukuru* work through their problems in an accessible and stigma-free environment. It's an incredibly simple, incredibly effective approach to caregiving: a give-and-take that transcends the realm of helper-helpless and, instead, roots itself in reciprocity, dialogue, and partnership.

In Zimbabwe today, there are hundreds of grandmothers offering services in more than seventy communities. As of 2021, more than 80,000 clients have been seen on Friendship Benches throughout the country. The program has also expanded to four other countries—Kenya, Tanzania, Malawi, and the United States, with programs in planning phases in other countries.[45] The program has proven to be a groundbreaking, low-tech solution that is rooted in local systems of care, support, and trust. More than that, it has utilized community to create belonging in ways that have reached beyond the Friendship Bench itself.

CIRCLE KUBATANA TOSE

SHORTLY AFTER THE LAUNCH of the Friendship Bench, Dixon's maternal grandmother, Edith, came up with a great idea to expand the teachings and wellness benefits of the program. What came to fruition were local community-based support groups called *Circle Kubatana Tose* (CKTs), which Dixon tells me means "holding hands together in a circle."[46] After attending four to six sessions on the Bench, a participant is referred to a community CKT group. In the meetings, everyone sits in a circle and passes a stone around, taking turns speaking about the problems they're facing.

Once everyone has a chance to speak, the participants decide which pressing issue to focus on through collective effort, such as helping people living with HIV get the right medication or helping single mothers get funds to pay their children's school fees. Oftentimes, those in the group are directly impacted by the issues under discussion, and their experiences help guide the proposed solutions. It's a way of listening to one another and shaping collective action.

Creating a truly safe space is critical to the circles. "People feel that the circles are a space where no one will judge them, even though they are coming from different backgrounds," Charmaine tells me. "Clients are given a platform to actually lead the support groups and come up with activities so that they take ownership of the group. It becomes part of their healing process rather than part of what the grandmothers would like them to experience," she says.[47]

Many of the Friendship Bench participants take part in the CKTs and learn how to plan out more independent livelihoods; the purpose of the circles extends beyond just counseling or social work. For many CKTs, activities include crocheting, gardening, and even making and selling laundry detergents, enabling the reach of CKTs to extend beyond mental health care, and enabling CKT participants to foster economic independence and practical life skills.[48] They have become embedded in the community, a continuous set of relationships that leads not only to the well-being of individuals, but also to healing within the community as a whole. What started out as having a chat on a bench with an elder has turned into something so much more, and the benefits will be felt for generations.

This is what it means to round the circle, as we discussed earlier. After the Grail Quest is realized, long after the *vazukuru* leave the Friendship Bench with solutions in hand, what happens next? As we learned through the stories of Parzival, Special Olympics, and now the Friendship Bench, it is only by passing on our teachings and creating a chain reaction of positive impact—fostering belonging for others—that we will truly round the circle. The lessons learned *must* transcend the initial interaction. The Friendship Bench and the CKTs are a model to be followed; this is reciprocity in action, and this is what it means to truly show up for the people around you.

For community becomes *of* community, and the circle rounds again.

AS WE'VE SEEN IN THIS CHAPTER, the act of giving and receiving care can take many forms. It can be through professional networks, like Caring for Caregivers. It can be in the personal, one-on-one dynamic between loved ones—similar to my experience with my sister Tammy, and the experiences of those who lose a partner to old age or ill health. Care can be community-driven, like we see with the community chorus, or it can be intergenerational, like we see with the Friendship Bench. All of these examples show us different ways of giving and receiving care. All are valid, all are important, and all do the essential work of rounding the circle and building a world in which we all belong.

CHAPTER NINE

SYSTEMS OF BELONGING

Now if you listen closely
I'll tell what I know
Storm clouds are gathering
The wind is gonna blow
The race of man is suffering
and I can hear the moan,
'Cause nobody,
But nobody
can make it out here alone.

—MAYA ANGELOU, "ALONE"[1]

WHEN I WAS NINE YEARS OLD, I was pretty certain of what I wanted to do with my life. My plan was twofold: I was going to be a teacher, and I was going to be a nun. Growing up, it happened that many of my teachers in grade school were nuns, so I assumed the two went hand in hand. While I never did pursue the latter, I got a chance to try my hand at the former, and it changed my life forever.

In fall 2016 and again in fall 2017, during my tenure as Professor of Practice, I taught a capstone seminar at McGill University's Institute for the Study of International Development, which I titled "Lessons of Community and Compassion: Overcoming Social Isolation and Building Social Connectedness Through Policy and Program Development." My goals were pragmatic: create a course that could be taught anywhere in the world, examine the structural manifestations of social isolation with serious academic rigor and study the practical applications of social connectedness, and lay the foundations for a novel field of inquiry.

Having studied these issues for much of my life, I knew the academic component would be relatively easy to map onto a syllabus. But before I set foot on campus, I gave a lot of thought as to what kind of classroom culture I wanted to create for students. I wanted the classroom to reflect the values embedded in the subject matter, and create a context in which students could not only study belonging, but also experience belonging. What I ultimately strived to create was a "caring classroom"—a place where dialogue was free-flowing, where the student-teacher relationship was built on reciprocity, and where students could bring their truest selves to class.

I'll never forget when I taught that first seminar. On the first day, students filed in, maybe a bit bewildered, but nevertheless intrigued at what this very unique-sounding course could offer them on their learning journey. We all got to know each other, sharing our names and some background information about ourselves, and our kickoff exercise was a reflection on social isolation. I walked away from that inaugural session and happiness washed over me. I was exactly where I was supposed to be—teaching was my calling profession. I had found my métier.

Throughout the course, I saw my job as that of a guide. I perceived my role as that of holding space for students to grow and flourish together. It was about cultivating safe and brave spaces, where the focus was on teaching the *whole* student and actively nurturing a sense of connection between peers, professor, and community.

Creating that kind of environment required doing things a little differently and curating the classroom experience for each student. One student had trouble finishing the assigned readings, so we worked together to create relevant weekly assignments that were centered around poetry and art—conducive to his learning style. Students that were particularly hesitant to speak up in class—due to shyness, lack of confidence, or any other reason—were given one-on-one options to engage with me directly and get full participation grades. This model of meeting students where they were at allowed us to co-develop assignments that met both their needs and rigorous academic standards—and the work they completed was incredible.

I'd bring in guest speakers from around the world to share their expertise and lived experience with our group. Working with my co-lecturers, my students sought to understand the work of building connectedness and belonging across sectors and disciplines.

These lessons were then shared outside the class through a forum series I convened at the Jeanne Sauvé Foundation, not far from campus. Guest speakers from class were invited to build on what they had shared through a public seminar series, open to all. Where the real magic of belonging came to life was through the relationships the students formed with each other. They became friends and confidants, bonded by their shared learning of a subject that centered on the importance of relationship-building. They started a Facebook group to talk about the course, and my always-busy office hours inevitably turned into animated hallway discussions among peers-turned-friends. Some students would bring visiting family to attend class with them, and two of my guest lecturers even returned to attend the class regularly to learn alongside my students. At our community dinners, I watched as ritual pleasantries evolved into comfortable dialogue.

For many young people, the transition to campus life is profoundly stressful. Many are leaving their hometown or country, family, and friends for the first time. Students can feel invisible in lecture halls while surrounded by hundreds of peers. Any relative competition experienced in high school pales in comparison to the pressures of post-secondary academia. It's no wonder so many students end up feeling isolated, anxious, and alone. In 2019, research showed that 69.6 percent of university students in Canada felt "very lonely," and 63.6 percent reported feelings of hopelessness at some point in the last year.[2] In the United States, the most recent National College Health Assessment found that 53 percent of students had experienced loneliness, and around 40 percent had felt things were hopeless at some point or more in the past thirty days.[3] These feelings have only worsened amid the pandemic, which has turned cracks of isolation into fault lines for students around the world.

Professors and lecturers, too, juggle multiple obligations, from administrative duties to raising funds to cover their own research. New faculty members with a limited timeline to earn tenure must race against the clock to "publish or perish." And it isn't easy to nurture a sense of community and individualized attention when you find yourself standing before a lecture hall packed with more than a thousand students. Constraints like these make it challenging for professors to bring forward all of their many gifts as teachers. The end result is a post-secondary environment where faculty are encouraged to speak first about their publications and distinctions, and only second about their work with students.

What is at stake is not just the crucial relationship between teacher and student, but the emotionally safe space that the educator can create in class to nurture reciprocal bonds inside and outside the classroom. In short, we lose the larger experience of community on campus and in class. In order to build a Caring Classroom, "people have to be able to know a little bit about each other," shared another former student and colleague, Vino Landry. "The professor has to care about their students and their success. The subject matter should be something that students really feel they can engage with and would care about outside the classroom as well"—and, I would add, long after they graduate.[4]

The course was not only about applying lessons of compassion and community inside the classroom—it was also about understanding how these played out in larger political, social, and economic arenas. The work we did in building trust and communication within our class was echoed in the way we learned about the challenges posed by pervasive social isolation across systems.

Our systems—whether they be responsible for education, business, governance, food security, or healthcare—all contribute to our overall success and sense of belonging as human beings. But in the twenty-first century, in many nations around the world, these systems have failed us.

More than that, however, many of the systems that shape our lives are not designed to be human-centric; in essence, the systems cannot support people if they were not designed with people in mind. Consider many contemporary agricultural systems, designed around not the health of humans, nor the health of the land, but instead, for profit maximization; contrast such a system with, say, the Garry oak meadows of the Pacific Northwest, where the camas flower has been cultivated by Coast Salish peoples for time immemorial, and where a holistic approach to the peoples and the place allowed for a nourished ecosystem to flourish. Think of a city, designed not for people but for cars, an urban environment molded around efficiency, not connection, as another system that does not effectively meet human needs. Or think of education systems, filled with passionate and inspired teachers, yet often underfunded, and centered around relentless management of test scores and other measurement metrics. Systems shape our lives, yet more often than not, we have little say in how such systems are shaped.

Our post-secondary systems, in addition to the above-stated challenges, often fall short in providing outlets for student-community connection and fail to build belonging. Our economic model has prioritized the pursuit of profit at all costs, deepening an already cavernous divide between the rich and the poor. Hundreds of millions of people around the world go hungry every day. Unequal access to healthcare literally means the difference between life and death.

As a global community, we have to demand better, and loudly. We have to take action ourselves. Without system reform that addresses existing barriers, we'll see even more social isolation, more fragile communities, and the further deterioration of belonging. Luckily, there are good people doing good work to fix our broken systems, and more often than not, we find them at the grassroots level.

Let's start with education.

ACCESS TO EDUCATION

"ACCESS IS NOT A DIRTY WORD."[5]

Dr. Deborah Saucier shared this insight at the opening night of the 2019 Global Symposium on Overcoming Isolation and Deepening Social Connectedness. A Métis woman from Saskatoon, Professor Saucier is a psychologist who has built a career in STEM research as a neuroscience and psychology professor in universities across Canada. And since 2019, she has served as the president and vice-chancellor of Vancouver Island University.

Out in Nanaimo in British Columbia, Vancouver Island University (VIU) recognizes the value of a holistic education as key to the success of the students they support. Founded in 1969 as Malaspina College, VIU takes a holistic view of education—one that prioritizes community involvement and equitable access. According to Deb, at VIU, access "is part of its DNA. It has roots as a community college, and as a training college before that. With that in mind, it was not very hard for people to continue to believe, especially in the twenty-first century, that everybody deserves access to a post-secondary education."[6]

Being part of VIU means being part of a community. I've had the opportunity to lecture there on several occasions, and have seen firsthand the unwavering confidence they have in the potential of their students. I've seen how their university is enriched by the inclusion of many voices and the recognition of diverse forms of expertise. Across their three campuses, located on the traditional territories of the Snuneymuxw First Nation, Tla'amin First Nation, Snaw-naw-as First Nation, and the Cowichan Tribes, VIU embodies a spirit of welcome.

With a large cohort of Indigenous students, students coming out of foster care, first-generation students, and students from other underrepresented backgrounds, belonging on campus is supported through several programs. VIU seeks to bolster Indigenous recognition and representation on campus, and does so through ceremony, like the Semélshun Aboriginal Graduation Recognition Ceremony, and place, like the Shq'apthut (A Gathering Place) building on its Nanaimo campus, which houses Services for Aboriginal Students and is open to everyone on campus. VIU participates in the Inside-Out Prison Exchange Program, which we learned about earlier through the story of Joe Cramer's educational experience. It runs a summer program for adult community members who are interested in continuing their education. It offers university courses to students learning trades, such as hairdressing and construction. VIU delivers on what Deb so succinctly calls for: everyone having access to a university education.

Through three initiatives in particular—CBAIR (Community-Based Applied Interdisciplinary Research), Elders-in-Residence, and the Tuition-Waiver programs—VIU invites fresh perspectives and new knowledge onto its campus and into its curriculum, challenging conventional assumptions about who belongs in academia.

As Deb emphasized, "VIU has a strong commitment to Place, and in doing so, that means that you have to have a strong commitment to the people who actually really own the place." The CBAIR program is a key driver of collaboration between students and the wider Vancouver Island community. Students are empowered to design and manage academic projects that hinge on social research conducted in the community. They're given tremendous agency from beginning to end, with faculty across disciplines acting as guides when necessary. Through this program, students are valued for their ideas and the community is seen as a vital collaborator in the university's overall success. There is an element of reciprocity at play here, where the relationship between VIU and the community is dynamic, and where they nurture one another's development.

We see the same ethos enacted through the work of VIU's Elders-in-Residence program. Knowing the fundamental importance of incorporating Indigenous knowledge and teachings across the VIU curriculum, the university created the Elders-in-Residence program in the early 1990s. It's been going strong ever since. Deb explained the program to me this way: "The Elders-in-Residence Program is a way to provide culturally appropriate support for Indigenous People, but also to help non-Indigenous folks learn about the realities of Indigenous Peoples of Canada, which also is an important piece if we're really going to advance reconciliation."

Elders form a core part of the VIU faculty, and that's intentional. During our discussion, Deb reflected on our tendency in the Western world to recognize knowledge in education through a formal degree, which, as we know, is far from being the sole indicator of expertise: "Many of our Elders don't have doctorates but they're considered faculty at our university because, by virtue of being Elders, they have, in my mind, done the equivalent of a doctorate." She continues, "They have this long-held Indigenous knowledge that is recognized by their communities. . . . Not everybody who's old and Indigenous is an elder. An elder is recognized to have specific knowledge by their community, and as a result, that's one way of showing respect."

The Elders-in-Residence program has since been adopted by other academic institutions in Canada, giving Indigenous and non-Indigenous students alike the ability to learn about—and learn from—their teachings.

Understanding the intersectionality between poverty and access to education, VIU started the Tuition-Waiver program in 2013 for students aging out of the care system. For that inaugural year, VIU covered tuition costs for fifty-two students, and the number has since grown. Since the 2016–17 academic year, nearly 500 students have been supported through VIU's tuition waiver program, with 103 in the 2020–021 academic year alone.[7]

In April 2018, on one of my trips to Vancouver Island, I met a group of peer support navigators at VIU. Their leadership and spirit have stayed with me since, as a testament to the significance of meeting students where they are. They shared with me how the program not only eliminates the financial barrier to education facing post-care students, but also aims to support them all the way to graduation. And this support is not limited to financial and academic assistance. One peer support navigator would ask students to take a photo of what was inside their fridge, and bring them to the grocery store to ensure they had enough nutritious food to eat. She explained to me how students might feel isolated because they were unable to afford good clothes, and felt they stood out. Others would take them clothes shopping. This is what makes the VIU Tuition-Waiver program so unique—it's not just about getting students in the door. It's about supporting them multidimensionally throughout their time at VIU.

Former VIU president Ralph Nilson knows that VIU has a responsibility to the most vulnerable and undervalued: "We are committed to providing access to post-secondary education to former youth in care because we know that without family support and stability, youth in care in this province are much less likely to graduate high school, let alone go on to post-secondary education." He continued, "We also know that an education is one of the most powerful ways a person can create positive change and opportunities—for themselves, their families and their communities."[8]

Following the success of the Tuition-Waiver program at VIU, the province has followed suit. In 2018, the government of British Columbia announced the Youth Futures Education Fund, which gives post-secondary financial support to youth aging out of care. As of June 2020, nearly 1,200 students were benefiting from the provincial waiver in BC. Some post-secondary institutions in other provinces—including Manitoba, Alberta, and Ontario—have followed BC and VIU's lead, and now offer waivers as well.

Currently, VIU is working to ensure that students are supported not only while on campus, but far beyond as well. "We need to actually actively not just hand people the parchment and say, 'Okay, our job is done here,'"[9] Deb stressed. The work of belonging through education reform must also be to "bridge that gap," as Deb described it, ensuring students are empowered to bring the lessons from campus out into the wider world.

THE BUSINESS OF BELONGING

IN THE TWENTY-FIRST CENTURY, we know that having an education is a key driver in one's ability to participate fully in the economy. But the economic world many students are graduating into can be unkind at the best of times. We've grown accustomed to the pursuit of profits at all costs, without question. For too long, we have tolerated an economic model that demands a survival-of-the-fittest approach to navigating the world and accumulating wealth. We get real-time access to stock market fluctuations, new economic data streams in daily, and companies routinely make headlines for slashing jobs and employee benefits—all in the name of increasing shareholder value. While the current economic system promises infinite wealth for the lucky few, it has also widened the already cavernous inequality gap. More and more, people are falling further behind as wages remain stagnant and cost of living only marches upward. Belonging is eroding away.

But there is a better way. There is a model wherein the corporations that have become so ingrained in our daily lives truly give back to the communities in which they operate. I'm talking about nurturing a culture based on social responsibility and shared values, where words are met with tangible action. One company, Agrolíbano, is walking the talk in a big way.

Agrolíbano is a family-owned business in Honduras that grows melons for the export market. It's made a name for itself by taking an unconventional approach to measuring success. Agrolíbano's head of corporate social responsibility, Pamela Molina—whose father, Miguel, founded the company when she was seven years old—explained it to me this way: "At the Agrolíbano Group, we measure our performance and impact in three lines: economic, environmental, and social. We believe that there can be no successful companies in failed communities."[10] In our conversation, I've seen how deeply Pamela believes in this mission.

The company has long been engaged in tackling poverty and climate change at a local level. And in 2018, its approach to belonging and community-building became even more data-driven. It adapted the methodology of a Community Multidimensional Poverty Index (C-MPI) to study well-being in the nineteen communities in which it operates. The C-MPI is a locally adapted version of the Multidimensional Poverty Index (MPI), a framework for understanding and measuring poverty created by the Oxford Poverty & Human Development Initiative (OPHI) in 2007, and grounded in Amartya Sen's Capability Approach. Rather than just capturing the traditional income-related poverty, the MPI uses microeconomic household data to measure the percentage of households experiencing overlapping deprivations in multiple dimensions, such as health, education, and living conditions.

Agrolíbano's C-MPI covered five dimensions—quality of life, education, job, heritage, and health—with each containing a number of indicators for measurement. The inaugural C-MPI survey revealed a troubling reality: Eighty-nine percent of respondents were living in poverty; 98 percent of the homes had at least one person between fifteen and forty-nine years of age who had less than six years of schooling; 52 percent of the homes did not have potable water or a waste disposal system; 63 percent of the homes did not have an adequate floor, roof, or walls; and 87 percent of the homes cooked with wood without a chimney. These dramatic results were a lightning rod for Agrolíbano, pushing it to strengthen its work in communities to tackle these serious problems.[11]

Because of the 2018 C-MPI survey, Agrolíbano put forward a 2019–23 vision to "promote the wellbeing of those most left behind." This vision contained various programming proposals in the areas of health, quality of life, and education. Pamela knew this couldn't be a top-down effort—the solutions for improving worker and community well-being had to come from the community itself. The company identified local leaders and organized them into work groups, which were then charged with promoting and running community-based programs. Agrolíbano partnered with folks on the ground—tapping into core belonging dimensions of purpose and power—to ensure that the programming would be most effective for the people it was designed to serve.

As of 2020, Agrolíbano has contributed more than US$5.5 million for community-based social investments, through ten years of operation of the Agrolíbano Foundation. It's planted more than one hundred thousand trees to produce lumber sustainably, and is in the process of shifting the company's central office and production laboratories away from fossil-fuel energy and onto solar energy. This is very much in line with how Pamela sees the relationship between business and community. "The first responsibility of companies should be to manage their impacts, even if they are positive or negative, real or potential. They must identify, prevent, mitigate, and respond to the negative consequences of their activities in the communities, proceeding with due diligence. They must commit to protecting and respecting human rights and remedying the negative consequences of their actions or to which they have contributed."[12]

Agrolíbano is a great example of responsible corporate practice. It understands the intricate, reciprocal dynamic between employer and employee, workplace and community. By asking the right questions through the C-MPI, working in partnership to develop community-driven programming, and allocating the resources needed to improve people's well-being, the Agrolíbano Group is doing its part to fix a broken economic system and ensure its employees, and their families and communities, know they belong.

BELONGING IN GOVERNANCE

AGROLÍBANO SHOWS US HOW to use better tools to measure the things we value, then implement real change based on the results. Its use of the C-MPI was a visionary move for a corporation. But it's not alone in creating policy based on factors beyond the bottom line.

OPHI uses the MPI to work with national governments to translate the findings into targeted policies that reduce multidimensional poverty. The first country to adopt the precise MPI methodology was the small Himalayan nation of Bhutan. It has seen impressive results in a short period of time. In 2010, 28.6 percent of Bhutanese were MPI poor and by 2017, the percentage of MPI poor was just 5.8 percent.[13] But Bhutan was already ahead of the curve when it comes to measuring what we value.

Bhutan is the first country in the world to reorient its measures of economic, social, political, and environmental progress around well-being and happiness. In the early 1970s, His Majesty Jigme Singye Wangchuck, the fourth king of Bhutan, argued that GDP alone, as a measure of success, could not deliver on well-being and happiness. His words, along with Bhutan's ancient legal code of 1629—which states, "If the government cannot create happiness for its people, then there is no purpose for government to exist"—resonated with many of his successors.[14] As a result, new ways of measuring societal progress were developed over the decades, culminating in the Gross National Happiness (GNH) index, which actually adapted and implemented the OPHI methodology before even the first official national MPI, launching in 2008 using a version at the national level; it has since been updated in 2010 and 2015 and is now updating in 2021–22.

Bhutan's GNH Index measures nine domains: psychological well-being, health, education, time use, cultural diversity and resilience, good governance, community vitality, ecological diversity and resilience, and living standards. Within these nine equally weighted domains, there are thirty-three indicators, and the GNH seeks to measure the well-being of the population by starting with each person's achievements in each category. As Sabina Alkire, whom we met earlier, puts it, Bhutan's Gross National Happiness is a way to "give space for people to choose their own road to wellbeing."[15] Sabina explains that it's a measure that emphasizes not only improvements in material circumstances, but also the strength of community ties. At the societal level, it's a shift in seeing.

Dasho Karma Ura is the president of the Centre for Bhutan Studies and one of the people at the forefront in promoting national and global understanding of Bhutan's homegrown development philosophy—the Gross National Happiness index. He recently shared with me the issues with our most dominant measures of "progress": "The single-minded pursuit of growth, economic expansion, GDP, has been facilitated by establishment of disciplines devoted to it," said Karma Ura. "Measurements, offices and departments devoted to it. Manpower, armies of manpower devoted to it, so it will take a long time to adjust . . . ideologically, manpower-wise, budget-wise but my deduction is that it will face challenges. Challenges from sheer philosophical contention against merely focusing on material production."[16]

By collecting household data that prioritize belonging not only to the economy, but also to community and place, Bhutan has been able to draw new correlations between certain social and economic issues and perceived levels of community and belonging. With this new set of data collected over the years, the government has been able to tailor new and existing policies to address poverty and well-being in a holistic manner.

There are important policy implications of the GNH index, of which governments around the world should take note. The Index can be broken down by gender, or neighborhood, for example, to show how different groups perform on various indicators, indicating where governments need to enact policy reform. In January 2019, I had the privilege of hearing Dasho Karma Ura speak at the University of Oxford. He explained that the Bhutanese government uses the GNH index in the allocation of budget to local governments, and has used the index to create the country's national five-year plan. Additionally, the government has created a policy screen tool, which evaluates the impact of each policy on twenty-two indicators drawn from the GNH Index.[17]

I recently spoke with former prime minister Dasho Tshering Tobgay to better understand the role of belonging and the GNH in guiding policy and governance in Bhutan. Dasho Tshering Tobgay is the leader of the People's Democratic Party, the first registered political party of Bhutan. He shared with me the importance of governance in upholding belonging on a systems level: "Since governments have taken over the mantle of holding society together, and coming up with rules and regulations, and systems on how society must function, then, by extension, it is the role of governments to ensure that no one is deprived of belonging." Tobgay continued, "If we start from the premise that human beings need to belong, then the role of government is to protect and to nurture that belonging."[18]

Moreover, Tobgay continued, "If governments must nurture the sense of belonging, what are the detriments? It could be caste, it could be creed, it could be color, it could be ethnicity, it could be gender, it could be sexuality, it could be disease, it could be social biases. If these are the detriments to belonging, the role of government is to ensure that these detriments do not take hold."

One landmark success of Bhutan, as a direct result of the GNH index and the Buddhist philosophy that underpins it, has been an addition to its constitution to protect 60 percent of its land under forest cover, the largest percentage of any country in Asia.[19] The case of Bhutan demonstrates that it is possible for national governments to implement sustainable and holistic development measures when belonging is upheld. "GNH places an emphasis on the equitable distribution of wealth," Tobgay shared. "That is important for belonging. Whether you achieve that by providing free education and free healthcare or subsidizing the lot of the poor or eradicating poverty, the fact is these are tools to ensure a bit more equity in society." He shared that while the GDP is important, "we have to be mindful of economic growth, it has to be balanced with GNH. Economy must serve a purpose, and it is for the people."[20]

The GNH index has laid the groundwork for a global conversation on what truly constitutes human development and individual happiness, as well as collective happiness and flourishing—of people and other sentient beings on a shared planet. "I would like to imagine that gross national happiness and any definition of happiness transcends Buddhism and indeed any religion," Tobgay shared with me. "I think it can be relevant in any context, any spirituality." As the only carbon-negative country, Bhutan demonstrates how a nation, in shifting how it measures its success, might shift its policies to match, creating a nationwide atmosphere emphasizing happiness and belonging, rather than simply chasing material progress.

NOURISHING COMMUNITY

We are each other's harvest; we are each other's business;
we are each other's magnitude and bond.

—GWENDOLYN BROOKS[21]

FOOD INSECURITY is one of the most pressing problems facing our world today. In 2019, nearly 750 million people were exposed to severe levels of food insecurity.[22] When we cast that net slightly wider to include those who experience moderate levels of food insecurity, we see that an estimated two billion people in the world do not have access to safe, sufficient food.[23] Those numbers only get bigger when we add qualifiers like access to nutrient-dense foods that are necessary for a healthy diet.[24]

Access to healthy and culturally appropriate food is important to our well-being—both physically and mentally. Poverty and lack of access to appropriate foods are the main drivers of food insecurity at an individual level. At the global level, the problem stems from the unequal distribution of that food. This happens for many reasons, including an increasing number of conflicts and climate-related shocks that have the power to majorly disrupt food supply in already impoverished regions.[25] We also can't discount the lack of political will to ensure equal allocation of food to those who need it most. Right now, we have enough food to go around if we wanted to make it happen.[26] However, if unsustainable agriculture remains the norm, we'll be facing not only a lack of political will, but also a genuine scarcity in food resources.[27]

In 2021, the organization Feeding America estimated that one in eight people, including one in six children, would experience food insecurity. In total, 42 million Americans are considered to be at risk of going hungry.[28] In the United Kingdom, roughly 9 percent of adults reported experiences of food insecurity in 2021.[29] At times, the term itself, "food insecurity," can make the issue seem near-palatable. But let's call it what it is: hunger. Food insecurity is, at its heart, the raw, aching sense of hunger. In countries around the world, both higher income and lower income, this form of hunger is an everyday occurrence. However, whether we call it "food insecure" or simply "hungry," the experience, and the suffering, is the same.

In Canada, 4.4 million individuals—including 1.2 million children—experienced food insecurity at some point in 2017–18.[30] Moreover, inadequate food access is tied to a number of intersectional factors, including race—case in point, households where the respondent was Indigenous or Black reported the highest rates of food insecurity in Canada.[31] Thankfully, in communities around the world, organizations are striving to build a better country where everyone has enough to eat. The Stop Community Food Centre in Toronto immediately comes to mind.

The Stop has been a pillar of the city's West End since the 1980s. For nearly forty years, it has created connections, fostered belonging, and strengthened food security for low-income Torontonians through a plethora of initiatives like urban gardening, hot meal service, food bank programming, and advocacy.[32] It also runs a prenatal program called Healthy Beginnings, financial literacy workshops, anti-oppression training, and an Emotional Wellness Peer Support Group for community members who are isolated and living in poverty. This connects to its broader work of training clients and community members to serve as self-advocates for policy change, particularly with regard to poverty reduction.[33] The Stop also serves as a community resource hub, directing clients to other local services such as mental health supports and affordable housing.[34] It is guided by the fundamental belief that "when people are connected to the land and to each other, they can create significant change within themselves, throughout their neighborhoods, and across the city."[35] The Stop's work has always been important, and it's even more critical now. In 2017, nearly 20 percent of Toronto households experienced "marginal, moderate, or severe food insecurity."[36] And between 2018 and 2019, the cost of nutritious food in Toronto had risen 7.6 percent.[37]

The Stop is stepping up in a big way to counter this worrying trend, fostering connection to people and place along the way. In 2018, it provided nearly 52,000 healthy meals to drop-in participants. It served meals to almost 17,000 people, including more than 4,000 children. It hosted a series of community kitchen workshops that left 95 percent of participants feeling more confident in their ability to prepare healthy meals at home. And its advocacy office provided 1,300 referrals for community members in need.[38]

Like most other community organizations, COVID-19 has proven to be challenging for The Stop. The traditional meal drop-in service became a takeaway service; the community advocacy office shifted to providing virtual support, connecting members to resources via telephone and other alternative means; and the community garden had to suspend in-person programming. Still, The Stop has innovated and carried on much of its important work in the midst of a global pandemic, with good reason.

As Leigh Godbold, long-term staff member at The Stop, told me in a recent interview, "The sense of belonging . . . is a connection too. Through the pandemic, one of the things that's been really hard is that we've had to revert to practices like handouts of food and take-out food, and all of these things that make us feel like we're going back in time. But at the same time, the programs and the staff and the volunteers have been resourceful, really creative and making sure that that connection is still always there."[39]

This is a theme echoed within the research conducted by the Samuel Centre for Social Connectedness in partnership with The Stop. Our research on The Stop's community garden programs, programming that was heavily impacted by COVID-19, demonstrated that it was the loss of community that was the most challenging element of the pandemic: "For some program participants, the suspension of in-person programming was particularly devastating, since such programming acted as their primary form of social connection to others."[40]

Sharon, a former client of The Stop turned staff member, can attest to the social connectedness benefits firsthand: "When I came to The Stop, I had two contacts in my phone: my doctor, and my ex. Now, my contact list is full."[41] "The Stop seemed like my little piece of heaven," says Ani, a former participant in the Healthy Beginnings prenatal program who later became a staff member at The Stop. "I felt welcomed, cared for, and uplifted. I was inspired to work with my community. I didn't know exactly how, but I knew that The Stop would be the place to start."[42]

The Stop is building food security by tapping into the community's most precious resource—its members' care and compassion for one another. "I'm making the case for social solidarity," said Rachel Gray, former executive director of The Stop. "I am suggesting that forty years on, certainly, the response to food insecurity does not lie in food banks. More importantly, what forty years of food bank drives tells us is that there is leveraging that we can do with people who actually want to make their community stronger."[43]

Not only that, but The Stop has built partnerships with the wider community to drive its mission forward—for example, "Grow for The Stop" is a collaboration between The Stop and The New Farm, an organic vegetable farm based in Creemore, Ontario. The proceeds from its annual ticketed concert event allow The Stop to fund its food banks, hot meal programs, and community kitchens with fresh produce directly from The New Farm.[44] The New Farm also sells retail products under the "Grow for the Stop" label, with a percentage of proceeds from their retail sales being donated directly to The Stop, which, in turn, uses the proceeds to purchase additional food from the New Farm.[45]

Building community, fostering a network of belonging, and sharing your time and teachings with others—as we discussed earlier, this is how you round the circle.

Rachel knows that food insecurity is inherently intersectional, and she realizes that the solution isn't changing symptoms but rather systems: "The problem with food banks is that they are trying to use food as a way of solving a problem, and the problem is actually income."[46] In its 2018–21 Strategic Plan, The Stop identified a key driver of food insecurity in the neighborhood, observing: "Gentrification is happening at a rapid pace, and while this can bring new opportunities, it also brings significant challenges to residents that are struggling to survive on insufficient incomes within an increasingly unaffordable area. The combination of poverty and social isolation puts their health at great risk."[47]

Thankfully, places like The Stop are challenging a broken system and working hard to ensure that, regardless of socioeconomic status, everyone has access to safe and healthy food.

HEALING HEALTHCARE

DR. PAUL FARMER, who departed this world on February 21, 2022, left behind a living legacy that has forever improved our understanding about the moral imperative for health equity and the systems needed to bring it about. I was blessed to call him my friend and role model. As the visionary cofounder and chief strategist of Partners in Health (PIH), Paul made the invisible visible with his unrelenting battle cry about the inequality and injustices underlying the lack of basic, let alone optimal, health care for people living in poverty. Through PIH, he created a world-class system of health care delivery, powered by excellence, dignity, and grace. And he transformed the idea of health as a human right by making it real. Butaro District Hospital, located in Bulawayo, Rwanda, today stands as one of the many testaments to Paul's life's work, and as a living embodiment of circles of care and compassion rounding themselves.

Butaro is a rugged and remote section of the Burera District in Rwanda's Northern Province. Like much of Rwanda, it suffered unimaginable tragedy in the 1994 genocide and has experienced continuing physical, emotional, and structural hardship in its wake. As late as 2008, there was only one doctor living in the entire surrounding district—an area with a population of more than 300,000. Despite the region's natural beauty, life in Butaro is challenging.

Yet, when I visited Butaro in July 2012, I saw something that seemed miraculous: hope, on a globally significant scale. The Rwandan Ministry of Health, in collaboration with Partners In Health (PIH), a Boston-based NGO, was opening the Butaro Cancer Center of Excellence (BCCE), the first comprehensive cancer center in East Africa. The facility—an addition to the Butaro District Hospital, which had opened the year before—was built to administer IV chemotherapy, revolutionizing the treatment of life-threatening disease in the region. It was a moment of accomplishment for Rwanda's health system, the people of the region, and all whom the facility would serve.

As I toured the BCCE, the thoughtfulness of the design was apparent at every turn. Everything was seemingly optimized to minimize patients' risk of feeling isolated. The chairs for intravenous treatments were arranged in a circle around central pods so that people receiving treatment could stay connected with physicians and the other people present. Each patient would have immediate access to the outside world—to the beauty of the Virunga Mountain landscape—through a pivot door. A cutting-edge ventilation system neutralized the dangers of airborne germs while keeping the space fresh.

Butaro's significance was, to me, bigger than the new facility or even the incredible new capacity it would provide. It symbolized a systems change. Butaro represents a different model of medical service, based on what Paul Farmer, called the "principle of accompaniment." As I saw at the Butaro opening, and as he emphasized to me in a recent conversation, everything at Butaro was "consciously designed" to embody a spirit of partnership between those providing care and those receiving care.

"The worst thing about the world is that some people think that there are those less valuable than they are," Paul recently shared with me.[48] The driving impetus behind PIH is addressing the inequalities that plague our global healthcare systems. The intersections between inequality, poverty, and health are widely known. The difference in life expectancy between high- and low-income countries is eighteen years.[49] Each year, the majority of the fifteen million premature deaths due to noncommunicable diseases occur in low- and middle-income countries.[50] And the mortality rate for children under five years old is more than nine times higher in Africa than the European region.[51]

Accompaniment is not charity. It doesn't mean giving aid in a short-term, one-off way, or deploying outside experts to save the day. Rather, it means investing in a long-term relationship, based on listening and working together to understand and address the structural barriers to wellness, establishing services that respect the rights and dignity of the poor. As Paul described to me, a key priority is ensuring that the people most afflicted by a problem are involved in its resolution. Accompaniment is empowering local people to be their own resilient guardians of community health.

This approach to healthcare through partnership rests on two key pillars that are integral to PIH's work. The first pillar is a hermeneutic of generosity, or the "H of G," in Paul's pithy vernacular. The H of G holds that partnership be built on a foundation of trust and honesty. The second pillar challenges top-down approaches to healthcare, and seeks instead to put compassion and collaboration into practice: "ABC," says Paul, "anything but colonialism."[52]

Community health workers (CHWs) are the core of the "accompaniment" approach at Butaro. CHWs are local people with professional training who walk with their fellow community members in a journey through sickness to good health. Because they hail from the very communities that they serve, CHWs are uniquely credible and effective educators, caretakers, and advocates. They conduct home visits, teach preventive healthcare skills and practices, make case findings for medical providers, and keep track of people with specific needs, including children under five, pregnant women, orphans, and people with intellectual disabilities. They also help people with tuberculosis and HIV—diseases whose burden is often intensified by stigma and shame—to access and take their treatments. Crucially, CHWs work to address root causes of disease and ill health by linking people to assistance with food, water, education, housing, and employment. In keeping with PIH's vision, the work addresses all the diverse determinants of good health.

In a 2017 report, PIH recognized the contributions of CHWs as doing "what doctors cannot do." This is the crucial work of systems change through connection and belonging, from the community outward, "connecting people to health systems, systems to communities, and communities to each other."[53]

Butaro's opening was the culmination of years of accompaniment work in Rwanda. This approach to healthcare first came to the country in 2005 when the Ministry of Health invited PIH to support a pilot program in "grassroots" public health. Today, Rwanda is making the CHW model an integral part of its overall approach to healthcare—and it's working. The country has a unique participatory process of selecting CHWs: Elders in a village call a community meeting, where officials from the Ministry of Health explain the role of the community health worker and call for applicants. People are democratically elected to each position by community members; then they're trained, supported, and continually assessed. Butaro is proof positive that this community-based collective approach can be successfully woven into an effective, modern healthcare system.

CHWs use what is called the "Household Model" of service delivery, whereby they visit all households in a community regardless of whether or not a resident is sick. Dr. Agnes Binagwaho—a pediatrician and vice-chancellor and chief executive of the University of Global Health Equity (UGHE) in Rwanda—describes CHWs as "people who are providing care at the community level where people live."[54]

In Rwanda, the government employs nearly sixty thousand CHWs across the country to support health communication and prevention, provide care for less severe cases, and refer patients to higher levels of care as needed. They used this method for the COVID-19 national response, adopting a Household Model for COVID-19 isolation and quarantine, which has played a huge role in combating stigma in the community. It works because CHW home visits are not necessarily associated with a resident having a disease.

CHWs have become true agents of belonging by providing personalized, community-based service and social connection for residents who may have been rejected by loved ones due to their ailments. Paul Farmer explained it to me this way: "We've tried to formalize it [the model] for reasons around policy and around saying: you can't really treat chronic disease effectively without belonging. . . . If you don't belong in a family, if you've been expelled from your family . . . [you are] still going to need to belong somewhere."[55]

For Paul, accompaniment describes not just the CHW approach, but also the spirit of partnership that permeates PIH's work with families, local grassroots groups, and even government health ministries. With its roots as a community-based project for treating people living with HIV/AIDS in Haiti, PIH has been working to build trust-based empowering partnerships for more than thirty years, supporting health in contexts as diverse as Rwanda, Serbia, Peru, and the Navajo Nation in the southwestern United States. Their partnerships in Haiti now include broader engagement, building on the model of partnering with local leaders to provide healthcare through accompaniment.

With a healthcare system still reeling from the damage of the 2014–15 Ebola outbreak, Sierra Leone has greatly benefited in recent years from collaboration with Partners In Health.[56] Extreme poverty, inadequate healthcare infrastructure, and lack of supplies have all contributed to traditionally poor health outcomes across the country. Communicable diseases are the leading cause of death in Sierra Leone, and mental health disorders are increasingly leading to premature death and chronic disability. The country also has the highest maternal mortality ratio in the world.[57]

However, Partners In Health is playing a role in turning things around and contributing to system reform through collaboration and community mobilization. Today, PIH partners with the government to support six health facilities across three districts in Sierra Leone. CHWs serve as a link between patients and these health facilities, maintaining close relationships with families, conducting routine home visits, and connecting residents with other intersectional health supports provided by PIH and other local organizations (including food packages, housing repairs, transportation, and educational opportunities). The results have been impressive so far: a 50 percent reduction in the stillbirth rate at Koidu Government Hospital, a 52 percent increase of mothers served at PIH-supported facilities, and 99.9 percent of HIV patients participating in ongoing care.[58]

More recently, PIH has played a key role in fighting COVID-19 in Sierra Leone. Community member Aiah Jonah Yorpoi told me, "We managed in the pandemic because of advice from Partners In Health." He said that his community benefited from receiving clear public health information from PIH in terms of how to protect themselves and loved ones from the spread of COVID—information that was then passed on. "As we receive information from PIH, we filter it down to our children, our neighbors, so that we can be safe in the hands of this COVID. So it was challenging, but we managed because PIH strongly intervened . . . and then we were able to understand."[59]

"The myths and rumors were a huge issue during Ebola, and again, they were a huge issue during COVID,"[60] shared Leah Blezard, community-based programs associate at PIH Sierra Leone. Leah is a Canadian who completed her MSc in global health delivery at the UGHE and, as Dr. Agnes said, graduated as one of their top students. "The CHWs are really the ones that are able to address those types of things. Community based programming, it's essential, it's critical to pandemic response." Dr. Agnes sees the vast potential of community-based care to deliver lasting wellness and belonging benefits for people. "If you had people to care for you, to come and see how you are, the link between community and the hospital will be stronger," she told me. "People will use non-emergency care more often, total cost of care will be less costly. And the rate of survival wellness and happiness will be higher."[61]

As Paul Farmer shared with me, one of the dangers with responses to COVID-19 has been the tendency to frame the fight against the virus in deeply non-human terms: "That's what we're talking about now with COVID and . . . sterile terms like contact tracing, we're really talking about social connection." In re-centering the fight against COVID-19 as a human story of survival, we can make it easier for people to access critically needed healthcare.[62]

The relationships forged through PIH's collaborative approach to healthcare has created strong bonds of trust and community, across organizational and geographical lines. "One of the things that moved my spirit," Aiah shared about Leah's commitment to his community, "[was] when the pandemic was at its high peak in this country, realistically, I've never seen any other international intervention on the ground. . . . But, there was Leah with us, fighting with us, ready to die with us."[63]

As I saw in Butaro, this spirit of accompaniment is all-encompassing. Even its physical construction reflected the approach: The facility and much of the medical equipment was built with locally sourced materials and custom-assembled by local staff on-site. The process of building the overall Butaro Hospital created jobs and fostered new skills for more than 550 local people. And, as a teaching facility, the hospital aims to empower Rwanda with not only skilled CHWs but also homegrown doctors and nurses.

I have witnessed Paul on grand rounds at the hospitals with which PIH partners. When he is working with a patient, he rests his hand on their hand—a gentle act of reassurance. This simple gesture of care brings to mind Wendell Berry's words: "Connection is health."[64] The kindness with which Paul approaches his patient care is carried throughout PIH's spirit and structure, and rests at the heart of their success.

The principle of accompaniment means that no person on the path to healing can be left to walk alone. To me, it's a principle that goes well beyond the work of physical healing. It's a principle rooted in belonging that has the power to heal our systems.

"SUPPORT IS ABOUT changing structures," Hilary Cottam recently shared with me. Cottam is an author, entrepreneur, and innovator who focuses her work on understanding and reforming the welfare state. "It's not about helping people who've got stuck at one end of a structure," she continued. "This is something that we've really got to make a generational shift on, whether it's loneliness or Black Lives Matter. It's about completely changing the rules of the game so that this is not an issue anymore."[65]

What rules do we need to change, or even break, to bring about structures that nurture belonging in multifaceted ways, rather than reinforce cycles of isolation? We have inherited systems that largely disconnect us from the people around us, from the lands on which we live, systems that do not provide opportunities to participate meaningfully in spheres of power and influence and allow us to affect change in order to lead purpose driven and fulfilling lives. Getting both the spirit and the structure right leads us to systems change.

The stories and places introduced in this chapter—Vancouver Island University, Agrolíbano, Bhutan, The Stop, and Partners In Health—are shining examples of what can happen when we decide to put belonging first. While our interwoven social systems often fall short, we have seen what happens when we come together, across divides, and build relationships of trust, generosity, and reciprocity. The ideas are simple, and the results speak for themselves.

As we have seen, people *from* specific communities are best positioned to inform systems change *for* those communities, in partnership, from the ground up. We can all work together to better support individuals, combat social isolation, strengthen communities, and build belonging. The work of building belonging on a systems level requires the participation of each and every one of us, working together to foster connection to people, place, power, and purpose.

Indeed, as the VIU motto proclaims, "You matter here."

CHAPTER TEN

THE RIGHT TO BELONG

WHEN I MET EMINA ĆERIMOVIĆ in the summer of 2014, she was already a distinguished lawyer, public activist, and researcher in the Disability Rights Division at Human Rights Watch (HRW). Over years of friendship and partnership, I have learned about the path she has taken to find belonging for herself, and then round the circle to build belonging for others. Emina is a warrior and an inspiration.

When Emina was seven years old in 1992, the Bosnian civil war broke out. At the time, the country was home to people from multiple ethnicities—Bosnian Muslims, Orthodox Serbs, and Catholic Croats. As violence spread and the war progressed, the population was split into ethnically delineated spaces of belonging and exclusion. Muslims were targeted and cast as "the Other." Emina's father was killed, and amid the conflict, Emina, her mother, and her sister were internally displaced for two and a half years.

In 2016, Emina spoke at a lecture series I convened while teaching at McGill. "In the war, I lost my dad," she recalled. "Later on, I lost my grandparent, and then I lost my best friend. And at one point, you just stop counting the people you lose in your family and in your community. I didn't go to school for two years. My sister suffered from jaundice, and I, myself, had a roundworm infection and was malnourished. We would often be woken up in the middle of the night by the sound of artillery fire. And I knew what it really meant to be hungry. Winters were the worst because I remember you were not sure whether it was worse to feel hunger or to feel cold."[1] Day after day, for years on end, Emina was denied belonging.

Emina had an aunt living in Sweden who paid smugglers to get the family out of Bosnia. Facing the threat of discrimination at each border, Emina and her family carefully moved through Europe with false passports and fake identities, with the goal of ultimately arriving in Sweden as refugees. They hid their Bosnian Muslim identity at every turn, lest they be detained or even sent back to Bosnia. Emina recalls, "getting to Sweden took months of unspeakable hardship—hardship that's left an imprint of feeling inadequate and unwanted."[2]

When the family finally arrived in Sweden as refugees, they received access to healthcare, food, clothing, and housing, yet Emina never truly felt like she belonged. "Other people identify you and they label you and they decide to discriminate against you and isolate you on the basis of what you are," she reflects. She experienced horrific bullying in school and was labeled the pejorative "*flykting*" or refugee.[3]

While Emina was able to find pieces of belonging in Bosnian language classes and cultural events, she often felt isolated. As a former refugee, she felt constant pressure to be the "perfect" model newcomer. She was lucky to have her mother and sister throughout this experience, but she lacked community connection and support, and was othered because of her language, religion, poverty, and culture. Although she was allowed to belong in Sweden under the label of "refugee," she was seldom allowed to belong as her whole self.

During her time in Sweden, Emina met a child with a disability, and found herself deeply affected by the encounter. She recalled that in Bosnia, she had never met a person with a disability, and began wondering why this was the case. She asked her family members about it, receiving only a vague response about how people with disabilities didn't really exist back home. She knew that couldn't possibly be true, and became determined to get answers.

In 2003, Emina returned to Bosnia with her mother and sister, where she later started her law degree. Specializing in human rights law, Emina decided to devote herself to investigating the deeper elements of disability rights in countries like Bosnia. She is now a leading advocate and researcher on the rights of people with disabilities. Her work has taken her to many corners of the world, from investigating the rights of refugees with disabilities in transit to Europe—like Nujeen Mustafa, whom we met earlier—to researching human rights violations of children with disabilities in Serbia and Syria.

Over the course of her career, Emina has set foot in institutions where children with disabilities were hidden from the world and subjected to horrendous living conditions. She shares, "In orphanages, children with disabilities are over-represented. And the main reason why they live there is because they have a disability."[4] Emina recalls encountering "dark windowless rooms, wooden cages, children—many fed by tubes and in diapers—crammed in tiny rooms."[5] On one fact-finding mission, she met a seven-year-old boy, Mujo, living in a Serbian institution with HIV as well as a disability, confined to a fenced-off area, completely isolated from the other children. Denied the right to go to school, the right to grow up with family, the right to live in community, even the right to play and interact with other children, Mujo and countless other children were, ultimately, denied the right to belong.

Thankfully, Emina's meticulous documentation and advocacy is having an impact. In 2017, the UN Committee on the Rights of the Child accepted recommendations from Emina and her colleagues at Human Rights Watch. The Committee called for the government of Serbia to work to transfer young children from institutions to family-based care and, more broadly, to address the issues of neglect, poor medical care, limited privacy, and exclusion from education and play at orphanages and other institutions. It wasn't the first time Emina's work on these issues catalyzed global action. The UN Committee on the Rights of Persons with Disabilities has issued similar findings based on Emina's reporting and recommendations. These pronouncements are now translating into tangible change.

Emina recently visited an institution where she had previously seen some of the worst neglect, and she saw encouraging improvements. The director of the facility told her that the Human Rights Watch advocacy started a chain of events that led to improved standards of care. At the facility, Emina again met Mujo, the little boy living with HIV. She was delighted to see him smiling, playing with a bike near the other children. While he was still "strongly supervised," he was no longer confined to a fenced-off area by himself.

Lately, Emina is focused on addressing one of the most severe forms of forced isolation imaginable: the shackling of thousands of people with psychosocial disabilities in countries around the world. Emina, along with over a dozen HRW researchers, has worked to investigate and end this practice, which they found evidence of in over sixty countries, including Afghanistan, Burkina Faso, Cambodia, Ghana, Indonesia, Kenya, Liberia, Mexico, Mozambique, Nigeria, Sierra Leone, Palestine, Russia, South Sudan, and Yemen.[6] In the fall of 2020, in partnership with other organizations including the Samuel Centre for Social Connectedness, Human Rights Watch launched a worldwide #BreakTheChains campaign, which has put pressure on governments and faith groups to end this horrific and deeply isolating practice. As Emina argues in her report, "people with mental health conditions should be supported and provided with effective services in their communities, not chained and abused."[7]

Emina—a child of war, an internally displaced person, an asylum seeker, a migrant refugee, a scholar, a warrior—is passing her experience and lessons on to people navigating desperate conditions of deprived belonging. By listening, investigating, calling out, and helping to correct severe injustices in her home region of the Balkans and well beyond, Emina is rounding the circle, doing the hard but lifesaving work of building belonging through human rights protection.

She's not the only one. The global community started working together on this in earnest over a hundred years ago.

A THEORY OF CHANGE

Perhaps we should not talk about a movement, or movements, but about movement: to apprehend these wild changes is as though to see many, many groups of people get up and move around from the positions they sat in for so long.

—REBECCA SOLNIT, *HOPE IN THE DARK*[8]

MORE THAN A CENTURY AGO, some of the world's brightest minds were assembled in the French countryside to try to achieve something unprecedented: a global legal framework for the defense of human rights. Europe had just emerged from the ravages of World War I, and the diplomats, planners, and scholars assembled in Versailles in 1919 saw their work as nothing short of essential for human survival.

They were right.

While the League of Nations—which was formally proposed in June of that year—did not ultimately succeed, it did lay the groundwork for vital future human rights compacts. It's a legacy that's been crucial to preventing and defusing conflicts, defending the environment, and promoting dignity around the world.

More than a hundred years after the conception of the League of Nations in 1919, it's increasingly clear that we've reached yet another inflection point—similar in magnitude to the end of WWI or the end of WWII, which brought the creation of the United Nations and the Universal Declaration of Human Rights.

While we have thankfully avoided conflict on the scale of the world wars in recent times, we, as a human family, nonetheless face a global challenge on par with those of the last century: We're facing a crisis of social isolation that's pervasive, systemic, and threatening our very survival.

In a time of unprecedented connectivity, people are increasingly alienated from meaningful work, a sense of community, connection to land and nature, a sense of *mattering* with respect to political and economic institutions, and—ultimately—a sense of being a part of a greater whole. The result of all this isolation is anxiety, depression, violence, othering, and environmental degradation on a global scale. It's a comprehensive challenge to humanity's future.

The world today looks very different from the world of 1919. But we're still in need of a revolution in terms of human rights. Political philosopher Dr. Henry Shue—perhaps best known for his foundational work on Basic Rights—argues that rights can arise in response to newly understood threats, which can shift over time.[9] We currently have a crisis in belonging, constituting a significant change in circumstance. I believe that what is required to meet this moment is the design and defense of a new kind of holistic rights framework for the twenty-first century—the Right to Belong.

Every person, by simple virtue of the fact that they are born, has the Right to Belong. That is the bedrock principle underpinning the Right to Belong. But notably, the Right to Belong isn't a singular legal entitlement. Rather, it is a constellation of both existing and yet-to-be-recognized rights—from the rights of people with disabilities and older persons to avoid discrimination, to the rights of refugees to a nationality. It's a framework for thinking about the rights of people to love whom they choose or to maintain a living cultural heritage as a minority community. It's a framework to be applied as we work to build dignity across the social, economic, and political domains. And it's a framework for enshrining the deep value of our human connection to people, to place, to power, and to purpose.

Ken Roth, the executive director of Human Rights Watch, whose counsel I've often sought as I've worked to define the Right to Belong and explore other rights issues, notes that the Right to Belong has the potential to "lift up a whole group of neglected rights." He also shared with me his view that this value of belonging is already embedded in many of the world's most fundamental legal rights: for example, the right to assemble, or to avoid discrimination as a member of an ethnic or religious or political minority.[10]

Many conventions and rights theories draw from this undercurrent of belonging. The Universal Declaration of Human Rights touches on belonging, speaking of "the free and full development of one's personality." We see belonging in the associational rights of the International Covenant on Civil and Political Rights, and in the rights to family and culture found in the International Covenant on Economic, Social and Cultural Rights. We also see it within Article 19 of the Convention on the Rights of Persons with Disabilities (CRPD), which includes the seminal right to live independently and be included in the community.

Belonging is present in all of these existing frameworks and ideas, and indeed, many others. It is long past time that we as a global community take this concept a step further and recognize that all people have an inalienable, universal Right to Belong.

Crucially, I will note that the Right to Belong is more than an entitlement—rather, for this framework to succeed in facilitating widespread change, we must recognize that we all have corresponding responsibilities to our fellow human beings. There is a deep sense of reciprocity central to the Right to Belong that ultimately removes the divide between the individual and the collective.

Professor William Alford, legal scholar and co-chair of the Harvard Law School Project on Disability, mentioned in a conversation we had recently that the focus of current human rights discourse on the individual ought not to diminish our collective and community responsibilities.[11] I wholeheartedly agree. Individuals who possess the capacity to build belonging for others have an inherent responsibility to do so.

The importance of responsibilities was also touched on in a 2021 UN side event on belonging, on which I served as a panelist. On that panel I was joined by the aforementioned Henry Shue, who explained the duality of rights and responsibilities this way: "Rights constitute our social compact in which the strong shield the weak, the able protect the vulnerable. This is why correlative duties are integral to rights. It's meaningless to say that the vulnerable have rights if the able don't have corresponding duties. Any given individual is likely to find, over the course of her life, that she's at some times one of the strong and at other times one of the weak; sometimes healthy, sometimes ill. We each put in our unpredictable stint as right holder and as duty bearer."[12]

As we think through the Right to Belong, the words of both Alford and Shue ring true. This new framework is a right in name, but also, notably, a responsibility in practice. This is the work of rounding the circle—using our capacity and positions of privilege to build belonging and uphold the rights of others.

FROM THEORY TO PRACTICE

OF COURSE, enshrining a specific Right to Belong is an ambitious aspiration because it runs up against the very limits of law and public policy. If, for example, an older person is socially isolated because her friends have passed away or her family has had to move for work, that isolation isn't directly the result of governmental abuse or failing. Such a situation isn't necessarily in the realm of traditional human rights.

Tim Shriver, whom we met through his work with Special Olympics International, is also the co-founder of US-based UNITE, a growing collaborative made up of Americans from all walks of life, empowered by the singular goal of bringing people together across differences. Belonging is one of the core beliefs underlying the Call to Unite, stated as follows, "Everyone belongs—we are each an irreplaceable part of an interconnected reality." Tim boldly—though I believe accurately—once put it to me this way: "Belonging isn't simply tactical, or I dare say legal. It's deep, it's visceral, it's about ultimate meaning and value in all of the many languages of the earth and of history. It beckons, it summons soul type questions."[13]

So, as we look to develop a new holistic rights framework for the twenty-first century, the question becomes: How do we root it in the practical? If we are not enshrining a new, specific legal right, how do we realize the Right to Belong? I believe that our approach must be two-pronged. First, we must mitigate existing harm. Second, we must change attitudes and norms so that laws and regulations will follow.

Let's start with the first prong. Realizing the Right to Belong should start with conscious and concerted efforts to address the most extreme and pernicious forms of social isolation that exist on the face of the earth—these include shackling, solitary confinement, the separation of migrant families, homelessness, the denial of marriage equality rights, lack of birth registration for vulnerable children, modern-day slavery, human trafficking, and the plight of climate migrants.

In 2016, Human Rights Watch found that an estimated 18,000 people with psychosocial disabilities in Indonesia were physically shackled—to beds, cement blocks, or in animal pens.[14] While exposure of this treatment forced the government to act, there are still an estimated 15,000 people in such conditions in that country today.[15] Realizing a Right to Belong means working systematically to free people from these circumstances.

Solitary confinement is another example. Holding incarcerated people for twenty-two hours or more a day without meaningful human contact is an instance of explicit and intentional social isolation. In the US, an estimated 80,000 incarcerated people are held in solitary isolation annually. Being in solitary confinement increases one's susceptibility to psychotic behavior and suicidal ideation.[16] Realizing a Right to Belong means changing the policies and procedures that enable solitary confinement.

We also see the violation of belonging in detention at our borders and the separation of migrant families. The US paints a vivid picture of this policy failure. The Trump administration made headlines in 2018 with its zero-tolerance family separation policies, which were intended to deter immigration across the southern US border. However, the policy failed in curbing undocumented immigration.[17] Though the Biden administration has attempted to reunite families, it has proven to be incredibly difficult. Today, there are hundreds—if not thousands—of children who were taken from their parents years ago that remain separated from their families because of the actions bolstered by the Trump administration.[18] Realizing a Right to Belong means fighting back against dangerous policies that tear apart families in the name of law and order.

The COVID-19 crisis has exacerbated many of our existing inequalities, deepening the belonging deficit among vulnerable groups. Consider people experiencing homelessness in Ontario. A study published by the *Canadian Medical Association Journal* found that those living without a home were more likely to test positive for COVID, face hospitalization, experience greater medical complications, and die from the virus. Because they face greater difficulties in self-isolating, those experiencing homelessness were "over 20 times more likely to be hospitalized for COVID-19, over 10 times more likely to receive intensive care, and they were over five times more likely to die within 21 days of a positive test."[19] Realizing a Right to Belong means recognizing the stark intersection between health and housing, and pushing our elected representatives to do something about it.

For generations, minority groups around the world have had to fight for their right to marry. In 1959, the overwhelming majority of white Americans considered the rejection of interracial marriage essential to preserve the nation. It took decades of societal progress to reach a point in 2017 where 91 percent of Americans considered interracial marriage to be a good or at least benign thing.[20] Disabled people can face significant financial burdens at the hands of the state when they marry. When disabled people in America get married, for example, it often triggers a bundle of Social Security rules that lead to a reduction or complete loss in income and health benefits for the disabled person.[21] And the fight to marriage equality for LGBTQIA+ couples in countries around the world has been a long, hard battle with varying degrees of success. Countries like Canada, the Netherlands, Belgium, and Spain were among the first to legalize marriage for same-sex couples; conversely, in countries like Iran, Saudi Arabia, and Yemen, same-sex relations are illegal and punishable by death.[22] As of June 2021, only twenty-eight countries in the world, including the United States, have legalized same-sex marriage.[23] Realizing a Right to Belong means pushing for marriage equality for all consenting adults around the world, regardless of gender, sexuality, race, or ability.

There are an estimated 237 million children under five who do not have birth certificates or other birth records. That's about 35 percent of the world's total population in that age range. Those without a birth record are fundamentally invisible to the state.[24] A child without a birth record often can't access healthcare, immunization, or other vital services. A child without a birth record can't prove their age, and therefore faces increased risk of labor exploitation, forcible conscription into the military, child marriage, or trafficking. This is the essence of not belonging. The SDGs—from which I draw inspiration as I work on the Right to Belong—call for progress toward counting and registering people. Realizing a Right to Belong can be as straightforward and clear as the work of building civil registration and vital statistics programs, ultimately ensuring meaningful universal birth records.

And finally, around the world today we see destructive social isolation in the ways that whole peoples are being made landless and stateless by climate change and other forces.[25] We see how forced migration requires people to disconnect from their families, their traditions, their ties to land and culture and community. Realizing a Right to Belong means focusing all our energies on reversing these trends, providing support for refugees while fighting climate change and disruptive regional conflicts with the urgency they demand.

At the same time, the Right to Belong demands that we look beyond simply mitigating damage. After all, this new framework offers us, at its core, a hopeful, positive vision of the world we can build together. If, at the same time as mitigating damage, we work to reorient attitudes and norms toward belonging, then laws and regulations that uphold the Right to Belong will follow.

What if every person believed that the state owes its citizens a minimum standard when it comes to medical care, transportation, and accessible public spaces? What if every person recognized the inherent rights of Indigenous peoples to live on and care for their lands and waters, speak their languages, and pass their knowledge on to future generations without the threat of assimilation? What if we acknowledge the impact of nurturing equitable participation in the economy, regardless of gender or ethnicity? What if we champion equal and consistent access to nutritious food for all, regardless of socioeconomic status? What if we recognized the right we all share to participate fully in spheres of power and influence, including voting rights and equal political participation and representation? What if every person believed that refugees are entitled to certain automatic basic protections? What if we value the notion that those requiring assistance should never lose the ability to live independently, and that they should be able to retain their dignity, agency, and choice? What if we accept as fact that older persons should not be allowed to languish alone?

The creation of substantive rights that protect and uphold belonging will find their genesis in changing attitudes and norms. When we drive global conversations toward notions of fairness and inclusion, we change individual hearts and minds, which allows us to then, in turn, harness our collective voice to demand laws and regulations that reflect our values. It is through cultural change that we can and will inspire action.

IT'S POSSIBLE, AND IT'S ALREADY HAPPENING

THE RIGHT TO BELONG isn't just a vision for wealthy industrialized countries. It's a vision for everyone. Over my two decades of exploration and study within this topic, I've found more and more reason for hope. I've seen heroes prioritizing the value of deep human connection—building a Right to Belong—in real, tangible ways.

I've seen Indigenous teachers from Canada's First Nations empowering young people to know their land and restore their sense of union through culture. I've seen arts programs enabling people coming out of conflict or oppression to find their bliss through song and creative expression. I've seen city planners and architects working to humanize and transform impersonal spaces into contexts for connection. I've seen inner-city farms, skill swaps, time banks, participatory city budgeting initiatives, community-owned art spaces, and intergenerational co-living programs bringing people together in service of something greater.

The work of building belonging isn't only about designing and implementing policies and programs. It's again about reexamining and reimagining our answer to this most fundamental question: *What do we value?*

The periods after World War I and World War II were so filled with possibility because the old systems and frameworks had broken down. People were not merely ready for change, they were also crying out for something new. At this moment—more than a century after the start of a global experiment in human rights—we are again ripe for renewal. As Martin Luther King Jr. would say, *what we need is a "revolution of values."*[26]

This work of renewal through the Right to Belong isn't confined to treaty halls like Versailles, or centers of legal scholarship—it happens in our streets, in our schools, in our most fundamental ways of seeing and sensing the world. It's about reordering our priorities: consciously determining whether we structure our societies to maximize economic growth, efficiency, and competitiveness, or—rather—to elevate community, connection, and belonging.

In reflecting on the necessity of a values-driven framework for mobilizing human rights in the twenty-first century, I think fondly of Sethu.

SETHU'S STORY

PICTURE THIS: a South African camp for homeless men in the throes of a global pandemic. A fashion show with gorgeous makeshift gowns, makeup, and jewelry. A local TV crew filming the celebration. An angel dressed all in white. A pervasive and enveloping sense of harmony and belonging. The event is called LOVE, and the place is dubbed Camp COVID.

In this moment, Sethu, a brilliant non-binary twenty-seven-year-old with a radiant smile, surrounded by people like them, felt beautiful, free, and accepted. "It was a day where we wanted to show that we are different in how we feel, we are different in how we think. We were celebrating diversity." According to Sethu, "There was love everywhere that day."[27]

But things weren't always like this.

"Being a homosexual in a homophobic society is like walking on thorns. An unrelenting marathon."[28] Ethan Sesethu Xabanisa grew up in the Eastern Cape in South Africa. Their mother died when they were young, and while they were still growing up, their grandmother died, too. Sethu recalls being inspired by their mother, who was a teacher. Born a biological male, Sethu knew throughout childhood and adolescence that they were different. They aspired to be a mother in a household one day. Sethu recalled, "I saw no male or boy in me, and I preferred to be addressed as a female."[29] In their teens, they were diagnosed with congenital bilateral retinal degeneration, a severe form of visual impairment. They have experienced physical and emotional abuse, as well as homelessness—they shared with me recently, "I was homeless because of my sexual orientation, and because no one could accommodate my disability."[30]

The pandemic compounded Sethu's problems. That's how they ended up at Camp COVID. But they recall the experience fondly, telling me, "I met my sisters at the camp and we built up a community." It was there that Sethu met Joey Monane, the founder of Ikusasalethu Youth Development Project—an organization focused on reducing the impact of HIV/AIDS through education. Joey immediately saw in Sethu their brilliance. "We saw [their] capabilities," says Joey, "so we brought [them] in so that [they could] become somebody, and [they're] doing that now. It's not just a person. [They are] visually impaired, but can see with [their] mind."[31]

Sethu now works as head of corporate affairs at Ikusasalethu, and is the founding director of Smartbutton Technologies, a telecommunications company that creates and develops systems for persons with disabilities.

Sethu no longer lives at the camp, but remains a strong voice for people living with disabilities and displaced persons—especially those from the LGBTQIA+ community. Sethu thoughtfully offered this reflection on the systemic violation of LGBTQIA+ rights: "LGBTQIA+ communities are at the receiving end of hate crimes and brutality," they write. "It's a global phenomenon; members of the LGBTQIA+ community are stripped of their human dignity, robbed of their right to life and perpetually humiliated, even by the very structures that are holding a crucial responsibility and mandate to protect their rights."[32]

Sethu goes on to elaborate on the state of LGBTQIA+ rights in Africa: "Doctrines of 'procreation' are some of the issues causing tensions between the LGBTQIA+ community members and heterosexual members of society, which mostly apply in conservative African countries such as Nigeria, Zambia, Namibia, Uganda, and many others. In some African countries, homosexuals are subject to thirty years of imprisonment or, worse, sentenced to death. This demonstrates a clear picture of how deeply entrenched the hate directed toward homosexuals is on the African continent. While South Africa is one of the many countries that has legalized same sex relationships and marriages, hate crimes against LGBTQIA+ community members continue unabated."[33]

I'm struck, in particular, by the last part of Sethu's quote. It reinforces the sad truth that even though certain communities may enjoy rights or freedoms on paper, those rights do not automatically translate into the experience of belonging. This is where existing rights frameworks fail, and subsequently, where I believe that the Right to Belong would make a real difference.

Graeme Reid is the director of the Lesbian, Gay, Bisexual, and Transgender Rights Program at Human Rights Watch. An expert on LGBTQIA+ rights, Reid was also the founding director of the Gay and Lesbian Archives of South Africa. In our conversation, Reid echoed Sethu's observation about how notions of religion and "traditional values" are often manipulated to justify violating the rights of LGBTQIA+ people. "Gay people or lesbians or transgender people are often seen as being the opposite of the family; they're put in opposition to the family, like traditional values, family values, are so often used as the counterpoint to LGBT identities. And so, they are seen to be the antitheses of the building blocks of society."[34]

In discussing the Right to Belong, Graeme told me, "To me, the concept of belonging provides a positive framing, a kind of aspirational vision with which to look at the LGBT rights issues."[35] As someone who has lived through oppression and othering on many fronts, Sethu said they would have benefited from a Right to Belong that protects our ability to be our truest selves. "You've got your own normal. And just because your normal is different, it doesn't make you less of a human being . . . Identity is an important aspect. That's where you find belonging."[36]

Sethu also speaks eloquently on the important duality of both rights and responsibilities, saying, "As human beings, we are designed on foundations of kindness and philanthropy. It is our collective responsibility to extend our helping hands to our brothers and sisters in times of need. There should be no room left for unfair discrimination, genderism, racism and homophobia." Sethu says simply of people like them: "We deserve the same rights as everyone else. We deserve to belong."[37]

Through their work, Sethu is fighting for the belonging of their sisters in the LGBTQIA+ community, and for the rights and independence of those living with disabilities in South Africa. Their fierce self-advocacy and care for others illuminates what the Right to Belong looks like in practice.

THE PLURALISM OF IDENTITY

I was singing all along in a corner, when the melody caught your ear.

—RABINDRANATH TAGORE[38]

DISTINGUISHED ECONOMIST AND PHILOSOPHER Amartya Sen, whom we met earlier in the book, was born in Shantiniketan, West Bengal, on the campus of Visva-Bharati University, where his mother was a student, and her father, a lecturer. As a child, Sen received a robust education and recalls being inspired by luminary Rabindranath Tagore's open approach to cultural diversity in the world, which was well reflected in the school curriculum. However, during his adolescence, things in India were changing—Sen recalls coming of age in India at a time of great divisiveness and oppression, driven in large part by political othering.

In his 1998 Nobel lecture, Professor Sen notes of the political and social upheaval in 1940s India, "People's identities as Indians, as Asians, or as members of the human race, seemed to give way—quite suddenly—to sectarian identification with Hindu, Muslim, or Sikh communities." He continues, "The broadly Indian of January was rapidly and unquestioningly transformed into the narrowly Hindu or finely Muslim of March. The carnage that followed had much to do with unreasoned herd behavior by which people, as it were, 'discovered' their new divisive and belligerent identities, and failed to take note of the diversity that makes Indian culture so powerfully mixed. The same people were suddenly different."[39]

Professor Sen has spoken about a particular moment in his life when he was witness to the horrific violation of another's rights simply because they were different. He was with his father in Dhaka when a man came through the gate, badly beaten. He was a Muslim in desperate need of work, and had made the mistake of entering a predominantly Hindu area to find employment at a neighboring house. He was attacked by locals and stabbed. Sen's father took the man to the hospital with Sen in tow, but it was too late. The man died there. "The experience was devastating for me," Sen recalled, "and suddenly made me aware of the dangers of narrowly defined identities, and also of the divisiveness that can lie buried in communitarian politics."

Indeed, Sen's story reminds us that our rights are fragile and too often subject to the whims of the dominant, ruling class. The Right to Belong firmly rejects the notion that our freedoms—to expression, to religion—can be used to violate the rights of others at any point for any reason.

I see echoes of this divisiveness in my own country through, for example, the mistreatment of newcomers, or the enduring legacy of colonization. Recognizing the Right to Belong means overcoming the shadow side of belonging in order to ensure we belong as our whole selves. As Ovide Mercredi, whom we met earlier, once proclaimed, "I will share with you my hopes and dreams for a true human country that is founded on the values of justice, fairness, inclusion, equality, diversity, and the two basic human rights: the right to be different and the right to belong. In my imaginary Canada I see the Indigenous people and Nations occupying a fundamental place of belonging as distinct Nations with rights of self-determination and freedom from want or need. In my vision of Canada I see no racism. I see no poverty. I see no prejudice nor discrimination. I see no economic or social disparity. And I don't see one group occupying a greater space for generating and acquiring wealth as a preferential right over other groups in society."[40]

The Right to Belong is rooted in the truth that we cannot belong at the direct exclusion of others. Human rights are absolute only if we are all entitled to them, all the time, and only if we work to protect and uphold them for one another as fiercely as for ourselves.

THE RIGHTS OF OLDER PEOPLE

Into the nothingness of scorn and noise
into the living sea of waking dream,
where there is neither sense of life, nor joys,
but the huge shipwreck of my own esteem

—JOHN CLARE, "WRITTEN IN NORTHAMPTON COUNTY ASYLUM"[41]

"YOU CAN'T BE PART OF SOCIETY if you're in an institution."[42]

When Loretta Claiborne, whom we met through her leadership with Special Olympics International, recently shared this reflection, I thought immediately of my father.

My dad was principled and fearless, kind of heart, and undaunted by challenge. At the beginning of 1997, he suffered a severe brain injury and fell into a three-month coma. When he woke up, my family turned to his workplace insurance for help. We were appalled when the insurance company would not consider rehabilitation because he had reached the age of sixty-five—in their words, he was in his "sunset years."

What insurance would happily do was put him in a long-term care facility, a nursing home where he was expected to live out his days in a hospital bed, with no hope of regaining his independence.

My father's story prompted a powerful image in my mind—one I've referenced throughout this book. I began to see a person sitting all alone at the bottom of a well. This is social isolation. It's the deprivation of social connectedness, a loss of agency and dignity, and a distinct lack of belonging. I remember thinking that it must be incredibly lonely to grow old in a world that gives up on you while you're still here.

His experience isn't unusual. In fact, the mistreatment and neglect of older people is all too common. As people age in our society, they're faced with myriad challenges. For many, it starts in the workplace—some countries have mandatory age-defined retirement policies, while some people experience age-based discrimination in hiring and promotion as they mature in their careers. The risks to belonging compound from there: death of a spouse, poverty, illness, inadequate housing, food insecurity, elder abuse, and loneliness, just to name a few.

On top of that, older people are now facing a new set of challenges unique to just the past few years. The COVID-19 pandemic, for example, exposed some of our deepest failures in healthcare, as we saw a devastating onslaught of preventable deaths in long-term care facilities. And climate change has brought about unimaginable heat waves and corresponding heat-related deaths—highest among older adults.[43]

Bethany Brown is a human rights advisor for the International Disability Alliance, a network of fourteen global and regional organizations of persons with disabilities, and a former researcher on the rights of older people at Human Rights Watch. She notes that we're at a crisis point when it comes to protecting the rights of older persons. "Never before in human history have so many older people been alive at the same time as people of other ages," she shared. "What that means is that issues of ageism, discrimination against people based on their perceived older age or their actual older age, become magnified."[44]

The Right to Belong is offered in direct response to the unique twenty-first-century challenges we are facing—that includes all people, regardless of age or circumstance. As it stands currently, in Canada, the US, and around the world, providing adequate support for us as we age is not a priority for our governments and within broader society. Brilliant activists and advocates have been campaigning for a Convention on the Rights of Older People for more than a decade, to no avail. Time and time again, we see the rights of individuals violated simply because they have reached a certain age. They become an afterthought, not worthy of government or social support. Make no mistake—this should not be dismissed as a matter of "resource allocation" and scarcity.

When we do begrudgingly get around to thinking about older people, we're so often focused on the idea of protecting them that we strip away their right to agency in the process. We incorrectly treat these concepts—protection and autonomy—as mutually exclusive, creating this push-pull dichotomy where we can have one or the other, but never both. It's ageism, it's a blatant violation of older persons' rights, and it's rampant.

The 2021 Global Report on Ageism tells us that, globally, one in two people are ageist against older persons.[45] And ageism is known to increase social isolation and loneliness, which affects more than one million older Canadians[46] and many millions more around the world. This is an unacceptable violation of older persons' fundamental Right to Belong. We have to course correct, and fast.

"We don't change our human rights as we grow old," Bethany Brown remarked recently. "We're born with them, and we hold them until the day we die. Think about what it is to be locked away from the rest of the world. Think about what it is to be told, 'What you have to offer, we don't want that.' "[47]

Over the years, I've spoken with many incredible colleagues about what it means to build and uphold belonging for older persons. Bridget Sleap is a senior researcher on the rights of older people at Human Rights Watch. Before that, she was a senior advisor at HelpAge International—a network of 158 partner organizations in 86 countries focused on supporting the rights of older people around the world. Bridget's work is international and intersectional. In a recent discussion, she told me that for us to experience belonging as we get older, "it is absolutely critical to maintain a sense of purpose."[48] On this point, I think of Judi Aubel.

Judi Aubel is the founder of the Grandmother Project—a Senegal-based NGO that upholds older people's Right to Belong through intergenerational connection, linking grandmother "mentors" with young girls in the community for culture-informed counseling. "My understanding of belonging," Judi tells me, "has to do with feeling that one's experience and role is valued by others, in the family and in the community. And then, as a result of that, being actively engaged in facing everyday challenges and working with others to come up with strategies for not only solving problems, but also promoting the well-being of the people that are important within the family and the community."[49]

I couldn't agree more. In 2018, I had a conversation with my colleague Kimberley Brownlee, professor of philosophy at the University of British Columbia, about conceptualizing the right to belong. She framed it eloquently, stating, "When we belong, it's not just that we're tolerated or accepted. Belonging signals that this person isn't just accepted, they're valuable, they have a purpose, they have a function, they are useful to other people."[50]

There is a long way to go in ensuring that our fundamental human rights do not become more vulnerable with each passing year. Recognizing that everyone has an inherent Right to Belong would better support human beings at every stage of their lives. Older people need to be there for these discussions, too, in leadership positions, representing their interests. On this, I am sometimes reminded of Margaret Laurence, Canadian author of the 1964 classic *The Stone Angel*, which relates the story of Hagar Shipley, a ninety-year-old woman reflecting back on her life as she fights against being placed in a long-term care facility.

Laurence beseeches us, "if this were indeed my Final Hour, these would be my words to you. I would not claim to pass on any secret of life, for there is none, or any wisdom except the passionate plea of caring. . . . Try to feel, in your heart's core, the reality of others. This is the most painful thing in the world, probably, and the most necessary. In times of personal adversity, know that you are not alone. Know that although in the eternal scheme of things you are small, you are also unique and irreplaceable, as are all of your fellow humans everywhere in the world. Know that your commitment is above all to life itself."[51]

The work of building belonging is necessarily guided by the tenet: *with, not for*. Belonging is, as Laurence suggests, a commitment to ourselves and to one another. By overcoming the structures that isolate and divide us, we can work together to reimagine them, and co-create bold, new systems that nurture and protect our innate Right to Belong.

EVERY PERSON, by simple virtue of the fact that they are born, has the Right to Belong.

This simple statement, if accepted as fact, has the power to change the world. It can change our institutions, our governments, our systems, our communities, and our interactions with one another. We see glimpses in the work of people taking up space and driving change for refugees, for children with disabilities, for the LGBTQIA+ community, for older people. But the potential to impact all lives is there—the Right to Belong has a broad application and a deep significance for every human being.

"This Right to Belong is a supply problem, not a demand problem," Tim Shriver said to me recently. "The demand is enormous for belonging. The hunger to be seen, to be heard, to express yourself, to connect—is massive."[52]

The undercurrent of belonging is already there in our existing rights legislation, conventions, frameworks, and theories. The Right to Belong would provide us with an explicit, values-driven rights framework for the modern era. As we look at the current state of the world, in which we are confronted with compounding and intersectional challenges, we must be united in our efforts toward positive change. But we will unite only if we feel a connection to something bigger than ourselves. We need to feel less isolated and less lonely, more connected and more like we belong. In recognizing a universal, inalienable Right to Belong, we will be challenged to build better, more inclusive societies that value everyone for their varied gifts and abilities.

I believe that we can shape the world into a place where the most marginalized and most vulnerable among us are treated as equals in every sense of the word. Where everyone knows that, regardless of who they are or where they come from, they, too, have a Right to Belong.

This is not an impossible dream; as we've seen throughout this book, the work of belonging is already underway.

CHAPTER ELEVEN

BELONGING TO A SHARED GLOBAL FUTURE

A Lighter Shade of Darkness

CAITLIN SAMUEL, 2014

WHEN I WAS TEN YEARS OLD, my elementary school class went on a field trip to the McLaughlin Planetarium at the Royal Ontario Museum in Toronto. I was a shy, timid kid who never quite felt like I belonged. Almost nobody could tell. I remember looking up at the breathtaking display of the universe, and having total awe wash over me. The sheer magnitude of what was before my eyes was astounding. I located Earth, a tiny spec amid a huge sea of stars and planets. It was a strikingly beautiful sight, not because Earth is the center of the universe—indeed, it is not. It was beautiful because in that moment I realized that we, the human race, are connected to everything. Our world today wrongly defaults to organizing people into hierarchies and categories that are largely indicative of our relative power and status. Our relationships with one another are neatly laid out in workplace org charts, our abilities jammed into the confines of the box filled with preconceived ideas that accompany a given role or place in society. The hard work of building belonging requires us to revert to our more natural, intrinsic human state—one where we model our relationships and societies after a circle, which I see as circles of belonging.

Operating at its best, the center of each circle of belonging is our wholeness, our common energy, passion, goodwill, and effort toward a given goal. This is where we create and hold intentional space for others, and there is magic at this center. Every point on the circumference is the same distance from the middle—these points are the people and programs that hold the circle up. Every individual point has the responsibility to hold that gravity, hold that fixed point where it is, and ensure that it doesn't shift, casting some aside—indeed, we belong only if we belong together. The points along the circumference are intrinsically connected with all other points, which in turn, each create their own circles of belonging. When we rid ourselves of our egocentric views, we realize that we as individuals needn't be in the middle of that circle—it's just enough to be in the orbit of that magic that holds us all in place.

I want the circle
Broken.

—MARGARET ATWOOD, *THE CIRCLE GAME*[1]

HOWEVER, not all circles are benevolent—some circles need to be broken. Some circles hold people in negative spaces where poverty, hate, and othering sit at the center. Luckily, there are good people doing good work to break these negative circles and replace them with circles of belonging; we've met many of them throughout this book. These everyday heroes have time and time again had their actions and efforts guided by reflecting on the biggest question of all: What do we value?

Key to breaking these negative circles is the realization that we are connected to so many facets of the world around us, and having society, in turn, prioritize our well-being and belonging. This is easier said than done. When we feel alone and isolated at the bottom of the well, we lose sight of the core fact that *there is no other—the other is only ever us*. If we have not felt deep connection, nor felt the deep sense of belonging, the darkness can easily blind us to this truth. It's not the darkness of our circumstance to be feared, but the lack of connection that often accompanies it. We think we are alone at the bottom of that well on our most difficult days. But if we know that we belong, if we feel it in our deepest state of being, and if others are willing and able to help us on our path toward belonging, there will be a way up from the bottom of the well.

We feel connection and belonging when we root our relationships in reciprocity, knowing that sometimes we're the giver, and sometimes we're the receiver, and core to this ebb and flow is the underlying beauty of humanity and all of Nature. We feel connected to others when we all do our part to round the circle—taking the lessons we've learned and passing them forward to others in our orbit. Remember, a gift that sits with the receiver forever without being passed to another is incomplete.

When we feel belonging, we can stand up at the bottom of that dark well, climb to the top, look to the sky, and realize how deeply we are interconnected with everything and everyone, unified in a common spirit. If, in our times of despair, we know that we belong, we won't fear the darkness, because we'll know that we're not alone. There is light all around us if we have been conditioned to see it—even the dark night sky graces us with the light of the stars.

Some circles of belonging are literal, like when we stand in circular formation to open and close our Global Symposia. Others are figurative, where the concept of "rounding the circle" is beautifully front and center—the Circle Kubatana Tose support groups that follow the Friendship Bench, the Community Health Workers of Partners in Health, or our friend Parzival, who, upon asking the Healing Question, became king and ruled with compassion and empathy after his epic quest.

In 2002, I started on a path that resulted in a co-creation that, in my mind, beautifully encapsulates the themes and lessons we've discussed in this book. Focused on combating social isolation and delivering better outcomes for people—especially children—living in poverty across southern Africa, this program is an ever-evolving network of support and empowerment, forever holding space and inviting others into circles of belonging. It reminds me of the planetarium—a vast universe of planets, stars, and moons, all working to a common end and catalyzing change in perfect, deliberate coexistence. Embodying both the spirit and the structure of belonging is a living, breathing model for belonging that can be replicated around the world.

THE SOCIAL CONNECTEDNESS PROGRAMME

"Of course, you would know all about isolation."
"No. I have never been isolated."
"Never isolated—not even on Robben Island?"
"No. On Robben Island, we were all brothers working together
    with a common purpose. I was never alone."

That exchange with Nelson Mandela in New York in 2002 transformed my understanding of isolation, of belonging, of community, of life itself. If Mandela, the most famous political prisoner of his time, didn't feel isolated in the confines of a South African prison, what, then, was isolation? And to the contrary, what did it mean to belong? It was at this dinner that an idea began taking shape. How could we counter isolation and foster connection at the same time? And how could we co-create solutions with the individuals and communities that are most marginalized?

Years later, in 2007, over afternoon tea at the home of Graça Machel and Nelson Mandela in Johannesburg, this vision solidified in my mind and later took flight as a full-fledged initiative.

FOR DECADES, Graça Machel has been working to counter multidimensional poverty and to transform systemic forms of isolation. Before becoming the first lady of South Africa, she was also a government minister and first lady in her home country of Mozambique. There, centuries of colonial oppression and decades of civil war had destroyed families and ravaged both the physical infrastructure and social fabric. Many of the country's children had seen the experience of childhood stolen away—by war, by poverty, and, increasingly, by the scourge of HIV/AIDS.

Graça had come to realize that repairing what had been broken required much more than the normal modes of altruism, like, for example, bringing a child soldier home from the front lines, or providing food, shelter, and schooling for a child who had none. There was a further need for emotional reconnection to draw marginalized children back to the community. This process couldn't be forced. By definition, it had to be participatory; it had to engage and embrace the child, the family, and the society of which they were all part. Graça shared with me that she created the Foundation for Community Development (FDC) in recognition of "the pain of isolation—and the promise of community-based interventions that enable children to be embraced by others, achieve their full potential, and become contributing members of the society."[2] "Without meaningful social connections, people often feel unsafe and as if they do not belong, which weakens the social fabric that holds us together, and enables us to develop inner resilience and the ability to thrive."

"Together," Graça says, "with the people living with chronic isolation, we must look at how to creatively re-knead the fabric which connects people to community and show them that they are held in a space that is safe and secure, and larger than themselves." With the goal of helping communities bring marginalized children back into circles of care, I drew upon my friend's inspirational leadership and wisdom as I worked to launch the Social Connectedness Programme in southern Africa in 2009.

The Synergos Institute, with which I had long been involved in a board and program capacity, was the obvious partner in helping me structure this new, ambitious initiative. Founded in 1986 by another decades-long friend and great mentor of mine, Peggy Dulany, to address a diverse range of social, economic, and environmental challenges toward the eradication of poverty, Synergos pioneered a model of service called Bridging Leadership: an approach that centers on incorporating diverse stakeholders into development projects as genuine partners. The essence of the approach is building trust—both within and between organizations—as well as empowering individuals to overcome their fears and other internal obstacles to effective service. Peggy recently summarized this process: "Where trust is built, connections are strengthened," she told me. "The issue of isolation and the importance of social connectedness is becoming clearer. Inclusive partnerships as a strategy for solutions are increasingly being looked at as a way to go."[3]

At the beginning, I brought together a handful of core partners to form the bedrock of the Social Connectedness Programme (SC Programme)—Synergos Institute, Foundation for Community Development (FDC), Nelson Mandela Children's Foundation (NMCF), and my family's Samuel Family Foundation (SFF). I later brought in my colleagues at the Oxford Poverty & Human Development Initiative (OPHI) to conduct on-site research and analysis. At the outset, I had three overarching inspirations, rooted in my own life journey: (1) to better identify and understand social isolation, (2) to call it out and destigmatize it, (3) to build collaborative partnerships to overcome it.

Our 2009 program and the report that followed—gave detail and texture to the sentiment that Mandela had shared with me about the nature of isolation: "I have seen isolation. I have seen it in the child with AIDS whom no one in the village will love or care for or touch or feed or shelter. I have seen isolation—and it is very bad."

Called *Imbeleko* in the Tsonga language in southern Africa, meaning "caring for children," the pilot program documented not only the pervasiveness of the problem of social isolation, but also its implications: for example, its lifelong debilitating effects on a child's ability to trust, seek and receive support, engage academically, forge functional relationships, and develop needed social skills. The research pointed to the effects of isolation on anxiety and depression, as well as other mental and physical health conditions, while also underscoring the ways that social isolation exacerbates the effects of poverty. The Imbeleko report also sought to build an understanding of Indigenous ways of responding to vulnerability among young people and, in turn, to develop new approaches, based on Indigenous knowledge and practices, that could enable new kinds of advocacy and practice among donors, governments, NGOs, and communities.

Marlene Ogawa, country director for Synergos in South Africa and long-term manager of the Social Connectedness Programme, is someone to whom I have often referred as the weaver behind the myriad threads of this tapestry. "Social connectedness speaks to the notion of *ubuntu*,"[4] she told me, referring to the South African concept of interconnectedness that we discussed earlier. "I am because you are. I'm connected to you, and because we are so connected, if you are not doing well, I am not doing well. Within the local context, for communities it's important to create local solutions, and so part of the local solutions is about reclaiming that ubuntu that's eroding."[5]

In our conversations, Marlene has highlighted how our inaugural Imbeleko report looked at ways to balance "individualism and collectivism," pointing, in her words, to essential principles for addressing poverty and isolation: "Everyone has purpose and there is a cycle of giving and needing. When someone doesn't have that sense of purpose, we shouldn't walk away, but do something. As social beings, it's inherent to help."[6]

Through the Imbeleko process, we found many organizations doing valiant work to address poverty. However, we found too few with the capacity to prioritize matters like emotional and psychosocial support, cornerstones of the work of social connectedness. Still, just as important, we found an abundance of community-led solutions that could help bring this kind of rootedness, resilience, and healing.

Over the years, the partnership has grown to include over a dozen organizations in South Africa, Mozambique, Namibia, Malawi, and Eswatini (formerly Swaziland) to help develop solutions to poverty centered on locally informed values of social connectedness. Between communities and within them, the leadership is at the grassroots level and not at the "top," because there is no top in a co-creation. Identifying grassroots organizations doing important work, we provide local grants and help them apply a vital social isolation and connectedness lens across their programming efforts. We've served to facilitate linkages between people and within organizations, all to the end of building belonging where it's needed most. The result is more holistic, belonging-centric outcomes for individuals and communities.

Through this journey together, we've uncovered strategies for disentangling the complex interplays between social isolation and poverty, as well as for addressing what I call the "first cousins" of social isolation: shame, stigma, alienation, and humiliation. Over the life of this program, I have seen communities rounding the circle to pass on their gifts to others. I've seen individuals building lasting connections, embracing the idea that we only belong if we belong together. Leaders are yielding space for others, breathing life into what I see as the crucial mantra of "empower, not power." Decisions are being made in a way that honors the central question that we should all be reflecting on, always—that is, *what do we value?* With belonging and connection at its very core, it's not hyperbole to say that the work being done by the Social Connectedness Programme partners and stakeholders on the ground is changing lives, one day at a time.

CITY YEAR

CITY YEAR SOUTH AFRICA, for example, shows us what can happen when we entrust youth with positions of leadership. The City Year South Africa program is run by a diverse group of eighteen- to twenty-five-year-olds acting as youth service leaders and site leaders at various locations across Johannesburg. These leaders work in schools as teaching assistants, supporting classroom work and running after-school sports and skills programming. They offer mentorship to children and teenagers in their community, helping them connect to education or work. They also participate in big community-building projects, helping to construct low-income housing, new schools, and recreation centers that often serve as cultural hubs for engagement and belonging.

Many of these young leaders have survived some of the toughest situations of social and economic marginalization, violence, and poverty, ultimately transforming their circumstances to become leaders and community-builders without sacrificing their authentic selves. When I visited in 2014, I saw firsthand these young people creating common purpose and renewal in their community so that others would not have to experience the social isolation with which they were all too well acquainted.

It was through City Year South Africa that I met the incredible Simangele "Smash" Shoyisa. From the township of Soweto in Johannesburg, Smash was a Service Leader with City Year, who expressed to me the joy she felt serving her community, whom, she said, was her source of resilience. Even though she identified as a lesbian, her parents and elders in their Muslim community supported her. They gave her the space to be herself. In a township community where many lesbian women were ostracized and even violently attacked, she wanted to pass on the care and support she had received—rounding the circle by helping isolated younger people to cultivate their own resilience.

"It is very satisfying work," she told me when she came to Toronto to participate in our first Global Symposium in 2014. "Especially when we walk into a school and the kids come running to us and give us a hug. They hardly do that with their teachers. We realized that the kids were connecting with us in a different way. They don't have anyone else to talk to, so we make it easy for them to come to us and speak to us." She recounted: "It was moving, but that's when we started to realize that they were suffering isolation and that we were bringing them connectedness."[7]

Nelson Mandela's influence on the City Year South Africa program cannot be overstated. Often referred to by his Thembu clan name "Madiba" out of respect, Daylene Van Buuren—who is executive director and a former service leader herself—said this of Mandela: "Madiba was a symbol of change in our society. Madiba taught us. He came out saying 'How do we restore? How do we rebuild? How do we connect?'" In reflecting on our collective responsibility to drive change, Daylene says, "I think for us and in our responsibility as the younger generation, I need to do more to help others feel connected and be in a community where we can make a difference."[8]

Asked about why she was determined to round the circle and build belonging for isolated youth in her community, Smash echoes Daylene's sentiments: "If not me, then who? If I don't do it, then who else would do it?" She went on, "I think a lot of how we grew up is that it takes a village to raise a child. If I don't do it, then that means it's going to be a vicious cycle that we will be unable to break. So why do I do what I do? It's because I want to inspire the next coming generation to do good. If you have something to offer, offer."[9] Smash has since left City Year and continues to courageously fight for LGBTQIA+ rights in very tough spaces.

City Year South Africa demonstrates to us the power of young leaders, and the force with which they can drive positive, inclusive change for their communities. We need more of this as we build a world where everyone belongs.

NACOSA AND YABONGA

NETWORKING HIV AND AIDS COMMUNITY OF SOUTH AFRICA (NACOSA), another partner of the Social Connectedness Programme, is a group that has built a network of more than 1,900 civil society organizations in southern Africa. One of NACOSA's implementing partners, Yabonga, is entrusted with running an incredible initiative called Circles of Support. Through this program, children who have been badly neglected or abused are taken to a safe and nurturing environment and provided with proper care and support for a set period of time. At the same time, the parents and guardians are offered multiple practical training sessions. They learn how to better care for their children, and build up the capacity to provide what their children need, both emotionally and socially.

Circles of Support is a place for parents to receive support from staff but, also, from each other. This program breaks negative cycles of abuse by providing compassionate care and healing for entire families—both neglected children and their parents simultaneously. Indeed, this program ultimately replaces malevolent circles with circles of belonging. As Yabonga's program manager, Siphokazi Hlati tells me, the Circles of Support are inherently about "belonging and connectedness."[10]

As we look to support families and build belonging in countries around the world, let us take a page out of the Circles of Support book. Protect the vulnerable, always, and couple that with education and programming so that families can become strong enough to stay together. This is how we round the circle, and support families in bringing forth compassion from one generation to the next.

OTHANDWENI GOGOS

THE OTHANDWENI FAMILY CARE CENTRE, located in Soweto, is a place for children who have been neglected, abandoned, abused, or orphaned. Othandweni runs the Granny Programme, which trains volunteer childcare workers—older women affectionately referred to as Gogos—and matches them with a young child up to the age of seven who is living at the Centre.[11]

Five days a week, each Gogo spends two hours a day with each of her assigned children. They often develop a deep one-on-one connection, rooted in the stimulation, support, love, and warmth that are often missing in residential care. This type of caregiving is reciprocal, which is a core tenet of belonging—the children benefit from improved development and functioning, the Gogos feel a strong sense of purpose in their work, and both the children and the Gogos benefit from powerful social connection.

Evidence from a program evaluation shows that this practice provides skills and opportunities for children to build meaningful social connections—with other children, with sector practitioners, and with their own families. It also helps children in residential care develop greater self-confidence and self-esteem—essential to combating social isolation and building toward belonging.

The late Patience Mokgadi, one of the Gogos, explained it to me this way: "You find children who have experienced such social disconnect that upon your first interaction with the child they are withdrawn, sad, blank, and unemotional. Social interaction or social connectedness that is consistent and planned is very important in a child's life, especially in those early stages because children begin to learn that kind of behavior. They open up. They become trusting, especially if it's done on a consistent level with an elderly person. I've seen children blossom from when they came in initially to be a child that me or you find at home."[12]

The Othandweni Granny Programme teaches us that connection is key for a child's development, and that love and attention can go a long way in setting all of our kids up for a healthy, emotionally-resilient future where they can nurture belonging for themselves and others.

THE SOCIAL CONNECTEDNESS PROGRAMME IS, at its heart, about building belonging and social resilience so that even in the most difficult of times, people are not isolated—instead, they can pull together to overcome extreme challenges. I've been struck in particular by the stories I've heard throughout the COVID-19 pandemic. Our partner organizations on the ground in southern Africa are doing absolutely lifesaving work to support their communities. There is unity, there is sense of purpose, there is connection, and there is no doubt in my mind that the seeds planted before the pandemic via the Social Connectedness Programme have played a role in mitigating the devastating impacts of the pandemic for African families. While it's been difficult to gather people together, organizations are still finding ways to connect, both with the people in their communities and with other Social Connectedness leaders—indeed, caring for the caregivers. They've developed incredible social resilience over the years, and they are innovating to deliver the programming that so many rely on.

Ikusasalethu—founded by Joey Monane, whom we met earlier, and which roughly translates to "Our Future"—runs a number of important programming initiatives for the community. Their work has only intensified during the pandemic. One of their programs is the Gogo/Khulu initiative, which provides seniors with both psychological and physical assistance, including help with bathing, getting medicines, and accessing grants as needed. Ikusasalethu is continuing its important work of caring for these Gogos in a time of greater isolation, and doing even more to support people experiencing homelessness. Program officers are getting people into camps, into shelters, into rehabilitation programs, and even reuniting families after decades apart. Even in these challenging times, Ikusasalethu is drawing on the capacity they've already built to take care of their community. As we discussed earlier, we need to show up *early* and *often*, laying the groundwork of belonging in the good times so that we can pull together in the bad times.

Lynette Mudekunye is the head of programs at the Regional Psychosocial Support Initiative (REPSSI), another one of the Social Connectedness Programme's partner organizations. REPSSI provides psychosocial help for young people in thirteen countries across eastern and southern Africa. They take a holistic approach to their work, applying integrative psychological, economic, and social support to those in need. In conversation, Lynette mentioned to me that COVID-19 has brought about new challenges, like children not being in school and those living in poverty losing the ability to interact with others in their community, which had provided connection and purpose for so many.

Of these unprecedented times, Lynette asks, "How do we find new ways of connecting across the physical distancing, across the need to wear a mask and not show your expressions, all of those things? And how do you make wearing a mask an act of social solidarity, rather than an act of social division?" But she sees hope on the horizon, and unity is key. "That's been a major message of all of our presentations in this time of COVID: We will not win by ourselves. We need to come together across different divides in new ways, in different ways."[13] REPSSI shows us the importance of championing unity and connection when crises threaten to divide us.

Rex Molefe, whom we met earlier, currently serves as director and trustee at Motheo, a South Africa–based public benefit trust that offers direct services and trains practitioners in the field of early childhood development. Through his work at Motheo, Rex and his team help children to understand that they are, in fact, "appreciated," worthy of respect and connection. He wants to ensure that young people are empowered—not through violence as he was—but rather through community.

Rex told me that Motheo continues to run programs and activities related to social connectedness during the pandemic. "Advocacy is not an event," he said. "It's something that is on an ongoing basis. Even now, during the middle of COVID-19 and in this place now locked down, we are continuously advocating that early child development be taken seriously." He framed the rationale beautifully: "We are running various campaigns, trying to bring communities together because we believe that community itself, when it is united, can become a powerful resource to fight anything."[14]

THE SOCIAL CONNECTEDNESS PROGRAMME will only grow from here, and the question, in my mind, is this: How do we expand from applying a targeted lens of social isolation and connection, to applying a broader lens of belonging? As I've outlined in this book, recognizing a Right to Belong has the potential to drive massive change in our communities. How do we continue to shine a light outward, highlighting and supporting the incredible work already happening in countries around the world? As we look at challenges like the COVID-19 recovery, climate change, and enduring political and social unrest, how can we expand the scope of the Social Connectedness Programme to build belonging for everyone?

To this end, I foresee the Samuel Centre for Social Connectedness (SCSC) taking on an even bigger role within our partnership with the Social Connectedness Programme. We are working in collaboration with our partners to develop community-driven research, guided by co-creative and Indigenous research methodologies and shared values.

In recent years, SCSC has done important cross-sector work on belonging, particularly through our Social Connectedness Fellowship Program. Seeking out methods of adaptive, hands-on learning, the Fellowship formed around the idea of cultivating partnerships between promising scholars and innovative practitioners and organizations, known as Fellowship partners. The Fellowship partner programs—many of which can be found throughout this book, including Human Rights Watch, Misipawistik Cree Nation, the Friendship Bench, Special Olympics International, the Harvard Project on Disability, and The Stop—are a core element of the Fellowship, working tirelessly to support SC Fellows in their research. Social Connectedness Fellows research a diverse range of topics, from disability rights and food security to climate change adaptation—topics tied together with the golden thread of belonging. For many SC Fellows, it is their first opportunity to engage deeply with topics beyond a traditional classroom setting, and to migrate beyond the limits of academia and into real-world practice. Many of the SC Fellows have continued on to become key members of the SCSC research team. Their important work will only intensify and expand in scope in the years ahead, cultivating a rich atmosphere within which SCSC can further support the essential work of the Social Connectedness Programme.

What started as a meaningful conversation with Graça Machel and Nelson Mandela twenty years ago has grown into something bigger than I ever could have imagined. Joey Monane told me recently, "Social connectedness, it's ubuntu. You are taking everybody with. You're not selfish. Ubuntu means sharing."[15] That's what we're doing with these partnerships—bringing others with us as we build our lives and lift our communities up through the power of belonging.

IN THESE PAGES, I've offered up the Right to Belong as a theory of change. As a way of building the kind of future we not only want, but so desperately need.

Kathleen Raine has deeply influenced my thinking on this topic over the years. As I said at the outset of this book, I often find myself returning to one core idea that permeated our conversations: There is crisis all around us, people have been left behind, and our society must be woken up to what it has forgotten.

It is suitable given Kathleen's status as a scholar of William Blake that this notion of "waking people up to what they have forgotten" couples with a famous quote from Blake himself. In *The Marriage of Heaven and Hell*, Blake wrote, "If the doors of perception were cleansed everything would appear to man as it is, infinite. For man has closed himself up, till he sees all things through narrow chinks of his cavern."[16]

This idea has spoken to me my whole life. It forces me to reflect on how the things we see as separate and without overlap—me versus you, them versus us, good versus bad—are not mutually exclusive. Humans do not exist at just two ends of the pole; rather, we all exist along various points of the same cyclical continuum. We all have good and bad within us, and we are all connected to the best and worst of humanity; we all have the innate capability to create a world that reflects the best of us. As Kathleen said, "We have created our nightmare world in the image of our ideologies; but with the awakening of our humanity we will see a different world, and create a different world."[17]

Indeed, we've lost sight of the fact that our survival, our happiness, the very notion of being human has never truly been about *me*, but always, rather, about *us*. Our relationships, our interconnectedness, our future has always been rooted in interdependence. I count on you, and you count on me. Your worst day affects me, and my worst day affects you.

Margaret Atwood wrote to me once,

In a We society you are rarely alone/
In a Me society you are rarely "with."[18]

We must remember that our responsibilities to ourselves and our responsibilities to others are not, in fact, different—they are part of the *same* responsibility.

I think I understand horses—and they don't judge me.

GEORGINA MATON, EQUESTRIAN ATHLETE,
SPECIAL OLYMPICS GB[19]

As a competitive horseback rider, I spent a lot of my childhood on my family's farm in Milton, Ontario. I loved tending to the ponies and horses, spending endless hours with them in the stables and out in the fields. They were my most trusted friends, my closest confidants—and they never judged. In many ways, I had an idyllic childhood. But don't be fooled—my parents ran a tight ship. With several brooms strategically placed around the barn, my father would harp on me and my siblings the responsibilities that came with such a great privilege, and sweeping up the stables was one of them. The brooms were stiff, and my hands were too small to get a good grip, but my dad told us, "If you don't do the sweeping up at the end of the day, does the work just disappear? No. It's still there the next morning, and it becomes someone else's problem." Throughout my life, at various points, I've thought back on this lesson from my father, always fondly.

Just because we ignore our responsibilities doesn't make them go away.

I've reflected on this a lot lately as we're confronted with the stark, complex, seemingly insurmountable challenges of our time.

As we've discussed throughout this book, we're pillaging our planet for profit, and a century of intense environmental destruction is coming home to roost. Entire communities and Nation Island states are sinking into the ocean. The inherent rights of Indigenous peoples are still violated in the name of the national economic interest. Wars, conflict, and climate change have driven the refugee crisis to a breaking point. Inequality is rampant, and the "haves" seem increasingly indifferent to the "have-nots." Shameless othering and blatant hatred have worked their way into the dominant discourse. We've never been more connected in terms of sheer technical connectivity, and yet we're lonelier than ever.

The fissures are widening.

The pressure is building.

We need to change, and we need to change now.

We must reimagine a world where people really and truly belong. But how?

Here's the really simple answer: We need to do the work. Not alone, but together.

Looking at the world around us and tolerating instead of engaging, choosing to believe that it's not our fight, ignoring the impetus to act . . . that's exactly what my father was talking about when we were kids. If you shirk your responsibilities, you're leaving twice as much for the next person. If we all—every one of us—play a role, alter our behavior, and think about belonging in our interactions, we can begin to turn the tide on the myriad challenges facing this generation and those that follow. While it may seem daunting, we've learned some important lessons about what belonging is, what happens when we do it wrong, but perhaps more importantly, what happens when we do it right.

Kluane Adamek, Yukon Regional Chief at the Assembly of First Nations (AFN), and the youngest regional chief in the AFN's history, guest-lectured in one of my classes at McGill. She told my students that belonging "is about how you show up for your community."[20] She couldn't have been more on point. In the pages of this book, together we've met extraordinary people and organizations who are showing up every day. They're doing the work of building belonging. We can do the work, too.

YOU MAY BE ASKING, *How can I be an agent of change? What can I do, right now, to build belonging?* But the better question to ask is "What can *we* do to build belonging?"

The Right to Belong is a movement for everybody, and one where people of all identities have a role to play. Perhaps you're a member of the LGBTQIA+ community in a country where people are persecuted for their sexual orientation and gender identity. You could be living on the streets, dealing with intersectional struggles around addiction, poverty, mental health, and gender. Maybe you've been institutionalized because of Alzheimer's, or are serving time in a correctional institution and feeling like belonging isn't something you can give or receive. Perhaps you are a girl or a woman in a country where your dignity and most basic rights are not recognized or respected, or someone living with a disability who is struggling to find meaningful employment or equitable access to healthcare. Maybe you don't have a country to call home, the safety to freely practice your religion, or are oppressed on the basis of the color of your skin.

We are multidimensional beings with so much to give, and deserving of so much from this life and the societies we inhabit.

Even if you don't feel whole, remember that you *belong*, you deserve *compassion*, and with the right support systems, you can help build belonging for others, too. If we recognize the basic premise behind a universal Right to Belong, we all have a right to inherent belonging and responsibility to honor this right for everyone, not tomorrow, but *today*. Take up space and embrace who you are, because it gives you a window into the world that perfection never could.

We build belonging along four core dimensions: connection to people, place, power, and purpose. This 4Ps framework is about interconnectedness; they are most effective when working in tandem toward the common goal. Our job now is to turn these dimensions—and the lessons we've learned in this book—into tangible outcomes for ourselves and others. What your journey toward belonging looks like will be up to you. Maybe upholding belonging means committing to a solemn purpose, or doing things with greater intention, listening more, increasing awareness, forging stronger connections, or asking the Healing Question like Parzival and leading a life rich in compassion for the people around you. Whatever you do, you can use the four dimensions of belonging as your guideposts to navigate this world and your place and interactions within it.

AS WE'VE DISCUSSED THROUGHOUT THE BOOK, belonging manifests perhaps most obviously through our relationship with people. We are social beings, and we require connection with one another to survive. Fostering belonging requires, among many other facets, a baseline recognition of one another's humanity. A baseline recognition that we are all multidimensional, complicated, and have diverse gifts and abilities. To build a world in which we all belong, we must meet people where they are, and ensure that we are building relationships rooted in reciprocity—sometimes we will give, at other times, we will receive, but the important thing is that we continue to grow and nurture those relationships, ensuring that the circle of belonging is never static but, instead, moving constantly.

Take inspiration from the work of Radosveta Stamenkova, who has spent years caring for and connecting with those who are vulnerable and isolated. Rada is the executive director of the Bulgarian Family Planning and Sexual Health Association (BFPA), a nonprofit organization based in Bulgaria and the Balkans with a focus on sexual and reproductive health, peer education, and preventive health for marginalized groups. She talks about the importance of walking toward those who differ from us in mutual respect and in recognition of our basic, shared humanity—she puts this principle into practice through her work at the local level with members of the Romani community, also known as Roma, a highly persecuted minority group, particularly within Europe, and young people at risk. On overcoming social isolation, Rada tells me, "If we want integration, if we want communities to live together, all the communities have to make steps towards the other. We all have to walk to the others, not to stay and to wait for the other people to come to you."[21]

We also see this common element of belonging—recognizing the humanity of all people—in the work of Juan Manuel Santos, former president of Colombia. During his presidency, President Santos successfully ended the decades-long conflict between the Colombian government and the Revolutionary Armed Forces of Colombia (FARC). Awarded the Nobel Peace Prize for his role in the peace process, President Santos told me recently about the sage advice given to him by a former army commander: "He said, 'We are Colombians, we're human beings, and military honor is not destroying your enemy, but beating your adversary and, therefore, lead the war with that in mind and then lead the peace with that in mind.'"[22] President Santos saw the common humanity in the FARC and treated them with corresponding dignity.

I first met President Santos while I was researching at Oxford, and his humanity shone through. I saw in him a leader who had incredible grace and self-awareness—features that undoubtedly influenced his style of leadership and approach to governance. Indeed, he shows us that respect for humanity is not limited to a one-on-one personal interaction between family members, or neighbors. Rather, it's powerfully scalable, and has the ability to change geopolitics and the world as we know it.

The eternal reciprocity of tears.

WILFRED OWEN[23]

DEREK BLACK WAS BORN into one of America's most prominent white supremacist families. His father was the founder of Stormfront, arguably the biggest hate website on the Internet, with more than 300,000 registered users. His mother was once married to David Duke, perhaps the most notorious "white nationalist" in the United States, who became Derek's godfather and an important mentor. By the time Derek was nineteen, he had founded a Stormfront website for young people, hosted his own radio show, and become a member of the Republican Party committee in Palm Beach County, Florida. He was considered part of a vanguard of white supremacists who were committed to leaving the fringes of society and infiltrating mainstream politics. With his skills as an orator, family connections, and zealous ideology, Derek came to be known in white supremacist circles as "the heir."

Derek attended university at the notably left-leaning New College of Florida, where his identity was quickly found out and he became a social pariah on campus. Matthew Stephenson was determined to change Derek's hateful views through connection, not ostracization. Matthew was the only Orthodox Jewish student on campus, and he hosted weekly Shabbat dinners for a diverse group of mostly non-Jewish students. One week, Matthew invited Derek to attend. "One of the most central concepts that was drilled into me growing up was the concept of human dignity," Matthew explained. "That I have the ability and the right to disagree with people, to protest against what they're doing, but I don't have the right to treat somebody without human dignity."[24]

Derek, perplexed by the invite and show of kindness, decided to show up—that first night, then every week. At these dinners, friendships were slowly and cautiously built, Derek had his views respectfully and methodically challenged, and, over time, Derek publicly disavowed his white supremacist views and defected from the movement his parents had helped to build. All of this happened because Matthew Stephenson extended care to someone he vehemently disagreed with. Caregiving can take many forms, and it needn't take place between agreeable parties. There is incredible power in extending care and compassion to those who hold hate in their hearts. By treating all people with inherent dignity, we forge connections through respect, dialogue, and the creation of spaces of belonging.

Indeed, we see similar values at work in the policies inspired by the late Jo Cox, British Member of Parliament who was widely known as a passionate advocate for tackling the pervasive issue of loneliness and for her powerful message at the time of Brexit: "We are far more united and have far more in common than that which divides us."[25] After her assassination, the Jo Cox Foundation was established in her memory. In 2017, the Foundation organized the first Great Get Together—a celebration for people across the UK to gather, form new community connections, and honor Jo's message of unity and inclusion. Jo's advocacy also laid the groundwork for the UK's first Minister for Loneliness in 2018, a role tasked with gaining a better understanding of the widespread issue of loneliness and developing policy solutions in turn. Japan has recently followed suit with their own Minister for Loneliness.

If we root our interactions with people in the common element of recognizing one another's humanity, we must also look at the intersections between people and place. Our connection to place happens through our relationship with the lands on which we live. On this, I take lessons from the Eden Project.

The Eden Project is located at an exhausted clay pit site in Cornwall, UK. It's since been rejuvenated with lush biodiversity and is home to several community-based initiatives that seek to reconnect people with nature. Perhaps its most well-known event is the Big Lunch—the largest annual community picnic across the UK, with on average six million people participating each year. During the pandemic, the Big Lunch allowed for hybrid online and in-person convening—nine million people participated virtually or at a safe distance. Known as an event where people can create friendships and combat loneliness, Peter Stewart, executive director, also describes it as an opportunity for people to "make positive local connections in their communities."[26] The Eden Project shows us how people can transform a place, and then that place can, in turn, transform people.

Place is so central to our identities because it, in many ways, shapes us and makes us who we are. If we nurture the relationships we have with the places we call home and encourage people to develop strong connection to place, we can build belonging for ourselves and those around us. That's precisely what we're doing with the Common Threads program of the Samuel Centre for Social Connectedness. One of my former McGill students and subsequent colleagues, Jessica Farber, observed a few years ago that asylum seekers were disconnected from the larger Montreal community. Later that same year, Common Threads was born, with Jessica taking on the role of its first program manager.

Engaging in research, storytelling, awareness building, and outreach, the aim of the Common Threads program is to create a positive narrative around forced migration and ease the social isolation felt by asylum seekers upon arrival. Through weekly Welcome Sessions, our program provides newcomers to Montreal with access to resettlement resources like housing information and language classes, while also fostering discussion about neighborhood events and community festivals. The goal is to help newcomers transition from Canada as *host* country to Canada as *home* country. Since the start of the Welcome Sessions, we have welcomed more than 1,200 newcomers and developed a strong volunteer base of 150 people and counting.

Connecting through these sessions helps newcomers gain a more intimate understanding of their new home through the collective knowledge shared by local residents, and helps volunteers develop a nuanced understanding of different cultures, backgrounds, and the realities of forced migration. What's more, many former newcomers are also able to share their own experiences and stories from when they first arrived in Montreal, developing special relationships of support with newly arrived participants, too. Banji Oguntayo from Nigeria has said, "We have become like a family."[27] By extending compassion and asking the Healing Question, we're building belonging for people in our community.

Power—the third core dimension of belonging—comes from being able to exert agency and participate meaningfully in the decision-making structures that govern us. Canadian-based nonprofit FORA: Network for Change is one such example of an organization engaged in the crucial work of connecting people to power. Through their program Girls on Boards, they provide women aged eighteen to twenty-five with leadership training, and ultimately, support participants in joining boards of directors for various organizations around the country. Women, particularly those of marginalized backgrounds, have faced a long history of exclusion from positions of power—this is an issue that FORA addresses, by empowering women to advocate for themselves and by helping to place those women in positions of power.[28]

Earlier we met Julianne Holt Lunstad, a professor and researcher whose work focuses on the long-term health effects of social isolation and loneliness. In discussing how we can empower people to build belonging, she told me recently, "What any individual can do, I would say, is to support others. There's so much research on social support. By supporting others, helping others, you can actually help yourself. Individuals can approach this from a sense of empowerment. You don't need to wait for someone else to do something. Anyone can do it."[29]

However, empowerment is just one part of the power equation—it must be followed by the ability to set agendas and shape outcomes. Dr. Michael

Stein is visiting professor at the Harvard Law School and the co-founder and executive director of the Harvard Law School Project on Disability (HPOD). He is an expert on disability law and policy and a powerful self-advocate who has worked with organizations advocating for people living with disabilities, notably championing the United Nations Convention on the Rights of Persons with Disabilities. When we spoke about how to drive structural change, Michael pointed to participatory justice, which he described as "being part of decisions about you, being part of decisions about your world, is to me part of the rights to inclusion, right to belonging."[30]

The Harvard Law School Project on Disability has been driving such structural change in many ways, though one particularly notable example is their work as Samuel Centre for Social Connectedness Fellowship partners, where, alongside the organization Massachusetts Advocates Standing Strong (MASS), they have been working on the issue of self-advocacy. During the 2021 Social Connectedness Fellowship, disability rights advocate and fellow Chester Finn, conducted research with HPOD and MASS to support people living with disabilities in gaining the legal power to make their own decisions, a process that is integral to both reducing isolation and connecting people to power.

As Chester wrote, "When one group takes control over another group, you create isolation and people are cut off. You want to give people an opportunity, and that's what Supported Decision-Making will do. It will give people independence, freedom, and the support to create a life of their own."[31]

We see participatory justice at work in the dominant, youth-driven movements of today—think of the global climate marches catalyzed by Greta Thunberg, Autumn Peltier, and other young climate activists, or the crucial advocacy work being done by Black Lives Matter. Today's young people are speaking up, taking leadership roles, and using their voices and agency to demand better outcomes where previous generations and systems have failed. In building movements and effecting policies, young citizens are creating space for participatory justice and the realization of long-withheld power.

Bill Drayton, the brilliant and passionate founder of social entrepreneurship organization Ashoka: Innovators for the Public, once said to me,

"Imagine when everyone is a changemaker and everyone is helping everyone else be that to the maximum extent." "The greatest gift," he went on, "is giving people the power to give, to imagine a different life of giving, of being powerful, of expressing love and respect in action."[32] Each year, the innovative work of Ashoka Fellows addresses global challenges, influences policy and seeks to bring about systems change through the ethos of "Everyone a Changemaker."

Acknowledging everyone's power and agency is at the heart of Bitty & Beau's Coffee. Amy Wright and her husband, Ben, are the proud parents of four children—the two youngest, Bitty and Beau, have Down syndrome. The Wrights founded Beau's Coffee in 2016 in Wilmington, North Carolina. Since renamed Bitty & Beau's Coffee at Beau's request to include his younger sister's name, the business now has multiple locations across the US. Fundamental to their operation is the employment of people with intellectual and developmental disabilities, providing jobs and creating space for young people with disabilities to be accepted and valued. As of writing, Bitty & Beau's employs 120 people with disabilities, providing opportunities for only empowerment but also purpose to so many—dimensions of belonging that we all deserve.

Purpose, you'll remember, refers to our ability to create meaning in our lives and share our gifts with the world. For many of us, it's the answer to life's big "Why?" Some people find their purpose through faith. Some find purpose in serving others. Others find purpose in pursuing a goal or walking a particular life path with intention.

Waukomaun Pawis is Ojibwe from Wasauksing First Nation and the Indigenous education coordinator at Connected North, a program that fosters student engagement and enhanced education outcomes in remote Indigenous communities. He spoke with me recently about the role of the program in helping youth find belonging through purpose. "Everyone in Creation has a gift, has something to provide, has a role in society, has a role in Creation," Waukomaun told me. "And so that's something that I want the youth to know, when we connect, that we have to help them find their purpose in life, give them these experiences to learn and to grow, no matter what they do."[33]

If you want to make the world a better place
Take a look at yourself, and then make a change
MICHAEL JACKSON, "MAN IN THE MIRROR"[34]

FINDING OUR PURPOSE is easier said than done. It takes an incredible amount of self-reflection, but when we find what we're meant to do, and who we're meant to be, the result is something powerful. I think of Quincy Jones and how he not only found his purpose in life, but has helped others discover their purpose and come to belonging through music.

Quincy Jones treats everyone around him with unconditional love, dignity, and respect. I've known him for more than twenty years, starting around the time my dad passed away. Quincy has been a beloved friend, cherished mentor, and true exemplar of belonging in my life ever since. He's also the only person who has ever made me feel cool and hep, even though it is widely known that I really can't hang, no matter how hard I try. Whether taking a group of youth from South Central LA to South Africa to find common ground together, bringing mayors from all over the world to Rome for a musical celebration to highlight the unifying role that cities can play in peacebuilding, and making sure that music education, including "America's classical music"—jazz—is taught in schools, Quincy is the builder of his own community, and he builds on a global scale.

Over the years he's told me the story of his incredible life, including the night he found his purpose through music. One night in 1944 when he was eleven years old, Quincy snuck into the armory near his family's house in Bremerton, Washington, close to Seattle. A group of what Quincy called "baby gang-bangers," they were there to vandalize the space and steal a fresh shipment of lemon meringue pies. He broke into a small room and found himself standing in front of a tiny stage and an old spinet piano. When he put his hands on those ivory keys, he says it was like a higher power talking to him, showing him that from that day forward, his purpose in life was tied to making music. In that moment, he discovered belonging in a world where belonging was scarce. Quincy went on to build a genre-spanning career eight decades and counting, as one of the most skillful composers and producers of all time. He's thrived and found purpose in the challenge of creation. He told me once, "Music is so subjective, honey. And everybody's different. But that's what connects us though. Same twelve notes for 710 years. What's that mean? It's a challenge, and you gotta figure out a way to make it yours."[35] I see his philosophy of life embodied in what he calls "global gumbo," an homage to the famed Creole dish, combining dozens of ingredients from different places to create a sumptuous stew, a world where every person is celebrated not in spite of, but precisely because of, the diversity of the one human race to which we all belong.

Over the years, Quincy has helped countless young musicians discover their purpose and belonging through music too. In 2011, he founded Global Gumbo as a mentoring program that brings together promising musicians from around the world to showcase cutting edge music and its deep roots. They are influenced by, and infused with, many different cultural and historical traditions, no matter where they come from. It's a purposeful approach that refuses to silo creativity into specific categories, instead taking its inspiration from a mosaic approach to live music performance, whereby an infinite number of individual and seemingly disparate voices and instruments connect to make a beautiful sound that didn't exist before. While he is known for pushing talented individuals outside their comfort zones in their drive towards greatness, Quincy truly cares for each artist as a whole person, embracing all their gifts, fully supporting them along the way as they pursue their purpose in life, not only in music. I think that's where the magic comes from. "You need your booty kicked sometimes to change, don't you? You gotta make mistakes," he said to me, "a lot of them. You gotta take a lot of chances though. You can't be afraid of an F if you want an A."

QUINCY EXUDES UNCONDITIONAL LOVE and compassion. He's magnetic, and, over our decades of friendship, I've always felt a deep sense belonging in his presence. Quincy has always made me feel seen. When he looks me in the eye and says he believes in me, I know he means it to his core.

Likewise, dear reader, I see *you* and I believe in *you*. You know that the dimensions of people, place, power, and purpose can work together to build a better world—a world in which we all belong. You *know* how you can contribute, because you *know* your intrinsic gifts and abilities. We've met some incredible people in this book who are putting in the work. Learn from them and draw inspiration from them as you chart your own path toward belonging—for yourself and for the world around you.

MORE THAN A DECADE AGO, I attended a roundtable in New York City hosted by Quincy. A dozen or so people had gathered to learn more about his Listen Up Foundation, dedicated to the power of music to change the world. We were at the outset of the meeting, going around the table one at a time, and everyone said who they were. The default structure for these kinds of introductions generally tends to be something along the lines of, "*My name is . . .*" and "*I am . . .*". That's exactly what I did, and the other participants introduced themselves in a similar fashion—name, title, and organization.

Then we got to visionary jazz musician and composer Herbie Hancock. He paused for a moment, then said, "My name is Herbie Hancock, and I am a human being."

Silence washed over the room, followed by smiles and nods of profound acknowledgment. I was floored. So simple, but really, this was the most important feature of who he was.

This idea is echoed in Oliver Sacks's collection of essays penned before the end of his life. In *Gratitude*, Sacks spoke of holding profound thanks simply because he was "a sentient being, a thinking animal on this beautiful planet."[36]

Oliver Sacks was—like Herbie Hancock is—a person. Full stop. At the end of the day, what else matters?

I decided to try this myself at the next roundtable event I attended. "My name is Kim Samuel, and I am a human being." Silence again, but then quiet snickering. "That's funny, Kim. But really, what do you do?" implored the meeting chairperson. "Okay, my name is Kim Samuel, I'm from Canada, and I run the Samuel Family Foundation." I felt pretty silly and frankly, disappointed, but I left that meeting determined to push this conversation forward.

Simply being human *is* enough. It's enough for the world around us to care about what we want, or need, or think. We should all have a platform to speak—we shouldn't need titles or status to sit at the table.

We exist, we are human, and therefore, we belong.

> *Nothing exists for its own sake,*
> *but for a harmony greater than itself which includes it.*

—WENDELL BERRY, *STANDING BY WORDS*[37]

IT HASN'T BEEN THAT LONG since we understood our place in the universe.

As the Greek philosopher Aristotle, who advanced the geocentric model of the universe, claimed, "The latter is matter, the former is the essence of the composition."[38] Aristotle and fellow Greek philosopher Ptolemy believed that the Earth was at the center of the universe, with the sun, moon, stars, and planets all orbiting around us. Their theories on geocentrism and the geostatic model dominated for centuries.

It's no surprise, then, that a revised theory of the cosmos articulated by sixteenth-century Polish mathematician and astronomer Copernicus was met with incredible fury when released. In his 1543 magnum opus, *De revolutionibus orbium coelestium* (*On the Revolutions of the Heavenly Spheres*), Copernicus proclaimed, "The Sun is appropriately called the lantern of the universe. As though seated on a royal throne, the Sun governs the family of planets revolving around it,"[39] orbiting in what Copernicus called "The Great Circle."

The Copernican theory of heliocentrism rested on three principal ideas:

1. There is no center of all the celestial spheres.
2. The Earth is not the center of the universe. It is the center toward which heavy things tend.
3. All the spheres revolve about the Sun, as if the Sun were the center of the universe.[40]

THE NOTION THAT EARTH and the humans that inhabit it were not the center of everything was, at the time, blasphemous. Scholars refused to believe that while we were a part of a larger whole, we weren't the epicenter around which the rest of the universe calibrated itself.

The lesson for belonging, however, is exactly this: Whether we're talking about the cosmos, or human beings, or political structures, or belief systems, it is not the placement of things that matters most, but rather the interconnectedness. We needn't be perfect, we needn't be the best; it is enough that we are here, and that we belong, equally. We can and should learn to recognize different perspectives to our own as just that: different, but no less valid, since our thoughts and opinions are not the central anchor point against which all others must orbit.

A similar realignment of our thinking about our place in society will take time, too, but the outcome will be a better world in which belonging is fostered and upheld for everyone.

Copernicus was building on the groundwork that others had laid, long before his time; the Pythagoreans and ancient Greek astronomers, most notably Aristarchus. And it was not until the seventeenth-century Italian physicist and astronomer, Galileo Galilei, against the Catholic Church defended Copernicus's theory in his 1623 *Dialogue Concerning the Two Chief World Systems*, that the truth that we are not at the center of the universe came to be widely accepted.

Like Copernicus enlightening us to our true place in the universe, or like our friend Parzival contravening the prevailing social norms and customs by daring to ask the Healing Question of the King, the work of belonging takes a revolutionary reimagination of ancient truths. True progress often requires courageous conviction to challenge the structures and conventions that no longer serve us. The value of belonging has always been with us; is it our right from birth, it is at the very heart of our oldest stories and most fundamental beliefs. To paraphrase Kathleen Raine, we need only to wake up to what we have forgotten.

The future that we build will be the one that we imagine.

I see in Copernicus the same connection that I felt all those years ago sitting beneath the Sitka spruce, resting on its roots between the soil and the sky, enveloped by the grandeur of Creation.

We don't have to be the center of the universe; it is enough to be part of it.

It is enough that we belong.

Indeed, it is only everything.

IN GRATITUDE

I see myself as a passionate messenger of a powerful idea. Yet I'm only one of many messengers and this idea—*the Right to Belong*—has come through the wisdom of innumerable people over untold centuries. I offer my deepest gratitude to a long lineage of people who have championed the cause of belonging.

To Begin—In sharing my thanks to specific individuals here, I'll start with the two people who made this book possible: Dan Mandel, senior agent at Sanford J. Greenburger Associates, for embracing all the possibilities, and Jamison Stoltz, editorial director at Abrams Press, who believed in this book from the start and brilliantly guided me throughout the journey.

To The Extraordinarily Wise and Compassionate Human Beings who Comprise the Soul and Substance of this Book—the people who shared their myriad gifts through interviews and conversations with me over the past several years, including: Aakash Pawar, Agnes Binagwaho, Albert Marshall, Alex Beard, Alexandra Godfree, Alicia Bazzano, Amanda Klasing, Angel Hsu, Anita Nowak, Anne St. Pier, Annie Lennox, Banji Oguntayo, Becky Cook, Benjamin Haack, Bethany Brown, William Drayton, Bridget Sleap, Calvin Brook, Dr. Carl Hart, Caroline Casey, Catherine Martin, Cherie Nursalim, Crystal Williams, Dr. Daniel Palazuelos, Dasho Karma Ura, David St. Pier, Daylene Van Buuren, Dean Velentzas, Deborah Saucier, Diego

Zavaleta, Dikembe Mutombo, Dr. Dixon Chibanda, Dominic Richards, Don Tapscott, Eddie Barbanell, Elisha London, Emina Ćerimović, Emma Harries, Evan Constant, Fauziat Serunjogi, Geoff Cape, George Monbiot, Goldie Hawn, Graça Machel, Graeme Reid, Guillermo Penalosa, Hadiya Roderique, Hafsat Abiola, Hannerie White, Hilary Cottam, Ian Goldin, Ignace Nikwivuze, Jackie Bagwiza, James Charman, Jedidah Nabwangu, Jennifer Corriero, Jessica Posner Odede, Jimmy Vasquez, Joe Cramer, Joey Monane, John Helliwell, Joseph Kalt, Josina Z. Machel, Juan Manuel Santos, Judi Aubel, Julia Cleave, Julianne Holt-Lunstad, Kate Mulligan, Kateri Lucier-Laboucan, Kathy Calvin, Kennedy Odede, Kenneth Deer, Kenneth Roth, Kenryu Miyagi, Kevin Sullivan, Kim Boucher-Morin, Kimberley Brownlee, Regional Chief Kluane Adamek, Laura Pitter, Leah Blezard, Leigh Godbold, Liesel Ebersohn, Loretta Claiborne, Dr. Lori Plutchik, Lynette Mudekunye, Lynn Dean, Margaret Atwood, Maria Shriver, Dr. Marianna Strongin, Mark Williamson, Marlene Ogawa, Mary Jordan, Matthew Williams, Micah White, Dr. Michael Dooley, Michael Green, Michael Stein, Michelle Muschett, Dr. Mitch Besser, Mitch Holmes, MJ Gauthier, Morio Taira, Dr. Murali Doraiswamy, Musimbi Kanyoro, Natasha Karod, Nick Clegg, Nisreen Mustafa, Nujeen Mustafa, Nureddin Amro, Ovide Mercredi, Pamela Molina, Patrick Holden, the late Dr. Paul Farmer, Peggy Dulany, Quincy Jones, Rachel Kiddel-Monroe, Radosveta Stamenkova, Ralph Nilson, Ramaswami Balasubramaniam, Rehmah Kasule, Rex Molefe, Richard Dunne, Lord Richard Layard, Father Richard Rohr, Sabina Alkire, Sabrina Sassi, Sandra Bakatana, Sandra Thandi Twala, Satish Kumar, Ethan Sethu Xabanisa, Shantha Rau Barriga, Sierra Tasi-Baker, Simangele "Smash" Shoyisa, Siphokazi Hlati, Sophie Weldon, Stephen Kinnock, Sumiko Taira, Susan Aglukark, Susan Pinker, Suzanne Fortier, Tanya Woods, Timothy P. Shriver, Former Prime Minister Tshering Tobgay, Tyrell Ballantyne, Vandana Shiva, Vino Landry, Wade Davis, Waukomaun Pawis, Weeda Mehran, Wendell Berry, William Alford, Yoshihisa Shimabukuro, Zainab Salbi, and Zita Cobb.

To The Philosophers, Poets, Disrupters, Challengers, and Other Inspiring Forces in Writing a Book and in Life—the people with whom I've spent endless hours talking about what it means to feel lonely, isolated, included, and connected, in the quest of belonging. Including their wisdom and kindness, this book came to fruition:

Annie Lennox, who bestowed on us both the title of "non-fitters," thereby freeing me from the pressures of conformity, inspiring me to find my wings and soar.

Brittany Perreault, for contributing her brilliant sense of wit and words, for helping me to find magical threads, hone key messages and tighten my prose, and for encouraging me to tell my own story too.

Charles, Prince of Wales, a kindred spirit, for commiserating with me over the agony of the blank page, celebrating with me over the joy of the completed manuscript, and sharing his deep reverence for Mother Earth and all creatures great and small.

Cherie Nursalim, who has shown me, by her own example, how to lead with grit and grace, in equal measure, even though I am still working on it.

Diana and Barry Levinson, for standing by me with love and humor, at a time when everything was upside down. For Diana—special thanks for convincing me that I was a "creative" all along, and to Barry, for telling me that it was okay to write "long," and for teaching me about how to tell stories and pay close attention to history.

Emina Ćerimović, human rights defender and peace warrior, for being my brave and compassionate teacher without even knowing it.

Gabrielle Hughes, DPhil, a member of the Wampanoag Nation and specialist in cultural heritage law, for sharing her knowledge about Indigenous research methodologies and for being a skilled researcher and superb mentor on the research team.

Graça Machel, a phenomenal woman with an indomitable spirit, a compassionate leader, peace builder, and fierce advocate on behalf of children and women around the world, for inspiring me and for seeing me. And to Josina Machel, another phenomenal woman with an indomitable spirit, whose bravery inspires me every day of my life.

Gloria Jones, in loving memory, my wise, salt-of-the-earth Sister-Friend, who was a great listener and sage advisor, and with whom I enjoyed many long kitchen breakfasts while everyone else was sleeping, combined with an equal number of late nights talking, listening to music, dancing, and celebrating life . . . all the way up till ten PM, and once we even made it to midnight!

Hugh Hudson, for introducing me to Wilfrid Owen, and for making *Chariots of Fire* forty years earlier; when sitting alone in the back of a movie theatre somewhere in Florida, Eric Liddel looked out from the movie screen right into my eyes and asked, "Where does the power come from, to see the race to its end? From within." I knew in that moment that I had such power inside me, and that everything would turn out okay.

Jennifer Corriero, for her true partnership, for becoming my mentor years after I had been hers, and for never hesitating to dump a rainbow of sharpies in my lap, secure in the knowledge that color restores my equilibrium like nothing else.

Jo Ann Harris, who, when I lamented the daunting task of starting this book, gave me the very best advice, saying simply: "Write shit." So I did, for a while, and then things got better.

Justin Talbot-Zorn, for sharing his wisdom on structure and flow, policy and strategy, and for doing all of this while bringing his own book into the world. To Meredy Talbot-Zorn, for helping me set high goals and low goals at the outset. And to Tierra Talbot-Zorn, my youngest friend, for reminding me that unicorns are real.

Ken Roth, for encouraging me to envision "the right to belong" as a way of illuminating a constellation of neglected human rights, rather than as a right unto itself.

Linda Potter and Tim Shriver, life partners to each other, and lifelong friends to me. For Linda—special thanks for some of my best philosophical discussions at the dumpster behind Politics and Prose Bookstore. For Tim—special thanks for always reminding me about the power of faith, and for his wild and crazy dance moves from Montreal to Washington, Davos to PyeongChang, convincing me that anything is possible.

Loretta Claiborne, for her wisdom, resilience, and grit, for sharing the serious things and the silly things too, making me laugh out loud whenever we get together, and for always being in my corner.

Margaret Atwood, for encouraging me to dive deep into the flora and fauna of loneliness and social isolation, to honor the teachings from imaginary realms, to examine light and dark and all the shadows in between, and to ask myself what it means to be part of an intelligent species.

Marlene Ogawa, Soul Sister, for holding the firestone in her hands always, and for always passing it round the ever-widening circle, to ensure that nobody is ever left out.

Mary Jordan and Kevin Sullivan, for believing in this book when it was little more than the words "Bottom of the Well" scribbled on a scrap of paper and for impressing upon me the importance of knowing the rules of grammar in order to break them effectively.

Matt and Crystal Williams, for being my family in BC for a special honor, in DC for a special birthday, and for bringing many sweet surprises my way.

Matthew Bishop, for believing in my idea for a book years before I articulated it, and for caring enough to provide me with constructive criticism and sharp corrections.

Michael Hawes and Robin McLay, for supporting the work of building belonging, and to Fulbright Canada for giving me the opportunity to expand my commitment to diversity and social connectedness.

Michael Pawluch, for helping me overcome countless technical challenges that rivaled the mental block I had about math in high school.

Nelson Mandela, in loving memory, who once told me he had never been isolated, and in that moment, I knew what I would be doing for the rest of my life.

Ovide Mercredi, a member and former Chief of the Misipawistik Cree Nation and former National Chief of the Assembly of First Nations, for helping me to understand his story and to understand my own story better too, for being a warrior and a poet, and for teaching me there is no contradiction here.

Paul Farmer, in loving memory, visionary and exemplar of the hermeneutic of generosity, and especially for one beautiful conversation about why we plant trees.

Peggy Dulany, fellow seeker, for inspiring me in the inner work of building belonging and the outer work of bridging leadership, and for helping me to see how everything connects.

Quincy Jones, for showing me a kindness decades ago that blossomed into family, for being proud of me in everything I undertake, even the things that don't work out, and for christening me "Sammy J" in the secular sense—a cool, free spirit with rhythm who can hang and dance all night long, and with whom unconditional love is shared eternally.

Richard Jeo, conservationist, educator, and guide, for taking the time to help identify and learn about species of trees in the Great Bear Rainforest, especially one magical Sitka spruce I met on the banks of the Elcho River twenty years ago.

Rod Temperton, in loving memory, for making beautiful music and for teaching me to trust in the melody, because if the melody is right, the words will always follow.

Sabina Alkire, for showing the world that poverty is multidimensional and that the voices of the poor matter most in bringing about change, for being my academic mentor, and for guiding me in my own faith and belonging journey.

Saoirse Kennedy Hill, in loving memory, for her shrieks of joy when jumping off a deep-water pier, always the first, then others would follow; the pure heart that spirited her to play with any child who wasn't included—she always knew—and then the other kids would join in; and for sharing her pain with courage and compassion; she was fully alive.

Satish Kumar, for walking with me, literally, for the past twenty years, in places like the high cliffs of Devon and the Rosedale Ravine Trail in Toronto, with me always taking four steps to his two steps just to keep up. And while I am ever grateful for our unending walks on the same path, I am also grateful to Satish for helping me to find my own.

Shelley Ambrose, for keeping me anchored at home, helping me to tell Canadian stories, for her zany sense of humor, and for our shared passion for homemade deviled eggs and summer picnics all year long.

Tom Stoppard, who asked me to place the first page of the book in his hands when I was ready. Little did I know at the time that this would be the last page I would complete, more than four years later; I thank him for his wisdom.

Wendell Berry, for his generosity, and for telling me, "Don't be prescriptive," words I have held close in writing ever since; and to Tanya Berry, for her generosity, and for explaining the "why" of it all while driving me from Lanes Landing back to the airport, worlds away.

To The Research Team—the wise and compassionate activists, learners, and movement-builders, all of whom have become my teachers, including: Ben Haack, Carmella Munyuzangabo, Caroline Shriver, Celine Thomas, Chester Finn, Claire Chauvel, Dean Velentzas, Eddie Barbanel, Eloïse O'Carroll, Emma Harries, Fauziat Serunjogi, Gabrielle Hughes, Genevieve Westgate, Illinca Gradea, Jessica Farber, Julia Pinchuk, Leeda Mehran, Mayumi Sato, MJ Gauthier, Morgane Ollier, Orla Magill, Priya Nair, Rebecca McLeod, Rossen Lee, Samuel McQuillen, Simone Jean-Marie Renault, and Vino Landry.

NOTES

INTRODUCTION

1. Nelson Mandela in discussion with the author, May 5, 2002.
2. Nelson Mandela, *Long Walk to Freedom* (New York: Little, Brown, 1994), 390.
3. Erich Fromm, *The Fear of Freedom* (London: Routledge, 1942), 15.
4. Johann Sebastian Bach, Chorale Prelude: *Wachet auf, ruft uns die Stimme*, Cantata BWV 140 (Leipzig, 1731), based on the hymn of the same name by Philipp Nicolai (Unna,1598).
5. Kathleen Raine, *The Collected Poems of Kathleen Raine* (London: Faber & Faber, 2019), 99.
6. Kathleen Raine in discussion with the author, July 4, 2003.
7. Walt Whitman, *Leaves of Grass, The Original 1855 Edition*, ed. Mary Carolyn Waldrep (New York: Dover Publications, 2007/1855), 35.
8. Kwame Anthony Appiah, *Cosmopolitanism: Ethics in a World of Strangers* (London: W. W. Norton, 2010), xi.
9. Martin Luther King Jr., *Where Do We Go from Here: Chaos or Community?* (New York: Harper & Row, 1967), 37.
10. Abraham Maslow, "A Theory of Human Motivation," *Psychological Review* 50, no. 4 (1943): 370–396.
11. E. M. Forster, *Howard's End* (New Jersey: J. J. Piper Books, 2013/1910), 172.

CHAPTER 1

1. Ruth Tittensor, *Shades of Green: An Environmental and Cultural History of Sitka Spruce* (Oxford: Oxbow Press, 2016), 24–26.
2. Tittensor, *Shades of Green*, 498–500.
3. Tittensor, *Shades of Green*, 112–114.

4. Eugene Richard Atleo, *Principles of Tsawalk: An Indigenous Approach to Global Crisis* (Vancouver: UBC Press, 2011), 140.
5. Albert Marshall in discussion with the author, June 23, 2020.
6. Robin Wall Kimmerer, *Braiding Sweetgrass: Indigenous Wisdom, Scientific Knowledge, and the Teachings of Plants* (Minneapolis: Milkweed Editions, 2013), 20.
7. Albert Marshall in discussion with the author, June 23, 2020.
8. Albert Marshall in Cheryl Bartlett, Albert Marshall, and Murdena Marshall, "Two-Eyed Seeing and Other Lessons Learned Within a Co-learning Journey of Bringing Together Indigenous and Mainstream Knowledges and Ways of Knowing," *Journal of Environmental Studies and Sciences* 2 (2012): 335.
9. Albert Marshall in discussion with the author, June 23, 2020.
10. Albert Marshall in discussion with the author, June 23, 2020.
11. Albert Marshall in Lorraine Coulter, "Recap and Reflections on the 2019 Global Symposium," *News and Articles*, Samuel Centre for Social Connectedness, December 2019, https://www.socialconnectedness.org/recap-and-reflections-on-the-2019-global-symposium/.
12. Albert Marshall in discussion with the author, June 23, 2020.
13. Rebecca Adamson, "First Nations and the Future of the Earth," in *Original Instructions: Indigenous Teachings for a Sustainable Future*, ed. Melissa Nelson (New York: Simon and Schuster, 2008), 47.
14. Winona LaDuke, "Traditional Ecological Knowledge and Environmental Futures," *Colorado Journal of International Environmental Law and Policy* 5, no. 127 (1994): 79.
15. Wendell Berry, *What Are People For?: Essays* (New York: Catapult, 2010).
16. Kathy Calvin in discussion with the author, February 26, 2021.
17. Cherie Nursalim in discussion with the author, December 23, 2020.
18. Sabina Alkire in discussion with the author, September 18, 2018.
19. T. J. VanderWeele, "On the Promotion of Human Flourishing." *Proceedings of the National Academy of Sciences of the United States of America* 114 (2017): 8149.
20. Richard Layard in discussion with the author, July 20, 2020.
21. John Helliwell in discussion with the author, July 24, 2020.
22. Michael Green in discussion with the author, April 30, 2021.
23. Elizabeth Barclay, "Eating to Break 100: Longevity Diet Tips from the Blue Zones," National Public Radio, April 11, 2015, https://www.npr.org/sections/thesalt/2015/04/11/398325030/eating-to-break-100-longevity-diet-tips-from-the-blue-zones.
24. Rob Goss, "This Island Unlocked the Secret to Long Life—and Knows How to Get Through the Tough Times," *National Geographic Magazine*, October 12, 2020, https://www.nationalgeographic.com/travel/article/uncover-the-secrets-of-longevity-in-this-japanese-village#:~:text hrough%20tough%20

times- ,This%20island%20unlocked%20the%20secret%20to%20long%20
life%E2%80%94and%20knows,good%20food%20may%20be%20why.

25. Sumi-san in discussion with the author, July 31, 2018.

26. Yoshihisa Shimabukuro in discussion with the author, July 31, 2018.

27. Robert Waldiger, "What Makes a Good Life? Lessons from the Longest Study on Happiness," November 2015, TEDxBeaconStreet, https://www.ted.com /talks/robert_waldinger_what_makes_a_good_life_lessons_from_the_longest _study_on_happiness.

28. Dan Buettner, "Blue Zones: The Secrets of Living Longer," *National Geographic*, November (2005): 9–26.

29. Julianne Holt-Lunstad et al., "Loneliness and Social Isolation as Risk Factors for Mortality," *Perspectives on Psychological Science* 10, no. 2 (2015): 227–237.

30. Louise C. Hawkley and John T. Cacioppo, "Loneliness Matters: A Theoretical and Empirical Review of Consequences and Mechanisms," *Annals of Behavioral Medicine* 40, no. 2 (2010): 218–227.

31. Steven W. Cole, "Social Regulation of Human Gene Expression: Mechanisms and Implications for Public Health," *American Journal of Public Health* 103 (2013): S84–S92.

32. Holt-Lunstad et al., "Loneliness and Social Isolation."227–237.

33. Hawkley and Cacioppo, "Loneliness Matters."

34. Cole, "Social Regulation of Human Gene Expression," S84–S92.

35. Kathleen Raine, *William Blake and the City*. Radio, (N.D.) 23:31.

36. Richard Rohr, "A Hidden Wholeness," *Daily Meditations*, Center for Action and Contemplation, March 2019, https://cac.org/a-hidden-wholeness -2019–03–27/.

CHAPTER 2

1. Fay Bound Alberti, "One Is the Loneliest Number: The History of a Western Problem," Aeon Ideas, September 2018, https://aeon.co/ideas/one-is-the -loneliest-number-the-history-of-a-western-problem.

2. Jill Lepore, "The History of Loneliness," March 2020, https://www.newyorker .com/magazine/2020/04/06/the-history-of-loneliness.

3. Fay Bound Alberti, *A Biography of Loneliness: The History of an Emotion* (USA: Oxford University Press, 2019), xi.

4. Alberti, *Biography of Loneliness*, 135.

5. Frieda Fromm-Reichmann, "Loneliness," *Psychiatry* 22, no. 1 (1959): 1–15. Cited in Jill Lepore, "The History of Loneliness."

6. Lepore, "The History of Loneliness."

7. Robert Weiss, *Loneliness: The Experience of Emotional and Social Isolation* (Cambridge: MIT Press, 1973).

8. Orlando Patterson "Trafficking, Gender and Slavery: Past and present," *The Legal Understanding of Slavery: From the Historical to the Contemporary* (2012), 3.

9. Edd Gent, "The Plight of Japan's Modern Hermits," BBC Future, BBC, January 2019, https://www.bbc.com/future/article/20190129-the-plight-of-japans-modern-hermits.

10. Bianca DiJulio et al., "Loneliness and Social Isolation in the United States, the United Kingdom, and Japan: An International Survey," KFF, August 2018, https://www.kff.org/report-section/loneliness-and-social-isolation-in-the-united-states-the-united-kingdom-and-japan-an-international-survey-section-1/.

11. "Social Isolation and Loneliness," Australian Institute of Health and Welfare, Australian Government, September 2019, https://www.aihw.gov.au/reports/australias-welfare/social-isolation-and-loneliness.

12. Desmond Ng and Sharifah Fadhilah, "The Loneliness of Old Age—and an Experiment to See If Instagram Can Be a Cure," CNA Insider, December 2020, https://www.channelnewsasia.com/cna-insider/loneliness-old-age-and-experiment-see-if-instagram-can-be-cure-794996.

13. "What Is the Prevalence of Social Isolation in Europe?" No Isolation, April 2019, https://www.noisolation.com/research/what-is-the-prevalence-of-social-isolation-in-europe/.

14. Gabrielle Denman, "All the Lonely People—the Epidemic of Loneliness and Its Consequences," Social Science Works, December 2020, https://socialscienceworks.org/all-the-lonely-people-the-epidemic-of-loneliness-and-its-consequences/.

15. Filipa Landeiro et al., "Reducing Social Isolation and Loneliness in Older People: A Systematic Review Protocol," *BMJ Open* 7, no. 5 (2016): 1–5.

16. Landeiro et al., "Reducing Social Isolation and Loneliness in Older People," 1–5.

17. "Children's and Young People's Experiences of Loneliness: 2018," Office for National Statistics, December 2018, ons.gov.uk/peoplepopulationandcommunity/wellbeing/articles/childrensandyoungpeoplesexperiencesofloneliness/2018.

18. Denman, "All the Lonely People."

19. Landeiro et al., "Reducing Social Isolation and Loneliness in Older People," 1–5.

20. K. D. M. Snell, "The Rise of Living Alone and Loneliness in History," *Social History* 42, no. 1 (2017): 2–28.

21. John Cacioppo and William Patrick, *Loneliness: Human Nature and the Need for Social Connection* (New York: W. W. Norton, 2008).

22. Denman, "All the Lonely People."

23. Denman, "All the Lonely People."

24. Denman, "All the Lonely People."

25. Tim Li and Paul W. C. Wong, "Youth Social Withdrawal Behavior (Hikikomori): A Systematic Review of Qualitative and Quantitative Studies," *Australian & New Zealand Journal of Psychiatry* 49, no. 7 (2015): 595–609.

26. "Loneliness Amongst Older People and the Impact of Family Connections," WRVS—Positive About Age, Practical About Life (2012).

27. Louise C. Hawkley and John T. Cacioppo, "Loneliness Matters: A Theoretical and Empirical Review of Consequences and Mechanisms," *Annals of Behavioral Medicine—Oxford Academic Journals* 40, no. 2 (2010).

28. Naomi Eisenberger et al., "Does Rejection Hurt? An fMRI Study of Social Exclusion," *Science* 302, no. 5643 (2003): 290–292.

29. John T. Cacioppo and Stephanie Cacioppo, "Older Adults Reporting Social Isolation or Loneliness Show Poorer Cognitive Function 4 Years Later," *Evidence-Based Nursing* 17, no. 2 (2014): 59–60.

30. Selby Frame, "Julianne Holt-Lunstad Probes Loneliness, Social Connections," *American Psychological Association*, October 2017.

31. Steven W. Cole et al., "Myeloid Differentiation Architecture of Leukocyte Transcriptome Dynamics in Perceived Social Isolation," *Proceedings of the National Academy of Sciences* 49, no. 112 (2015): 15142–15147.

32. Vivek Murthy, "Work and the Loneliness Epidemic," *Harvard Business Review*, September 2017, https://hbr.org/2017/09/work-and-the-loneliness-epidemic.

33. Julianne Holt-Lunstad et al., "Loneliness and Social Isolation as Risk Factors for Mortality: A Meta-analytic Review," *Perspectives on Psychological Science* 2, no. 10 (2015): 227–237.

34. Ashley Lewis, "Convening Examines the Intersection of Social Isolation, Health and Homelessness," San Diego Seniors Community Foundation, February 2021, https://sdscf.org/news/convening-examines-the-intersection-of-social-isolation-health-homelessness/.

35. Lewis, "Convening Examines the Intersection of Social Isolation, Health and Homelessness."

36. Laura Alejandra Rico-Uribe et al., "Association of Loneliness with All-Cause Mortality: A Meta-analysis," *PLoS ONE* 13 no. 1 (2018), https://doi.org/10.1371/journal.pone.0190033.

37. M. A. Tijhuis et al., "Changes in and Factors Related to Loneliness in Older Men. The Zutphen Elderly Study," *Age and Ageing* 28, no. 5 (1999): 491–495. Cited in Rico-Uribe et al., "Association of Loneliness with All-Cause Mortality."

38. V. Buffel et al., "Professional Care Seeking for Mental Health Problems Among Women and Men in Europe: The Role of Socioeconomic, Family-Related and Mental Health Status Factors in Explaining Gender Differences," *Social Psychiatry and Psychiatric Epidemiology* 49, no. 1(2014), 1641–1653. Cited in Rico-Uribe et al., "Association of Loneliness with All-Cause Mortality."

39. A. Stickley et al., "Loneliness: Its Correlates and Association with Health Behaviours and Outcomes in Nine Countries of the Former Soviet Union," *PLoS ONE* 8 no. 7 (2013). Cited in Rico-Uribe et al., "Association of Loneliness with All-Cause Mortality."

40. Louis Achterbergh, Alexandra Pitman, and Mary Birken et al., "The Experience of Loneliness Among Young People with Depression: A Qualitative Meta-synthesis of the Literature," *BMC Psychiatry* 20, no. 1 (2020).

41. Alan R. Teo et al., "Social Isolation and Loneliness: A Hidden Killer," *Journal of the American Geriatrics Society* 63, no. 10 (2015): 2014–2022.

42. Julianne Holt-Lunstad in discussion with the author, September 1, 2021.

43. Carola Suárez-Orozco et al., "I Felt Like My Heart Was Staying Behind: Psychological Implications of Family Separations and Reunifications for Immigrant Youth," *Journal of Adolescent Research* 26, no. 2 (2010): 222–257.

44. "Adolescent Mental Health," World Health Organization, September 2020, https://www.who.int/news-room/fact-sheets/detail/adolescent-mental-health.

45. Martha Butler and Melissa Pang, "Current Issues in Mental Health in Canada: Child and Youth Mental Health," Publication no. 2014–13, Parliamentary Information and Research Service, Library of Parliament, Ottawa, March 5, 2014.

46. Murali Doraiswamy in discussion with the author, October 9, 2018.

47. Michael C. Lu and Neal Halfon, "Racial and Ethnic Disparities in Birth Outcomes: A Life-Course Perspective," *Maternal and Child Health Journal* 7, no. 1 (2003): 13–30.

48. Lesley Russell, "Health Disparities by Race Ethnicity," Center for American Progress, December 2010, https://www.americanprogress.org/issues/healthcare/news/2010/12/16/8762/fact-sheet-health-disparities-by-race-and-ethnicity/.

49. Dhruv Khullar, "How Social Isolation Is Killing Us," *New York Times*, December 2016, https://www.nytimes.com/2016/12/22/upshot/how-social-isolation-is-killing-us.html.

50. Jessica Olien, "Loneliness Is Deadly," *Slate*, August 2013, https://slate.com/technology/2013/08/dangers-of-loneliness-social-isolation-is-deadlier-than-obesity.html.

51. Dhruv Khullar, "How Social Isolation Is Killing Us."

52. Kim Samuel et al., "Social Isolation and Its Relationship to Multidimensional Poverty," *Oxford Development Studies* 46, no. 1 (2017): 87.

53. Samuel et al., "Social Isolation and Its Relationship to Multidimensional Poverty," 87.

54. Amartya Sen, "Social Exclusion: Concept, Application, and Scrutiny," Asian Development Bank (2000).

55. Martha Nussbaum, *Creating Capabilities: Human Development Approach* (Cambridge, MA: Belknap Press of Harvard University Press, 2011), 39–40.

56. Nussbaum, *Creating Capabilities*.

57. "How the Census Bureau Measures Poverty," United States Census Bureau, accessed October 2021, https://www.census.gov/topics/income-poverty /poverty/guidance/poverty-measures.html.

58. Sabina Alkire and James Foster, "Understandings and Misunderstandings of Multidimensional Poverty Measurement," *Journal of Economic Inequality* 9, no. 2 (2011): 289–314.

59. R. Diprose, "Physical Safety and Security: A Proposal for Internationally Comparable Indicators of Violence," *Oxford Development Studies* 35 no. 4 (2007): 431–458.

60. S. Ibrahim and S. Alkire, "Agency and Empowerment: A Proposal for Internationally Comparable Indicators," *Oxford Development Studies* 35 no. 4 (2007): 379–403.

61. M. A. Lugo, "Employment: A Proposal for Internationally Comparable Indicators," *Oxford Development Studies*, 35, no. 4 (2007): 361–378.

62. Samuel et al., "Social Isolation and Its Relationship to Multidimensional Poverty."

63. Luis Galegos Chiriboga, "Panel Remarks," *The Right to Belong*, Samuel Centre for Social Connectedness, May 2020.

64. Deepa Narayan et al., *Voices of the Poor: Can Anyone Hear Us?*, Understanding Poverty, World Bank, March 2000.

65. Oxford Poverty & Human Development Initiative, "Social Isolation and Poverty in South Africa and Mozambique: A Fieldwork Report," *Oxford Poverty & Human Development Initiative* (2013): 3.

66. Oxford Poverty & Human Development Initiative, "Social Isolation and Poverty in South Africa and Mozambique," 6.

67. Oxford Poverty & Human Development Initiative, "Social Isolation and Poverty in South Africa and Mozambique," 5.

68. "Global Tuberculosis Report 2020," World Health Organization, October 2020.

69. "Global Tuberculosis Report 2020."

70. Yuhui Xu, "Investigation of Tuberculosis Outbreak in Nunavut, 2017," November 2017.

71. Public Health Agency of Canada, "Canadian Tuberculosis Standards," Centre for Communicable Diseases and Infection Control, 2014, https:// www.canada.ca/en/public-health/services/infectious-diseases/canadian -tuberculosis-standards-7th-edition.html.

72. Public Health Agency of Canada, "The Time Is Now—Chief Public Health Officer Spotlight on Eliminating Tuberculosis in Canada," Government of Canada, March 2018, https://www.canada.ca/en/public-health/corporate /publications/chief-public-health-officer-reports-state-public-health-canada /eliminating-tuberculosis.html.

73. Natan Obed, Speech at McGill International TB Centre event, June 2018.

74. Pat Sandiford Grygier, *A Long Way from Home: The Tuberculosis Epidemic Among the Inuit* (Montreal: McGill-Queen's University Press, 1994).

75. Stephen Lewis, "Press Statement by Stephen Lewis on TB in Nunavut, "AIDS-Free World, September 2017, https://aidsfreeworld.org/statements/2017/9/9/statement.

76. Lauren Vogel, "TB: Fighting a Forgotten Disease in Canada," *CMAJ: Canadian Medical Association Journal* 187, no. 8 (2015): 557.

77. Paula Arriagada, "Insights on Canadian Society: Food Insecurity Among Inuit Living in Inuit Nunangat," Statistics Canada, February 2017, https://www150.statcan.gc.ca/n1/pub/75–006-x/2017001/article/14774-eng.htm.

78. Standing Senate Committee on Aboriginal Peoples, "We Can Do Better: Housing in Inuit Nunangat," report by the Standing Senate Committee on Aboriginal Peoples, March 2017.

79. Stevie Smith, *Not Waving but Drowning* (Hamburg and New York: Peer Musikverlag, 1957).

80. Jean Twenge, "Have Smartphones Destroyed a Generation?," *The Atlantic*, September 2017, https://www.theatlantic.com/magazine/archive/2017/09/has-the-smartphone-destroyed-a-generation/534198/.

81. Twenge, "Have Smartphones Destroyed a Generation?"

82. Twenge, "Have Smartphones Destroyed a Generation?"

83. Yi-Ju Wu et al., "A Systematic Review of Recent Research on Adolescent Social Connectedness and Mental Health with Internet Technology Use," *Adolescent Research Review* 1 (2016): 153–162.

84. Brian Primack et al., "Social Media Use and Perceived Social Isolation Among Young Adults in the U.S.," *American Journal of Preventive Medicine* 53, no.1 (2017): 8.

85. Cal Newport, *Digital Minimalism: Choosing a Focused Life in a Noisy World* (London: Portfolio, 2019), 139.

86. Marlene Ogawa in discussion with the author, June 29, 2016.

87. Vivek Murthy, "Work and the Loneliness Epidemic," *Harvard Business Review*, September 2017, https://hbr.org/2017/09/work-and-the-loneliness-epidemic.

88. Kai-Fu Lee, "How AI Can Save Our Humanity," TEDxVancouver, April 2018, https://www.ted.com/talks/kai_fu_lee_how_ai_can_save_our_humanity?language=en

89. Julianne Holt-Lunstad in conversation with the author, September 2020.

90. Jena Hilliard, "Study Reveals Gen Z as the Loneliest Generation in America," Addiction Center, August 2019, https://www.addictioncenter.com/news/2019/08/gen-z-loneliest-generation/.

91. "UN/DESA Policy Brief #92: Leveraging Digital Technologies for Social Inclusion," Division for Inclusive Social Development, United Nations, February 2021.

92. "UN/DESA Policy Brief #92."

93. UNHCR Staff, "COVID-19 Crisis Underlines Need for Refugee Solidarity and Inclusion," United Nations High Commissioner for Refugees, October 2020, https://www.unhcr.org/news/latest/2020/10/5f7dfbc24/covid-19-crisis -underlines-need-refugee-solidarity-inclusion.html.

94. "Study Shows 76% of 5–16 Yr Olds Suffered from Loneliness During the COVID-19 Pandemic," FE News, August 2020, https://www.fenews.co.uk /press-releases/53395-study-shows-76-of-5–16yr-olds-suffered-from-loneliness -during-the-covid-19-pandemic.

95. "US: Concerns of Neglect in Nursing Homes," Human Rights Watch, March 2021, https://www.hrw.org/news/2021/03/25/us-concerns-neglect -nursing-homes.

96. Samir K. Sinha, Ryan Doherty, Rory McCleave, and Julie Dunning, "NIA Long Term Care COVID-19 Tracker," National Institute on Ageing, Ryerson University, accessed March 2021, https://ltc-covid19-tracker.ca/.

97. Nathan M. Stall et al., "Increased Prescribing of Psychotropic Medications to Ontario Nursing Home Residents during the COVID-19 Pandemic," medRxiv (2020): 1–6.

98. William Wan, "Pandemic Isolation Has Killed Thousands of Alzheimer's Patients While Families Watch from Afar," Washington Post, September 2020, https://www.washingtonpost.com/health/2020/09/16/coronavirus-dementia -alzheimers-deaths/.

99. Claire Ewing-Nelson, "Four Times More Women Than Men Dropped Out of the Labor Force in September," National Women's Law Center, October 2020.

100. Ewing-Nelson, "Four Times More Women Than Men."

101. Justine Jablonska, "Seven Charts That Show COVID-19's Impact on Women's Employment," McKinsey & Company, March 2021, https://www.mckinsey .com/featured-insights/diversity-and-inclusion/seven-charts-that-show-covid -19s-impact-on-womens-employment.

102. David Welna, "1 in 5 Child Care Jobs Were Lost Since Pandemic Started. Women Are Affected Most," NPR, August 2020, https://www.npr.org /sections/coronavirus-live-updates/2020/08/19/903913689/1-in-5-child-care -jobs-were-lost-since-pandemic-started-women-are-affected-most.

103. Carducci et al., "Food Systems, Diets and Nutrition in the Wake of COVID-19," Nature Food 2, no.2 (2021): 68.

104. Beatrice Mosello et al., "Spreading Disease, Spreading Conflict? COVID-19, Climate Change, and Security Risks," Adelphi, 2020, 5.

CHAPTER 3

1. W. B. Yeats, "The Second Coming," The Dial, 1920.

2. Rabindranath Tagore, "Nationalism in the West," Atlantic Monthly, March 1917.

3. Rex Molefe in discussion with the author, August 20, 2020.

4. Graça Machel, "Impact of Armed Conflict on Children," United Nations, August 1996, 17.

5. Sabina Alkire et al., "Changes over Time in the Global Multidimensional Poverty Index," *OPHI MPI Methodological Note 50*, Oxford Poverty & Human Development Initiative, July 2020.

6. Emeline Wuilbercq, "Factbox: Ten Facts About Child Soldiers Around the World," Reuters, February 12, 2021, https://www.reuters.com/article/us -global-childsoldiers-factbox-trfn-idUSKBN2ACoCB.

7. Rex Molefe in discussion with the author, August 20, 2020.

8. Weeda Mehran in discussion with the author, October 1, 2020.

9. Weeda Mehran in discussion with the author, October 4, 2018.

10. Weeda Mehran in discussion with the author, October 1, 2020.

11. Sabrina Sassi in discussion with the author, May 12, 2018.

12. Carl Hart in discussion with the author, September 25, 2018.

13. Carl Hart, *High Price: A Neuroscientist's Journey of Self-Discovery That Challenges Everything You Know About Drugs and Society* (New York: HarperCollins, 2013), 209.

14. Hart, *High Price*, 177.

15. Carl Hart in discussion with the author, September 25, 2018.

16. Institute for Economics and Peace, "Global Terrorism Index," November 2017.

17. G. W. F. Hegel, *Phenomenology of Mind*, translation of Hegel (1807) by J. B. Baillie (London: Harper & Row, 1967), 147–149.

18. Toni Morrison, *The Origin of Others* (Cambridge, MA: Harvard University Press, 2017), 3.

19. Ta-Nehisi Coates, Foreword to *The Origin of Others*, by Toni Morrison (Cambridge, MA: Harvard University Press, 2017).

20. Morrison, *Origin of Others*, 59.

21. John Powell and Stephen Menendian, "The Problem of Othering: Towards Inclusiveness and Belonging," Othering and Belonging, June 2017, https:// otheringandbelonging.org/the-problem-of-othering/.

22. Richard Rohr in discussion with the author, May 28, 2020.

23. Ta-Nehisi Coates, "The Case for Reparations," *Atlantic Monthly*, June 2014, https://www.theatlantic.com/magazine/archive/2014/06/the-case-for -reparations/361631/.

24. Coates, "Case for Reparations."

25. Kenneth Deer, "Panel Remarks," The Right to Belong, Samuel Centre for Social Connectedness (hosted remotely on Zoom), May 2020.

26. Kenneth Deer, "Movement Building Panel: From Local to Global," Global Symposium: Reimagining Community in the 21st Century, Samuel Centre for Social Connectedness, October 2019.

27. Kenneth Deer in discussion with the author, June 26, 2020.

28. Pamela Palmater, "Genocide, Indian Policy, and Legislated Elimination of Indians in Canada," *Aboriginal Policy Studies* 3, no. 3 (2014): 27–54.

CHAPTER 4

1. Joseph Campbell, *Romance of the Grail: The Magic and Mystery of Arthurian Myth* (Novato, CA: New World Library, 2015), xvii–xviii.
2. James Finley, "Our Compassionate God," *Centre for Action and Contemplation*, September 2021, https://cac.org/our-compassionate-god-2021–09–29/.
3. Cyril Edwards, *Wolfram von Eschenbach's Parzival and Titurel: A New Translation* (Oxford: Oxford University Press, 2009), 47–53.
4. Edwards, *Wolfram von Eschenbach's Parzival and Titurel*," 95–102.
5. Campbell, *Romance of the Grail*, 53.
6. Kim Samuel, "Re-imagining the Grail Quest: The Grail of Compassion," *Temenos Academy Review* 19 (2016): 78–95.
7. Edwards, *Wolfram von Eschenbach's Parzival and Titurel*, 105–108.
8. Claire Dunn, *Carl Jung: Wounded Healer of the Soul* (London: Watkins Publishing, 2000).
9. Edwards, *Wolfram von Eschenbach's Parzival and Titurel*, 310.
10. Roger Scruton, *Wagner's Parsifal: The Music of Redemption* (London: Penguin UK, 2020), 102.
11. Scruton, *Wagner's Parsifal*, 102.
12. Jules Cashford, "The Hero's Quest," Dartington College Spring Conference (1993), 40.
13. Lewis Hyde, *The Gift: How the Creative Spirit Transforms the World* (New York: Vintage Books), 12.
14. Cashford, "Hero's Quest," 9.
15. Hyde, *The Gift*, 18.
16. Cashford, "Hero's Quest," 35.
17. Eddie Barbanell—Biography," IMDb, accessed October 2021, https://www.imdb.com/name/nm1485809/bio.
18. Nelson Mandela, Opening Speech, International World Games, 2003.
19. Eunice Kennedy Shriver, "Remarks: 1968 World Games," Special Olympics, 1968, https://www.specialolympics.org/eunice-kennedy-shriver/media-library/remarks-1968-world-games.
20. "What Is Intellectual Disability?" Special Olympics, accessed September 2021, https://www.specialolympics.org/about/intellectual-disabilities/what-is-intellectual-disability.
21. "What Is Intellectual Disability?"
22. Gary N. Siperstein et al., "National Snapshot of Adults with Intellectual Disabilities in the Labor Force," *Journal of Vocational Rehabilitation* 39, no. 3 (2013): 157–165.

23. Lisa L. Christensen et al., "Bullying Adolescents with Intellectual Disability," *Journal of Mental Health Research in Intellectual Disabilities* 5, no. 1 (2012), 49–65.

24. "Camp Shriver—The Beginning of a Movement," Special Olympics, Accessed September 2021, https://www.specialolympics.org/about/history/camp-shriver.

25. Timothy Shriver, in "Special Olympics Founder Eunice Shriver Dies," *NonProfit Times*, August 2009, https://www.thenonprofittimes.com/npt_articles/special-olympics-founder-eunice-shriver-dies/.

26. Alice Walker, *The World Has Changed: Conversations with Alice Walker* (New York: New Press, 2010), 404–406.

27. Loretta Claiborne in discussion with the author, August 31, 2020.

28. Loretta Claiborne, "Let's Talk About Intellectual Disabilities," TedxMidAtlantic, December 11, 2012. 11:34. https://www.youtube.com/watch?v=oXXqr_ZSsMg&ab_channel EDxTalks.

29. Loretta Claiborne, "A Journey of Resilience," Global Symposium: Reimagining Community in the 21st Century, Samuel Centre for Social Connectedness, October 28, 2019.

30. Claiborne, "Journey of Resilience."

31. Loretta Claiborne in discussion with the author, October 2, 2014.

32. Loretta Claiborne in discussion with the author, August 31, 2020.

33. Loretta Claiborne in discussion with the author, May 8, 2016.

34. Loretta Claiborne in discussion with the author, August 31, 2020.

35. Claiborne, "Journey of Resilience."

36. Loretta Claiborne in discussion with the author, August 31, 2020.

37. Loretta Claiborne, "Game Changer: Loretta Claiborne," Special Olympics, January 6, 2019, YouTube Video, 06:28, https://www.youtube.com/watch?v=HaLvOZen-es&ab_channel=SpecialOlympics.

38. Matthew Williams in discussion with the author, October 10, 2020.

39. Matthew Williams, in "Beyond the Medal," Samuel Centre for Social Connectedness, December 4, 2015, https://www.socialconnectedness.org/beyond-the-medal/.

40. Matthew Williams, "Special Olympics Let Me Be Myself—a Champion," TEDx Vancouver, November 2015.

41. Matthew Williams, Movement Building Panel, 2019 Global Symposium, Samuel Centre for Social Connectedness, October 2019.

42. Matthew Williams in discussion with the author, October 10, 2020.

43. Matthew Williams, Movement Building Panel.

44. "Special Olympics Research Overview," Special Olympics, 2020.

45. Holly Jacobs et al., "The Special Olympics Unified Champion Schools Program: Year 8 Evaluation Report 2015—2016," *Center for Social Development and Education*, University of Massachusetts Boston (2016): 1–87.

46. Matthew Williams in discussion with the author, July 21, 2018.
47. "Kabuki Syndrome," National Organization for Rare Disorders, accessed September 2021, https://rarediseases.org/rare-diseases/kabuki-syndrome/.
48. Crystal Williams in discussion with the author, August 20, 2020.
49. Crystal Williams in discussion with the author, October 10, 2020.
50. Adrianna Vanos, "Social Connectedness, Self-Determination & Health at Home: An Examination of Special Olympics Athletes and Their Families' Experiences During the COVID-19 Pandemic," Samuel Centre for Social Connectedness, August 2021.
51. Alicia Bazzano, Chief Health Officer at Special Olympics International, citing internal 2021 SOI Athlete Survey.
52. Ben Haack, email correspondence, September 14, 2021.
53. Pablo Neruda, "Towards the Splendid City," Nobel Lecture, December 1971.

CHAPTER 5

1. Kate Torgovnick May, "I Am, Because of You: Further Reading on Ubuntu," *TED Blog*, December 9, 2013, https://blog.ted.com/further-reading-on-ubuntu/.
2. Desmond Tutu Peace Foundation, "Mission and Philosophy," accessed September 2021, http://www.tutufoundationusa.org/desmond-tutu-peace-foundation/.
3. Martin Luther King Jr., "Christmas Eve Sermon," December 1967.
4. Desmond Tutu, "Who We Are: Human Uniqueness and the African Spirit of Ubuntu," Templeton Prize Speech, April 2013.
5. Barack Obama, "Remarks by President Obama at Memorial Service for Former South African President Nelson Mandela," The White House: Office of the Press Secretary, December 2013.
6. Thomas Merton, *No Man Is an Island* (Boston: Shambhala, 2005), xvii.
7. Joe Cramer in discussion with the author, January 17, 2021.
8. "Guthrie House Therapeutic Community," John Howard Nanaimo Region John Howard Society, 2012.
9. "Nanaimo Correctional Centre Therapeutic Community Preliminary Impact Analysis," Ministry of Public Safety and Solicitor General of British Columbia, September 2010.
10. Joe Cramer in discussion with the author, January 17, 2021.
11. "Studying Criminal Justice from the Inside Out," Yale Law School, June 2019, https://law.yale.edu/yls-today/news/studying-criminal-justice-inside-out.
12. Joe Cramer in discussion with the author, January 17, 2021.
13. Natasha Karod in discussion with the author, January 16, 2021.
14. Joe Cramer in discussion with the author, January 17, 2021.

15. Walt Whitman, *Leaves of Grass, The Original 1855 Edition,* ed. Mary Carolyn Waldrep (New York: Dover Publications, 2007/1855), 81.
16. Goldie Hawn in discussion with the author, June 1, 2018.
17. Jacqueline E. Maloney et al., "A Mindfulness-Based Social and Emotional Learning Curriculum for School-Aged Children: The MindUP Program," in *Handbook of Mindfulness in Education, Mindfulness in Behavioral Health,* ed. K. A. Schonert Reichl and R. W. Roeser (New York: Springer, 2010), 313–334.
18. Claire V. Crooks et al., "Impact of MindUP Among Young Children: Improvements in Behavioral Problems, Adaptive Skills, and Executive Functioning," *Mindfulness* 11 (2020): 2433–2444.
19. Goldie Hawn in discussion with the author, June 1, 2018.
20. Caroline Casey in discussion with the author, July 7, 2020.
21. Caroline Casey, "Looking Past Limits," TEDWomen, December 2010.
22. Caroline Casey in discussion with the author, July 7, 2020.
23. Casey, "Looking Past Limits."
24. Caroline Casey in discussion with the author, July 7, 2020.
25. Casey, "Looking Past Limits."
26. Caroline Casey in discussion with the author, July 7, 2020.
27. Casey, "Looking Past Limits."
28. Casey, "Looking Past Limits."
29. "Disability Inclusion Overview," Understanding Poverty, World Bank, March 2021, https://www.worldbank.org/en/topic/disability.
30. "Disability and Health," World Health Organization, December 1, 2020, https://www.who.int/news-room/fact-sheets/detail/disability-and-health.
31. Caroline Casey in discussion with the author, July 7, 2020.
32. The Valuable 500, accessed September 2020, https://www.thevaluable500.com/.
33. "500 CEOs of Major Organizations Create the World's Biggest Community for Disability Business Inclusion," *The Valuable 500,* Press Release, May 18, 2021, https://www.thevaluable500.com/500-ceos-of-major-organisations-create -the-worlds-biggest-community-for-disability-business-inclusion-3/ content /uploads/2019/04/The_Valuable_500_release.pdf.
34. Caroline Casey in discussion with the author, July 7, 2020.
35. Josina Machel, "Josina's Thoughts on Pencil," August 2018, https:// josinazmachel.com/2018/08/24/josinas-thoughts-on-pencil/.
36. Machel, "Josina's Thoughts on Pencil."
37. Josina Machel, "Storytelling with Josina Machel," 2019 Global Symposium, Samuel Centre for Social Connectedness, October 2019.
38. Machel, "Josina's Thoughts on Pencil."
39. Machel, "Storytelling with Josina Machel."
40. "Mozambique: Justice for Gender-Based Violence Survivor: Josina Machel," Amnesty International, August 2020, https://www.amnesty.org/en /documents/afr41/2926/2020/en/.

41. "Mozambique."
42. "Mozambique."
43. Josina Machel, "Male Violence Against Women: The Next Frontier in Humanity," TEDxLytteltonWomen, February 2020.
44. United Nations Office on Drugs and Crime, *Global Study on Homicide 2019*, July 2019.
45. "Facts and Figures: Ending Violence Against Women," UN Women, accessed September 2021, https://www.unwomen.org/en/what-we-do/ending-violence-against-women/facts-and-figures#notes.
46. "The Economic Costs of Violence Against Women," UN Women, September 2016, https://www.unwomen.org/en/news/stories/2016/9/speech-by-lakshmi-puri-on-economic-costs-of-violence-against-women.
47. Instituto Nacional De Estatística; Ministério Da Saúde, *Moçambique: Inquérito Demográfi Co E De Saúde*, March 2011.
48. Josina Machel, "The Power Within You," August 2018, https://josinazmachel.com/2018/08/26/the-power-within-you-will-be-the-source-to-end-gbv-keynote/.
49. Machel, "Storytelling with Josina Machel."
50. Machel, "Storytelling with Josina Machel."
51. Josina Machel in discussion with the author, November 2018.
52. Machel, "Storytelling with Josina Machel."
53. Josina Machel in discussion with the author, November 2018.

CHAPTER 6

1. Wendell Berry in discussion with the author, June 14, 2018.
2. Wendell Berry, *The Unsettling of America: Culture and Agriculture* (Berkeley, CA: Counterpoint, 2015), 116.
3. Wendell Berry in discussion with the author, June 14, 2018.
4. Jonathan Sacks, *The Home We Build Together: Recreating Society* (United Kingdom: Bloomsbury Academic, 2007), 23.
5. Wendell Berry, Home Economics: Fourteen Essays (United States: North Point Press, 1994), ii.
6. Ovide Mercredi, "In Conversation with Zainab Salbi, 2014 Global Symposium, Samuel Centre for Social Connectedness," Toronto, October 1, 2014.
7. Ovide Mercredi, *My Silent Drum* (Winnipeg, MB: Aboriginal Issue Press, 2015), 146.
8. Ovide Mercredi, "In Conversation with Zainab Salbi."
9. Ovide Mercredi in discussion with the author, October 2, 2014.
10. Rita Joe, *I Lost My Talk* (Halifax, NS: Nimbus Publishing, 2019).
11. Nikki Wiart, "Lost Words: How Dozens of Indigenous Languages in Canada Are in Danger of Disappearing," University of Toronto News, July 2017,

https://www.utoronto.ca/news/lost-words-how-dozens-indigenous-languages
-canada-are-danger-disappearing.

12. Binesi Boulanger, "Fast Facts: Indigenous Language Revitalization and Child
    Care," Canadian Centre for Policy Alternatives, September 2018, https://www
    .policyalternatives.ca/publications/commentary/fast-facts-indigenous
    -language-revitalization-and-child-care.
13. Julie Siebens and Tiffany, "Native North American Languages Spoken at
    Home in the United States and Puerto Rico: 2006–2010," United States
    Census Bureau, December 1, 2011. https://www.census.gov/library
    /publications/2011/acs/acsbr10–10.html.
14. Becky Cook in discussion with the author, October 16, 2018.
15. Kahontakwas Diane Longboat, "Soul of Sovereignty: The Impact of Culturally
    Responsive Education on the Academic Achievement of First Nations
    Students," *Assembly of First Nations Education, Jurisdiction, and Governance*
    (2012): 71.
16. Evan Constant in discussion with the author, July 10, 2020.
17. Tyrell Ballantyne in discussion with the author, July 10, 2020.
18. Evan Constant in discussion with the author, July 10, 2020.
19. Tyrell Ballantyne in discussion with the author, July 10, 2020.
20. Becky Cook in discussion with the author, July 10, 2020.
21. Mercredi, *My Silent Drum.*
22. Becky Cook, "Kiskinomakewin, Pimatisikamik, Pimatisimihkiwap,
    Pimatisimeskanaw—Gathering Report," 2020.
23. Ovide Mercredi, Traditional Wisdom Panel, 2016 Global Symposium, Samuel
    Centre for Social Connectedness, Montreal, October 2016.
24. Nujeen Mustafa in discussion with the author, June 8, 2018.
25. Nujeen Mustafa, "The Situation of Children with Disabilities in Syria,"
    Human Rights Watch Private Briefing, June 2021.
26. Nujeen Mustafa in discussion with the author, June 8, 2018.
27. Nujeen Mustafa in discussion with the author, July 8, 2020.
28. Nujeen Mustafa, *I Am Not a Number: A Refugee's Tale,* TEDx Talk, 2017.
29. Nujeen Mustafa in discussion with the author, June 8, 2018.
30. Nujeen Mustafa, "The Situation of Children with Disabilities in Syria."
31. Human Rights Watch, "Nujeen Mustafa: First Woman with a Disability to
    Brief the UN Security Council," April 2019.
32. Mustafa, *I Am Not a Number.*
33. Nujeen Mustafa, "In Conversation with Emina Ćerimović, Nujeen and
    Nasrine Mustafa," Global Symposium: Reimagining Community in the 21st
    Century, Samuel Centre for Social Connectedness, October 2019.
34. Satish Kumar in discussion with the author, August 21, 2020.

35. Samuel McQuillen, "At the Bottom of a Coal Shaft," Samuel Centre for Social Connectedness, September 8, 2021, https://www.socialconnectedness.org /at-the-bottom-of-a-coal-shaft/.
36. Vandana Shiva in discussion with the author, September 25, 2020.

CHAPTER 7

1. Richard Sennett, *The Fall of Public Man* (New York: Knopf, 1977).
2. Kathleen Raine, *Golgonooza, City of Imagination: Last Studies in William Blake* (New York: Lindisfarne Press, 1991), 92.
3. Kathleen Raine, *William Blake and the City*, radio, (N.D.), 1:22.
4. William Blake, David V. Erdman, and Harold Bloom, *The Complete Poetry and Prose of William Blake*, newly rev. ed., 1st California ed. (Berkeley: University of California Press, 1982), 180.
5. Raine, *Golgonooza, City of Imagination*, 107.
6. Raine, *William Blake and the City*, 13:27.
7. Peter Hall, *Cities of Tomorrow: An Intellectual History of Urban Planning and Design Since 1880* (Hoboken, NJ: John Wiley & Sons, 2014).
8. Dan Stanislawski, "The Origin and Spread of the Grid Pattern Town," in *Gridded Worlds: An Urban Anthology*, ed. Reuben Rose Redwood and Liora Bigon (New York: Springer, 2018), 21–35.
9. Jane Jacobs, "The Missing Link in City Redevelopment," in *Vital Little Plans: The Short Works of Jane Jacobs*, ed. Samuel Zipp and Nathan Storring (New York: Random House, 2016).
10. Amy Bernstein, "Cities as Ideas," *Harvard Business Review*, April 2013, https:// hbr.org/2013/04/cities-as-ideas.
11. Dominic Richards in discussion with the author, November 5, 2018.
12. Jane Jacobs, *The Death and Life of Great American Cities* (New York: Vintage Books, 1992), 56–72. (Originally published 1961.)
13. Jonathan F. P. Rose, *The Well-Tempered City: Why Modern Science, Ancient Civilizations, and Human Nature Teach Us About the Future of Urban Life* (New York: Harper Wave, 2016), 1.
14. Department of Economic and Social Affairs Population Division, "World Urbanization Prospects 2018: Highlights," United Nations (2019): 1–33.
15. Dominic Richards in discussion with the author, November 5, 2018.
16. Natalie Bicknell, "Seattle's Resilience Roadmap Lacks a Cohesive Vision for the Future," *The Urbanist*, September 2019, https://www.theurbanist .org/2019/09/09/seattles-resilience-roadmap/.
17. Kwame Anthony Appiah, *Cosmopolitanism: Ethics in a World of Strangers* (New York: W. W. Norton, 2007), xi.
18. R. I. M. Dunbar, "Coevolution of Neocortical Size, Group Size and Language in Humans," *Behavioral and Brain Sciences* 16, no. 4 (1993): 681–694.

19. Jan-Emmanuel De Neve and Christian Krekel, *Cities and Happiness: A Global Ranking and Analysis*, World Happiness Report, Sustainable Development Solutions Network, chapter 3, March 2020.
20. Angel Hsu in discussion with the author, May 11, 2018.
21. Angel Hsu in Valériane Buslot, Social Connectedness Fellow, "Connecting Climate Change and Social Exclusion at the Neighbourhood Level: The UESI as a Solution to Fight Back," **Samuel Centre for Social Connectedness**, June 15, 2018, https://www.socialconnectedness.org/uesi-event/.
22. "Key Findings: Urban Environment and Social Inclusion Index," Data-Driven Lab, 2020, https://datadrivenlab.org/urban/report/key-findings/.
23. Jeremy Hoffman, "The Effects of Historical Housing Policies on Resident Exposure to Intra-Urban Heat: A Study of 108 US Urban Areas," *Climate* 8, no. 1 (2020): 12.
24. Angel Hsu, Glenn Sheriff, Tirthankar Chakraborty, and Diego Manya, "Disproportionate Exposure to Urban Heat Island Intensity Across Major US Cities," *Nature Communications* 12, 2721 (2021): https://doi.org/10.1038/s41467-021-22799-5
25. Tuviere Onookome-Okome, "Urban Heat Island: Mitigating the Worst of Increasing Temperatures in Montreal," Samuel Centre for Social Connectedness, August 2021.
26. Genevieve Westgate, "Equity and Green Space in Montreal: Potential for Healthier and More Inclusive Communities," Samuel Centre for Social Connectedness, August 2018.
27. Angel Hsu, "Cities Are Driving Climate Change. Here's How They Can Fix It," TED, October 2020.
28. Shawn Boburg and Beth Reinhard, "How Houston's 'Wild West' Growth May Have Contributed to Devastating Flooding," *Washington Post*, August 2017, https://www.washingtonpost.com/graphics/2017/investigations/harvey-urban-planning/.
29. Sarah Knapton, "Grenfell Tower refurbishment used cheaper cladding and tenants accused builders of shoddy workmanship," *The Telegraph*, June 2017, https://www.telegraph.co.uk/news/2017/06/16/grenfell-tower-refurbishment-used-cheaper-cladding-tenants-accused/.
30. Chikafusa Sato et al., "Land Subsidence and Groundwater Management in Tokyo," *International Review for Environmental Strategies* 6, no. 2 (2006): 403–424.
31. "Violent Eviction of Poor in Kampung Pulo," *Jakarta Post*, August 2015, https://www.thejakartapost.com/news/2015/08/20/violent-eviction-poor-kampung-pulo.html.
32. Dominic Richards in discussion with the author, November 5, 2018.
33. "Disability and Health—Key Facts," World Health Organization, December 2020, https://www.who.int/news-room/fact-sheets/detail/disability-and-health.

34. "What Is Universal Design? Definition and Overview," Centre for Excellence in Universal Design, May 2021, http://universaldesign.ie/what-is-universal -design/.

35. "Our Mission," *Enabling Village*, November 2020, https://enablingvillage.sg /the-enabling-village-2/.

36. "Cleveland Rated Poorest Big City in U.S.," Associated Press, September 23, 2004, https://www.nbcnews.com/id/wbna6080044.

37. S. Stolberg, "Sparkling and Blighted, Convention Cities Spotlight Ignored Urban Issues," *New York Times*, July 17, 2016.

38. Rodneya Ross, "Cleveland No. 1 with Highest Poverty Rate Among Larger U.S. Cities," *Spectrum News*, October 5, 2020, https://spectrumnews1.com/oh /columbus/news/2020/10/03/a-look-into-poverty-rates-in-ohio-cities.

39. Juliet Schor, *True Wealth: How and Why Millions of Americans Are Creating a Time-Rich, Ecologically Light, Small-Scale, High-Satisfaction Economy* (New York: Penguin, 2011), ix.

40. H. Sheffield, "The Preston Model: UK Takes Lessons in Recovery from Rust-Belt Cleveland," *The Guardian*, April 11, 2017, https://www.theguardian.com /cities/2017/apr/11/preston-cleveland-model-lessons-recovery-rust-belt.

41. Seana Irvine and Erin Elliott, "Transformation—The Story of Creating Evergreen Brick Works," Evergreen Canada, April 2018.

42. Irvine and Elliott, "Transformation."

43. "Why City Parks Matter," Park People, January 2018, https://parkpeople.ca /resource/why-city-parks-matter/.

44. Geoff Cape in discussion with the author, October 4, 2018.

45. "Who We Are: Rhonda Douglas," Women in Informal Employment: Globalizing and Organizing, accessed December 2020, https://www.wiego .org/specialists/rhonda-douglas.

46. Charles Prince of Wales, Tony Juniper, and Ian Skelly, *Harmony: A New Way of Looking at Our World* (London: Blue Door, 2010), 245.

47. West Dorset District Council, "Supplementary Planning Document: Poundbury Development Brief," December 2006.

48. HRH the Prince of Wales, "Facing Up to the Future: Princes of Wales on 21st Century Architecture," *Architectural Review*, December 20, 2014, https://www .architectural-review.com/essays/facing-up-to-the-future-prince-charles-on -21st-century-architecture.

49. Michelle Thompson-Fawcett, "'Urbanist' Lived Experience: Resident Observations on Life in Poundbury," *Urban Design International* 8 (2003): 67–84.

50. Roger Scruton, "Cities for Living: Antimodernist Léon Krier Designs Urban Environments to Human Scale," *City Journal*, Spring 2008, https://www.city -journal.org/html/cities-living-13088.html.

51. Scruton, "Cities for Living."

52. Marie-Claire Alfonso, "Doctor Is Royally Appointed to Become New High Sheriff of Dorset," Dorset ECHO, March 2021, https://www.dorsetecho.co.uk /news/19198668.doctor-royally-appointed-become-new-high-sheriff-dorset /ttps://highsheriffdorset.co.uk/the-modern-role.

53. Michael Dooley in discussion with the author, September 6, 2021.

54. Rebecca MacLeod, "An Education Transformation That Celebrates Learning," Samuel Centre for Social Connectedness, November 2019, https://www .socialconnectedness.org/an-education-transformation-that-celebrates -learning/.

55. Michael Dooley in discussion with the author, September 6, 2021.

CHAPTER 8

1. Michael Jackson, John Bettis, and Steve Porcaro, "Human Nature," *Thriller*, produced by Quincy Jones, Epic Records, and Columbia Records, 1983.

2. Joshua E. Cimmer, "Social Dimensions of Resilience in Social-Ecological Systems" *One Earth* 1, no. 1 (2019): 51–56.

3. António Guterres, "We Need to Take Action to Address the Mental Health Crisis in This Pandemic," United Nations Secretary-General, May 2020, https://www.un.org/sg/en/content/sg/articles/2020–05–21/we-need-take -action-address-the-mental-health-crisis-pandemic.

4. Daniel Lakoff, "By the Numbers: Physician Suicide," *ACEP Now*, September 2020, https://www.acepnow.com/article/by-the-numbers-physician-suicide/.

5. "At Height of COVID, Nurses and Doctors Reported High Levels of Distress," Columbia University Irving Medical Center, June 2020, https://www.cuimc .columbia.edu/news/height-covid-nurses-and-doctors-reported-high-levels -distress.

6. Lakoff, "By the Numbers."

7. Lori Plutchik in discussion with the author, January 25, 2021.

8. Lori Plutchik, email correspondence with the author, May 2021.

9. Lori Plutchik in discussion with the author, January 25, 2021.

10. Marianna Strongin in discussion with the author, January 25, 2021.

11. Annie Lennox in correspondence with the author, August 23, 2018.

12. "Parishes: Grays Thurrock," in *A History of the County of Essex*, vol. 8 (London: Victoria County History, 1983), 35–56. British History Online, http://www .british-history.ac.uk/vch/essex/vol8/pp35–56.

13. "Thurrock Facts and Statistics | Employment and Income," Thurrock Council, 2019, https://www.thurrock.gov.uk/thurrock-facts-and-statistics/employment -and-income.

14. "Labour Market Profile—Thurrock," *Office for National Statistics*, Report, 2021, https://www.nomisweb.co.uk/reports/lmp/la/1946157204/report.aspx.

15. Lizzy Davies, "'It's One Big Cesspit Here': Thurrock, the Country's Capital of Misery," *The Guardian*, July 2012, https://www.theguardian.com/lifeandstyle/2012/jul/25/thurrock-capital-misery.
16. Alex Beard in discussion with the author, July 6, 2021.
17. Martin French, Royal Opera House, "The Royal Opera House Thurrock Community Chorus Performing at Awake in Chorus!," YouTube video, 00:04:01, December 4, 2012, https://www.youtube.com/watch?v=a3krrLc4Oc8&t=14s&ab_channel=RoyalOperaHouse.
18. Eloïse O'Carroll, "How the Royal Opera House Thurrock Community Chorus Found Its Voice," Samuel Centre for Social Connectedness, July 2018, https://www.socialconnectedness.org/how-the-royal-opera-house-thurrock-community-chorus-found-its-voice/.
19. Daisy Fancourt et al., "Psychosocial Singing Interventions for the Mental Health and Well-Being of Family Carers of Patients with Cancer: Results from a Longitudinal Controlled Study," *BMJ Open* 9, no. 8 (2019): 7.
20. Ian Morrison and Stephen Clift, "Singing and Mental Health," Sidney De Haan Research Centre for Arts and Health, Canterbury Christ Church University, September 2012.
21. Jacques Launay, "Choir Singing Improves Health, Happiness—and Is the Perfect Icebreaker," The Conversation, October 2015, https://theconversation.com/choir-singing-improves-health-happiness-and-is-the-perfect-icebreaker-47619.
22. David St. Pier in discussion with the author, September 22, 2021.
23. Anne St. Pier in discussion with the author, September 22, 2021.
24. David St. Pier in discussion with the author, September 22, 2021.
25. Anne St. Pier in discussion with the author, September 22, 2021.
26. David St. Pier in discussion with the author, September 22, 2021.
27. O'Carroll, "How the Royal Opera House Thurrock Community Chorus Found Its Voice."
28. O'Carroll, "How the Royal Opera House Thurrock Community Chorus Found Its Voice."
29. Internal Report, Royal Opera House, 2017.
30. Alex Beard in discussion with the author, July 6, 2021.
31. "Philistines at the Gates? Future of Thurrock Community Choir in Doubt as Funding "Pulled," Your Thurrock: Local but Global, September 2020, https://www.yourthurrock.com/2020/09/05/philistines-at-the-gates-future-of-thurrock-community-choir-in-doubt-as-funding-pulled/.
32. David St. Pier in discussion with the author, September 22, 2021.
33. Anne St. Pier in discussion with the author, September 22, 2021.
34. David St. Pier in discussion with the author, September 22, 2021.
35. Dixon Chibanda, "How Can a Team of Grandmothers Make Therapy Accessible to All?," TED Radio Hour (National Public Radio), October 2019, https://www.npr.org/transcripts/764654028?t=1626792765430.

36. Dixon Chibanda, "Friendship Bench—GHLS 2019," London School of Hygiene and Tropical Medicine Lecture, December 2019, https://www.rev .com/transcript-editor/Edit?token=X5i4Xg4bc9WVFkHv9YKOHLy9S _FxAqhBieAGKA_la7qRnDnOnJxdAqARMaHiobXGDRbOa3WxQJwWelAge -9PsGOzz8A&loadFrom=DocumentDeeplink&ts=576.61.
37. Chibanda, "Friendship Bench."
38. Dixon Chibanda in discussion with the author, June 29, 2020.
39. Susan Chali in discussion with the author, July 20, 2020.
40. Chibanda, "Friendship Bench."
41. Charmaine Chitiyo in discussion with the author, July 20, 2020.
42. Sabinah Dovi in discussion with the author, July 20, 2020.
43. Dixon Chibanda et al., "Scaling Up Interventions for Depression in Sub-Saharan Africa: Lessons from Zimbabwe," *Global Mental Health* 3 (2016): e13.
44. Sabinah Dovi in discussion with the author, July 20, 2020.
45. "Home," The Friendship Bench, Accessed September 2021, www .friendshipbenchzimbabwe.org.
46. Dixon Chibanda in discussion with the author, June 29, 2020.
47. Charmaine Chitiyo in discussion with the author, July 20, 2020.
48. Simone Jean-Marie Renault, "Holding Hands Together: Preliminary Qualitative Findings of Mental Health Support Groups in Zimbabwe," Samuel Centre for Social Connectedness, August 2021, https://www .socialconnectedness.org/wp-content/uploads/2021/09/Renault_SCSC_Final -Report_Holding-Hands-Together.docx.pdf.

CHAPTER 9

1. Maya Angelou, *Oh Pray My Wings Are Gonna Fit Me Well: Poems* (New York: Random House, 2013), 26.
2. "Canadian Reference Group: Executive Summary," American College Health Association, Spring 2019.
3. "Spring 2021, Reference Group Data Report," American College Health Association, Spring 2021.
4. Vino Landry in discussion with the author, November 30, 2018.
5. Deborah Saucier, Global Symposium: Reimagining Community in the 21st Century, Samuel Centre for Social Connectedness, October 2019.
6. Deborah Saucier in discussion with the author, September 29, 2020.
7. OUPA dp5yr data point at October 1, 2021.
8. "Youth Aged Out of Care Funding: Tuition Waiver Program," Vancouver Island University, Accessed June 2020, https://services.viu.ca/financial-aid -awards/youth-care-tuition-waiver-program.
9. Deborah Saucier in discussion with the author, August 26, 2020.
10. Pamela Molina in discussion with the author, November 12, 2020.

11. John Hammock and OPHI, "Case Study: Agrolíbano, Honduras," Internal Report, Case Study, September 2020.
12. Pamela Molina in discussion with the author, November 12, 2020.
13. Oxford Poverty & Human Development Initiative (OPHI), *BHUTAN Multidimensional Poverty Index 2017*, National Statistics Bureau, Royal Government of Bhutan, 2017, vi.
14. "History of GNH," GNH Centre Bhutan, accessed July 2021, http://www .gnhcentrebhutan.org/what-is-gnh/history-of-gnh/.
15. Sabina Alkire in discussion with the author, September 18, 2018.
16. Dasho Karma Ura in discussion with the author, August 11, 2020.
17. Dasho Karma Ura, "ISBS 2019: Dasho Karma Ura—Development with Integrity: Bhutan's Gross National Happiness Index," OPHI Oxford, January 10, 2019, YouTube video, https://www.youtube.com /watch?v=da8fqUdHGoM.
18. Tshering Tobgay in discussion with the author, September 27 2021.
19. "Bhutan: Committed to Conservation," World Wildlife Foundation, accessed September 2021, https://www.worldwildlife.org/projects/bhutan-committed -to-conservation.
20. Tshering Tobgay in discussion with the author, September 2021.
21. Gwendolyn Brooks, *The Essential Gwendolyn Brooks (American Poets Project # 19)* (New York: Library of America, 2005).
22. "Part 1: Food Security and Nutrition Around the World in 2020," *The State of Food Security and Nutrition in the World 2020: Transforming Food Systems for Affordable Healthy Diets*, Food and Agriculture Organization of the United Nations, 2020, 18.
23. "Part 1: Food Security and Nutrition," 3.
24. "Part 1: Food Security and Nutrition," 65–66.
25. "Part 1: Food Security and Nutrition," 66.
26. "Part 1: Food Security and Nutrition," 69.
27. Leo Horrigan, Robert S. Lawrence, and Polly Walker, "How Sustainable Agriculture Can Address the Environmental and Human Health Harms of Industrial Agriculture," *Environmental Health Perspectives* 110, no. 5 (2002): 445–456.
28. Feeding America, *The Impact of the Coronavirus on Food Insecurity in 2020 & 2021*, Issue brief, March 2021, https://www.feedingamerica.org/sites/default /files/2021–03/National%20Projections%20Brief_3.9.2021_0.pdf.
29. Food Foundation, *A Crisis Within a Crisis: The Impact of Covid-19 on Household Food Security*, 2021, https://foodfoundation.org.uk/wp-content /uploads/2021/03/FF_Impact-of-Covid_FINAL.pdf.
30. Valerie Tarasuk and Andy Mitchell, "Household Food Insecurity in Canada 2017–2018," PROOF Initiative, University of Toronto, 2018.
31. Food Foundation, *A Crisis Within a Crisis*.

32. "What We Do: About Us," The Stop Community Food Centre, accessed July 2021, https://www.thestop.org/what-we-do/about-us/.
33. Brent Preston, *The New Farm* (New York: Abrams, 2018), 241.
34. Preston, *The New Farm*, 242.
35. "Growing Community: Feeding Change," *2018–2021: Three-Year Program Vision and Strategic Plan*, The Stop Community Food Centre, 2018, 9.
36. "Food in Toronto: Affordability, Accessibility, and Insecurity," *2019 Board of Health Report*, Toronto Board of Health, 2019.
37. "Food in Toronto."
38. "Roots of Food Justice," *The Stop's 2018/2019 Annual Report*, The Stop Community Food Centre, 2019.
39. Leigh Godbold in discussion with the author, September 15, 2021.
40. Rossen Lee, "Exploring the Influence of Publicly Accessible Green and Growing Spaces on Health Implications for Toronto During the COVID-19 Pandemic," Samuel Centre for Social Connectedness, August 2021.
41. "What We Do: Impact," The Stop Community Food Centre, accessed July 2021, https://www.thestop.org/what-we-do/impact/.
42. "What We Do: About Us," The Stop Community Food Centre, accessed July 2021, https://www.thestop.org/what-we-do/about-us/.
43. Rachel Gray, "Beyond Food Banks," Jeanne Sauvé Forum on Social Connectedness, April 3 2017.
44. Kristi Green, "New Farm Raises $40,000 for The Stop," The Creemore Echo, June 2014, https://creemore.com/new-farm-raises-40000-for-the-stop/.
45. Preston, *The New Farm*, 250.
46. Gray, "Beyond Food Banks," Jeanne Sauvé Forum on Social Connectedness, April 2017.
47. "Growing Community: Feeding Change," 10.
48. Paul Farmer in discussion with the author, June 24, 2020.
49. "Uneven Access to Health Services Drives Life Expectancy Gaps: WHO," World Health Organization, April 2019, https://www.who.int/news/item/04 –04–2019-uneven-access-to-health-services-drives-life-expectancy-gaps-who.
50. "Noncommunicable diseases," World Health Organization, April 2021, https://www.who.int/news-room/fact-sheets/detail/noncommunicable-diseases.
51. Global Health Observatory, "Under-Five Mortality Rate (Probability of Dying by Age 5 per 1000 Live Births)," World Health Organization, accessed October 24, 2021, https://www.who.int/data/gho/data/indicators/indicator -details/GHO/under-five-mortality-rate-(probability-of-dying-by-age-5-per 1000-live-births).
52. Paul Farmer in discussion with the author, May 14, 2018.
53. "Community Health Workers as Agents of Social Change and Social Connectedness: Rollout of the Household Model in Malawi and Liberia," Partners In Health, Internal Report, June 2017.

54. Agnes Binagwaho in discussion with the author, July 12, 2020.
55. Paul Farmer in discussion with the author, June 24, 2020.
56. "Sierra Leone," Partners In Health, accessed January 2021, https://www.pih.org/country/sierra-leone.
57. "Sierra Leone," *Country Cooperation Strategy at a Glance*, World Health Organization, May 2018, https://www.who.int/publications/i/item/WHO-CCU-18.02-SierraLeone.
58. "Sierra Leone," Partners In Health, accessed January 2021, https://www.pih.org/country/sierra-leone.
59. Mohammed Jara, Ramatulai Jalloh, Umaru Gbandequee, and Aiah Jonah Yopoi in discussion with the author, December 2020.
60. Leah Blezard in discussion with the author, August 10, 2020.
61. Agnes Binagwaho in discussion with the author, July 12, 2020.
62. Paul Farmer in discussion with the author, June 24, 2020.
63. Aiah Jonah Yorpoi in discussion with the author, December 2, 2020.
64. Wendell Berry, *The Art of the Commonplace: The Agrarian Essays of Wendell Berry*, ed. Norman Wirzba (Berkeley, CA: Counterpoint, 2002), 199.
65. Hilary Cottam in discussion with the author, July 15, 2020.

CHAPTER 10

1. Emina Ćerimović, "The Human Right to Belong: Unique Perspectives on Achieving the Elusive Goal of Peace," Jeanne Sauvé Forum on Social Connectedness September 16, 2016.
2. Emina Ćerimović, "In Conversation with Emina Ćerimović, Nujeen and Nasrine Mustafa," Global Symposium: Reimagining Community in the 21st Century, Samuel Centre for Social Connectedness, October 2019.
3. Emina Ćerimović, "Class Lecture," Lessons of Community and Compassion: Overcoming Social Isolation and Building Social Connectedness Through Policy and Program Development, September 2017.
4. Emina Ćerimović, "The Human Right to Belong," Unique Perspectives on Achieving the Elusive Goal of Peace," Jeanne Sauvé Forum on Social Connectedness, September, 2016.
5. Emina Ćerimović in email correspondence with the author, October 2018.
6. "Living in Chains: Shackling of People with Psychosocial Disabilities Worldwide," Disability Rights Division, Human Rights Watch, October 6, 2020, https://www.hrw.org/report/2020/10/06/living-chains/shackling-people-psychosocial-disabilities-worldwide.
7. "Nigeria: People with Mental Health Conditions Chained, Abused," Human Rights Watch, November 11, 2020, https://www.hrw.org/news/2019/11/11/nigeria-people-mental-health-conditions-chained-abused.

8. Rebecca Solnit, *Hope in the Dark: Untold Histories, Wild Possibilities*, 3rd ed. (Chicago: Haymarket Books, 2016), 91.

9. Henry Shue, *Basic Rights: Subsistence, Affluence, and U.S. Foreign Policy*, 40th Anniversary Edition (Princeton, NJ: Princeton University Press, 2020).

10. Ken Roth in discussion with the author, November 20, 2019.

11. William Alford in discussion with the author, August 26, 2020.

12. Henry Shue, "Remarks: COVID-19 and Older People's Rights: Social Connectedness and Belonging," 11th Session of the UN Open-Ended Working Group on Ageing Side Event, United Nations, March 2021.

13. Tim Shriver, "Panel Remarks," The Right to Belong, Samuel Centre for Social Connectedness (hosted remotely on Zoom), May 2020.

14. Philippa H Stewart, "Witness: Shackled for Years, Now Free," Human Rights Watch, October 2018, https://www.hrw.org/news/2018/10/02/witness-shackled-years-now-free.

15. "Living in Chains."

16. S. Dingfelder, "Psychologist Testifies About the Dangers of Solitary Confinement," *Monitor on Psychology* 43, no. 9 (2012): 10.

17. Tom K. Wong, "Do Family Separation and Detention Deter Immigration?," Center for American Progress, July 2018, https://www.americanprogress.org/issues/immigration/reports/2018/07/24/453660/family-separation-detention-deter-immigration/.

18. Maggie Jo Buchanan, Philip E. Wolgin, and Claudia Flores, "The Trump Administration's Family Separation Policy Is Over," Center for American Progress, April 2021, https://www.americanprogress.org/issues/immigration/reports/2021/04/12/497999/trump-administrations-family-separation-policy/.

19. Lucie Richards in Kate McGillivray, "Ontario's Homeless 5 Times More Likely to Die of COVID-19, Study Finds," CBC News, January 2021, https://www.cbc.ca/news/canada/toronto/ontario-s-homeless-5-times-more-likely-to-die-of-covid-19-study-finds-1.5869024.

20. Jessica Viñas-Nelson, "Interracial Marriage in 'Post-Racial' America," *Origins—Current Events in Historical Perspective* 10, no. 12, https://origins.osu.edu/article/interracial-marriage-post-racial-america/page/0/1.

21. Andrew Pulrang, "A Simple Fix for One of Disabled People's Most Persistent, Pointless Injustices," *Forbes*, August 2020, https://www.forbes.com/sites/andrewpulrang/2020/08/31/a-simple-fix-for-one-of-disabled-peoples-most-persistent-pointless-injustices/.

22. CFR Staff, "Marriage Equality: Global Comparisons," Council on Foreign Relations, June 2021, https://www.cfr.org/backgrounder/marriage-equality-global-comparisons.

23. CFR Staff, "Marriage Equality."

24. "Background Note on Sex Discrimination in Birth Registration," Coalition on Every Child's Right to a Nationality, UNHCR and UNICEF, July 2021.

25. United Nations High Commissioner for Refugees (UNHCR), "Climate Change and Statelessness: An Overview," 6th session of the Ad Hoc Working Group on Long-Term Cooperative Action (AWG-LCA 6) under the UN Framework Convention on Climate Change (UNFCCC) (2009): 1–4.

26. Martin Luther King Jr., "Beyond Vietnam: A Time to Break Silence," Riverside Church, New York City, April 4, 1967.

27. Ethan Sethu Xabanisa in discussion with the author, July 17, 2021.

28. Ethan Sethu Xabanisa, "Act Straight," Samuel Centre for Social Connectedness, July 2021, https://www.socialconnectedness.org/act-straight/.

29. Xabanisa, "Act Straight."

30. Ethan Sethu Xabanisa in discussion with the author, July 17, 2021.

31. Joey Monane in discussion with the author, October 19, 2020.

32. Ethan Sethu Xabanisa, "Act Straight."

33. Xabanisa, "Act Straight."

34. Graeme Reid in discussion with the author, October 28, 2018.

35. Graeme Reid, "Panel Remarks," The Right to Belong, Samuel Centre for Social Connectedness (hosted remotely on Zoom), May 2020.

36. Sethu Xabanisa in discussion with the author, July 17, 2020.

37. Xabanisa, "Act Straight."

38. Rabindranath Tagore, *Gitanjali* (New York: Macmillan, 1917), 42.

39. Amartya Sen, "The Possibility of Social Change," Nobel Lecture, Trinity College, December 1998.

40. Ovide Mercredi, Acceptance Speech of Honorary Doctorate of Law Degree from the Law Society of Ontario, 2019.

41. Arthur Quiller-Couch, *The Oxford Book of English Verse, 1250–1900* (Oxford: Clarendon Press, 1902), 720.

42. Loretta Claiborne, "Remarks," Special Olympics International Board Meeting, SOI, June 2021.

43. "Older People: Section 1—Who Are We Concerned About?," Climate Just, accessed July 2021, https://www.climatejust.org.uk/messages/older-people.

44. Bethany Brown, "Panel Remarks," The Right to Belong, Samuel Centre for Social Connectedness (hosted remotely on Zoom), May 2020.

45. "Global Report on Ageism," Global Campaign to Combat Ageism, World Health Organization, March 2021.

46. Heather Gilmour and Pamela L. Ramage-Morin, "Social Isolation and Mortality Among Canadian Seniors," Statistics Canada, June 2020, https://www150.statcan.gc.ca/n1/pub/82-003-x/2020003/article/00003-eng.htm.

47. Brown, "Panel Remarks."

48. Bridget Sleap in discussion with the author, September 17, 2020.
49. Judi Aubel in discussion with the author, November 20, 2018.
50. Kimberley Brownlee in discussion with the author, September 25, 2018.
51. Margaret Laurence, "My Final Hour," Address to the Philosophy Society, Trent University, January 26, 1987.
52. Tim Shriver, "Panel Remarks."

CHAPTER 11

1. Margaret Atwood, *The Circle Game* (Toronto: Contact Press, 1966), 41.
2. Graça Machel, "Remarks" at the Global Symposium: Overcoming Isolation and Deepening Social Connectedness, Samuel Centre for Social Connectedness, October 2014.
3. Peggy Dulany in discussion with the author, October 2, 2014.
4. Marlene Ogawa in discussion with the author, June 29, 2016.
5. Marlene Ogawa in discussion with the author, November 28, 2018.
6. Marlene Ogawa in discussion with the author, June 29, 2020.
7. Simangele "Smash" Shoyisa in discussion with the author, October 2, 2014.
8. Daylene Van Buuren in discussion with the author, January 29, 2018.
9. Simangele "Smash" Shoyisa in discussion with the author, October 2, 2014.
10. Siphokazi Hlati in discussion with the author, August 14, 2020.
11. "The Granny Programme: A Promising Practice," Jo'burg Child Welfare, Samuel Family Foundation and Synergos, 2016.
12. Patience Mokgadi, "In Conversation with the Othandweni Grannies," Global Symposium: Overcoming Isolation and Deepening Social Connectedness, Samuel Centre for Social Connectedness, October 2014, https://www .socialconnectedness.org/in-conversation-with-the-othandweni-grannies/.
13. Lynette Mudekunye in discussion with the author, August 12, 2020.
14. Rex Molefe in discussion with the author, August 20, 2020.
15. Joey Monane in discussion with the author, October 19, 2020.
16. William Blake, *The Marriage of Heaven and Hell* (London: Camden Hotten, 1906), 17.
17. Kathleen Raine, *Golgonooza, City of Imagination: Last Studies in William Blake* (New York: Lindisfarne Press, 1991), 177.
18. Margaret Atwood in email correspondence with the author, July 2018.
19. "Special Olympics GB: Dreams Do Come True!," *Able Magazine*, April 2018, https://ablemagazine.co.uk/special-olympics-gb-dreams-do-come-true/.
20. Kluane Adamek, "Class Lecture," Lessons of Community and Compassion: Overcoming Social Isolation and Building Social Connectedness Through Policy and Program Development, McGill University, October 2017.
21. Radosveta Stamenkova in discussion with the author, July 17, 2020.
22. Juan Manuel Santos in discussion with the author, November 12, 2018.

23. Wilfred Owen, *The Poems of Wildred Owen*, ed. Edmund Blunden (London: Chatto & Windus, 1931), 65.

24. Alexandra Lang, "The Concept of Understanding," *Hillel International*, 14 November 2019, https://www.hillel.org/about/news-views/news-views---blog /news-and-views/2019/11/14/the-concept-of-understanding.Alexandra

25. Jo Cox, ITV News, "Remembering Jo Cox MP: Her Maiden Speech," YouTube video, 00:05:55, June 2016, https://www.youtube.com /watch?v=u3OQRnJ1zrQ&ab_channel=ITVNews.

26. "The Big Lunch Join in Where You Live," CommunityNI, accessed July 2021, https://www.communityni.org/event/big-lunch-join-where-you-live.

27. Banji Oguntayo, in discussion with Common Threads, Samuel Centre for Social Connectedness, May 2019.

28. FORA: Network for Change, *Girls on Boards*, accessed October 24, 2021, https://www.foranetwork.org/programs/girls-on-boards.

29. Julianne Holt-Lunstad in discussion with the author, September 1, 2021.

30. Michael Stein in discussion with the author, August 8, 2020.

31. Chester Finn, "Supported Decision-Making: A Self-Advocate's Ten Commandments for Community Members," Samuel Centre for Social Connectedness, August 2021, https://www.socialconnectedness.org/wp -content/uploads/2021/09/Chester-Finn-Final-Output-with-cover-page-hez .docx.pdf.

32. Bill Drayton in discussion with the author, August 8, 2018.

33. Waukomaun Pawis in discussion with the author, July 16, 2020.

34. Lyrics by Siedah Garrett, music by Glen Ballard, "Man in the Mirror," from the record *Bad*, produced by Quincy Jones, Michael Jackson, and Epic Records, 1988.

35. Quincy Jones in discussion with the author, November 26, 2017.

36. Oliver Sacks, *Gratitude* (New York: Knopf, 2015), 10.

37. Wendell Berry, *Standing by Words: Essays* (San Francisco: North Point Press, 1983).

38. John Louis Emil Dreyer, *A History of Astronomy from Thales to Kepler* (Chelmsford, UK: Courier Corporation, 1953), 115.

39. Nicolaus Copernicus, *On the Revolutions*, ed. Jerzy Dobrzycki, trans. Edward Rosen. (Warsaw, Poland: Polish Scientific Publishers, 1978), cited in L. S. Fauber, *Heaven on Earth: How Copernicus, Brahe, Kepler, and Galileo Discovered the Modern World* (New York: Pegasus Books, 2019), 25.

40. Copernicus, *On the Revolutions*, 17.

INDEX